KU-539-461

IF THIS BE HERESY

A Study of Milton and Origen

6 00 140906 9   TELEPEN

This Book must be returned to
the Library on, or before the
      late sho

IF THIS BE HERESY

A Study of Milton and Origen

HARRY F. ROBINS

ILLINOIS STUDIES IN LANGUAGE AND LITERATURE

51

UNIVERSITY OF ILLINOIS PRESS, URBANA, 1963

LC6300T254

C

304010.

Board of Editors: BURTON A. MILLIGAN, JOHN R. FREY, AND PHILIP KOLB.

© 1963 by the Board of Trustees of the University of Illinois. Manufactured in the United States of America. Library of Congress Catalog Card No. 63-7254

To Gwynne Blakemore Evans

IN RECOGNITION OF A DECADE OF FRIENDSHIP AND ENCOURAGEMENT.

ACKNOWLEDGMENTS

To Professors Arthur E. Barker, Gwynne B. Evans, Burton A. Milligan, and Marcus S. Goldman, my associates in the English Department of the University of Illinois, who read this work in its several manuscript stages, I wish to express my gratitude for time generously given and for valuable critical suggestions.

To Merritt Y. Hughes, of the University of Wisconsin, I owe a special debt for wisely counseling changes which led to a complete reorganization of my materials, and for other sound advice.

To my father-in-law, Ben M. Scifres, attorney, of Lebanon, Indiana, for his aid in matters of style and for his enthusiastic interest, my thanks.

To the University of Illinois Research Board I am grateful for a fellowship which allowed me to devote the summer of 1957 exclusively to the subject of this work.

And, most of all, I wish to thank my wife, without whose encouragement and aid as audience, critic, editor, typist, and proofreader this book would not yet be done.

I alone am responsible for whatever errors in judgment or scholarship remain.

Urbana, Illinois   H.F.R.
April 28, 1962

CONTENTS

For my own part, I adhere to the Holy Scriptures alone — I follow no other heresy or sect. I had not even read any of the works of heretics, so called, when the mistakes of those who are reckoned for orthodox, and their incautious handling of Scripture first taught me to agree with their opponents whenever those opponents agreed with Scripture. If this be heresy, I confess with St. Paul, Acts xxiv. 14. "that after the way which they call heresy, so worship I the God of my fathers, believing all things which are written in the law and the prophets" — to which I add, whatever is written in the New Testament. Any other judges or paramount interpreters of the Christian belief, together with all implicit faith, as it is called, I, in common with the whole Protestant Church, refuse to recognise.

Dedication to *The Christian Doctrine*

CHAPTER ONE

INTRODUCTORY

A primary purpose of this study is to demonstrate that Milton as a theologian is deeply indebted to early Christian thought, of which Origen is, in some ways, the best representative. There will be objections, no doubt, to my singling out as standard-bearer for primitive Christianity a writer who was banished by his bishop from his native Alexandria after informal excommunication, who is sometimes spoken of as the spiritual father of Arius, whose name posthumously became all but synonymous with heresy, whose doctrines were considered scandalous by Jerome and by Augustine, and whose direct influence upon official Church doctrine did not extend beyond the sixth century. Yet Origen, excepting Augustine alone, is the most important theologian of ancient times: He created the dogmatic of the Church. He began the criticism of the Bible. He summed up the work of those who had preceded him — Justin, Tatian, Athenagoras, Pantaenus, and Clement. In doing so and in 'reconciling Greek culture with the Christian faith, he, more than any other man, won the ancient world to Christianity. According to Harnack, perhaps the greatest student of the development of Christian dogma, "Orthodox theology has never, in any of the confessions, ventured beyond the circle which the mind of Origen first measured out. It has suspected and amended its author, it has expunged his heresies; but whether it has put better or more tenable [doctrines] in their place may be gravely questioned." [1]

What Origen believed is interesting per se only to the ecclesiastical historian; what Milton believed, because it is couched in the imperishable language of great art, is interesting to all of us. It is my intent to use the thought of Origen as a gloss upon Milton's *De Doctrina*

---

[1] Adolf Harnack, "Origen," in *Encyclopaedia Britannica*, 11th ed. (New York, 1910), XX, 270.

Christiana and, therefore, ultimately and most importantly as a means of explaining the theological system which governs the structure of *Paradise Lost*. My summation of Origen's views in the following chapters will be deliberately limited. Only that which will contribute to the understanding of Milton will be set forth. I am concerned with the poet's conclusions upon questions which were to him inexhaustibly vital, urgent, and restorative. The answers which Milton laboriously put down in his "best and richest possession," *The Christian Doctrine*, were hopefully broadcast in *Paradise Lost*; but only a few readers recognized their existence before Bishop Sumner brought out the *De Doctrina* in 1825; and another hundred years intervened before Denis Saurat, in his *Milton: Man and Thinker*, dispatched forever the idle and condescending appraisal of the greatest epic in the English language as a peal of organ music. Still there lingers in some quarters, I am afraid, a certain cavalier disregard for Milton's seriousness of purpose in the poem, a reluctance to grant that he means what he seems to mean, a readiness to force his express opinion into conventional molds less disturbing to individual preference. I am persuaded that Milton's theology is coherent, philosophically sound, and consistently adhered to in both the treatise and the epic. Since the publication of Professor Maurice Kelley's *This Great Argument*, the fact that the views propounded in *The Christian Doctrine* are turned to account as ideological background in *Paradise Lost* needs, I should think, no further demonstration. Indeed, Professor Kelley sometimes disallows what seem to me patent similarities in doctrine. Though my interest is centered on the epic, I shall rely less upon it than upon the treatise in developing my explication of the Miltonic system, for the obvious reason that the subtleties of dogma tend to get lost in the pleasant labyrinth of poetic ornamentation. The subtleties are there, nevertheless; and upon a few occasions the epic is clearer than the treatise. Moreover, had the treatise never come to light, its major tenets could have been re-created by a careful reading of the poem.

As C. S. Lewis wisely remarks, "Milton's thought, when purged of its theology, does not exist." [2] This is surely the view of most, if not all, Miltonists today. But upon the precise nature of the poet's doctrine and upon its exact relationship to his epic, there is now, as there has been for almost three centuries, wide disagreement. The theology of *Paradise Lost* has been called Arian, Arminian, Puritan,

---

[2] C. S. Lewis, *A Preface to Paradise Lost* (London, New York, and Toronto, 1956), p. 64. Future reference will be to *Lewis*.

Presbyterian, Baptist, orthodox, heterodox, heretical, Catholic, Protestant, Hebraic, millenarian, cabalistic, mortalist, Platonic, neo-Platonic, materialistic, mystical, stoic, Epicurian, Socinian, atheistic, Quaker, Independent, quietist, humanitarian — my list is incomplete. Most of these epithets are justified in part at least. None of them, however, is comprehensive enough or accurate enough to describe the poet's theological system as a whole.

Historically, criticism of *Paradise Lost* has been swayed by party and by sect. Upon whether a critic was a Whig or Tory depended in large measure his attitude toward Milton and toward his writings. Not until about the middle of the nineteenth century was the poet's art likely to be judged apart from his political views. And still today religious affiliation tends to affect interpretations of the epic. Lewis condemns as mistaken any criticism which forces heretical elements into the foreground and asserts that "this poem was accepted as orthodox by many generations of acute readers well grounded in Theology." [3] But as most existing Christian sects follow, in the main, the Augustinian pattern, Lewis might with equal fairness apply his statement to practically all Protestant systems. Nor is it true, as he maintains, that acute readers grounded in theology have always accepted *Paradise Lost* as orthodox. Since the publication of the epic, and long before the discovery of *The Christian Doctrine*, critics of the poem in every generation have been aware of Milton's anti-Trinitarianism.

In 1732, a correspondent to *The Gentleman's Magazine*, signing himself "A.Z.," objects to Bentley's evaluation of Milton: "The kindest excuse I can make for him [Bentley] is, that he scatters both his Censures and Praises at random, has injudiciously condemned *Milton* for his Poetry, and praised him for his religious Principles." Seven years later, in a letter to the same magazine, "Theophilus" accuses Milton of Arianism: "Whether he was a Christian or no, could scarce be determined (I believe) by any thing that occurs in his Poem; much less could one determine, that Way, what Sect he was of; for he seems to shape his Religion so, as to give the most Scope for the Exercise of his own fine Imagination, and to leave the greatest Room for Scenery, and varied Amusement; but, whether for that Reason or no, I will not say, he has certainly adopted the *Arian Principle into his Paradise Lost*." The critic of Newton's edition of the epic for *The Monthly Review*, in 1749–50, says of Milton: "He was indeed led away from the church by early Prejudices; in his

---

[3] *Ibid.*, p. 81.

younger years he joined with the presbyterians, in his middle age he judged the independents and anabaptists to come nearest the primitive practice; and in his more advanced age was not a professed member of any particular sect, frequented no place of public worship, nor used any religious rite in his family. But if he was of any denomination, he was at last a sort of a quietist, and rather an enthusiast than an infidel."

The reviewer of Godwin's *Lives of Edward and John Philips* for *The British Critic* of 1816 evidently felt that Milton's writings had been used more than once as a bludgeon with which to belabor the Church. In his scurrilous and intensely partisan review of Godwin's biography, he writes: "We trust the Church is not yet in danger; but when an attack is insidiously made upon its fundamental discipline, and the authority of Milton is again made to bear against its bulwarks, we render good service to our country by attempting to show the value of that authority, and to expose the ascertained qualities of the person who adduces it."

Among early annotators of *Paradise Lost*, Newton, Bentley, the Richardsons, Colton, Joseph Warton, and Warburton suspected that the epic contained Arian views.

I do not, however, intend to imply that *Paradise Lost* has been thought heretical or even unorthodox by the great majority of its readers. Many men with religious training and considerable discernment have held the epic to be a bulwark of orthodoxy. The letter by "Theophilus" quoted above upon Milton's Arianism was shortly refuted by another in *The Gentleman's Magazine* in 1738, which answered the charge merely by citing Addison, who in his famous critique remarked that Milton chose "to confine himself to such thoughts as are drawn from the Books of the most Orthodox Divines, and to such Expressions as may be met with in Scripture." Dr. Samuel Johnson thought Milton "to have been untouched by any heretical peculiarity of opinion." Hayley, in his biography of the poet, asserted: "A devotional taste is as requisite for a full enjoyment of Milton, as a taste for poetry." Cowper, in his edition of the Latin and Italian poems, wrote: "Milton is the poet of Chrisitans: an Infidel may have an ear for the harmony of his numbers, may be aware of the dignity of his expressions, and in some degree of the sublimity of his conceptions, but the unaffected and masculine piety, which was his true inspirer, and is the very soul of his poem, he will either not perceive, or it will offend him." The defense of orthodoxy in *Paradise Lost* came to something of a climax in the outrage of the reviewer of Bryon's "Cain" for *The British Critic* in 1822.

But it has been argued that Lord B. has done no more than Milton did before him with universal applause; and upon one occasion, a challenge was thrown out that every passage in "Cain" could be paralleled, line by line, from the "Paradise Lost." Now, excepting the Bible, we know no book for which we feel so profound a veneration as we do for this latter poem, and to be told all at once that nothing in this outlawed pamphlet of blasphemy is worse than many things that are to be found in what we are accustomed to call a Divine work, is somewhat startling. That any one should dare to make this assertion, and that any one should believe it is another proof of the lamentable neglect into which Milton's writings have generally fallen, and shows that this mighty Poet, like Lord Bacon, though much talked of, is now little more than the shadow of a name.

Elsewhere in the review *Paradise Lost* is declared to be a book "which not seldom occupies the devout attention of our wives and sisters alternately even with the word of God itself."

With the discovery of *The Christian Doctrine* and its publication in Latin and in an English translation by Sumner in 1825, the scholarly world in general had cause to re-evaluate its conception of the Miltonic theology.[4] At least one critic denied that the work was Milton's.[5] Others were ready to weep at the poet's apostasy. Some felt that the *De Doctrina* should not have been published and that certainly printing a translation was ill-advised. Still, most reviewers took the discovery of Milton's true beliefs in stride, and many refused even to admit surprise. A writer for *The Oriental Herald* (1825), for example, seemed very well satisfied with the poet's newly revealed tenets.

I propose . . . to take an early opportunity of showing . . . by what arguments Milton had been led to conclusions in theology very opposite to those which have assumed the high-sounding appellation, *orthodox*. Nor will it be uninteresting to discover how he has occasionally anticipated the criticisms proposed by learned theologians of this later age.

Christians of all persuasions, and, indeed, all liberal-minded persons, must be gratified to mark the mental progress of an inquirer so disinterested as Milton.

The tolerance which characterizes this comment was echoed by re-

---

[4] For a review of critical opinion upon this occasion, see Francis Mineka, "The Critical Reception of Milton's *De Doctrina Christiana*," *University of Texas Studies in English* (Austin, 1943), pp. 115–47.

[5] *Milton Memorial Lectures, 1908*, ed. Percy W. Ames (London, 1909), p. 213; Thomas Burgess, *Protestant Union* (London, 1826), pp. xlvii–xlix. See also W. Carlos Martyn, *Life and Times of John Milton* (New York, 1866), p. 292.

viewers for *Blackwood's Magazine, The Gentleman's Magazine, The New Monthly Magazine,* and *The British Critic.* Macaulay, in his famous essay for *The Edinburgh Review* (August, 1825), did not grant the treatise any lasting importance.

> The book, were it far more orthodox or far more heretical than it is, would not much edify or corrupt the present generation. The men of our time are not to be converted or perverted by quartos. A few more days, and this essay will follow the *Defensio Populi* to the dust and silence of the upper shelf. The name of its author, and the remarkable circumstances attending its publication, will secure to it a certain degree of attention. For a month or two it will occupy a few minutes of chat in every drawing room, and a few columns in every magazine; and it will then, to borrow the elegant language of the play-bills, be withdrawn to make room for the forthcoming novelties.

When the *De Doctrina* was published, it was felt by many that, though the treatise might indeed be heterodox, perhaps even heretical, *Paradise Lost* was nevertheless impeccably orthodox. The opinion expressed in *Blackwood's Magazine* in 1825 was typical: "The entire scheme of Paradise Lost is, by fair interpretation, orthodox. Trapp pronounces it to be so in every part. . . . The sins against orthodoxy in our great epic, are those of omission, not commisssion."
In our own time there is by no means unanimous agreement as to the orthodoxy or lack of it in *Paradise Lost.* Saurat pronounced the epic daringly unorthodox; Tillyard, Conklin, Waldock, Kelley, Hughes, and Hanford affirm the heretical nature of elements in the poem. Lewis, who of course does not deny the recusancy of the treatise, yet insists that the heresies in *Paradise Lost* "reduce themselves to something very small and rather ambiguous." [6] What Lewis is willing to label heretical, however, appears rather difficult to say. By implication he defines orthodoxy as a collection of beliefs held "always and everywhere and by all." [7] But this definition is less than useful. The only functional one, which should be understood as consistently employed in this study, equates orthodoxy with acceptance of all doctrines formally articulated by an ecclesiastical authority; it equates unorthodoxy with opinions antagonistic to a fundamental article of the Christian faith and heresy with a willful and pertinacious adherence to such opinions in the face of warning, remonstrance, and rebuke. This is not Milton's view, nor is it possible for any reformist to subscribe to it; for where there is no authority other

---

[6] *Lewis,* p. 89.
[7] *Ibid.,* p. 81.

than personal exegesis there can be no orthodoxy and hence no heresy except, as Milton declares, "in the will and choice professedly against scripture." [8]

Those who judge *Paradise Lost* on the grounds of orthodoxy necessarily rely (for semantic convenience quite apart from personal conviction) upon dogma which is basically Roman Catholic. Accordingly, they must exclude from consideration any embellishment of the Christian story upon which no official position has been taken; in other words, matters of faith and matters of fiction must be kept separate. Just as the Church tolerated the traditional characterization of Noah's wife as a shrew in the mystery plays until interest in the character began to overshadow the didactic import of the drama, so no Catholic would be likely to take offense at extra-Biblical particulars in, for example, Milton's Hell, however pagan in origin. These are not "small heresies," to use Lewis' term; they are not heresies at all. It may be doubted that there is such a thing as a small heresy. For any deviation from authorized belief, if it is held responsibly and reasonably, must be reconciled with the whole of a theology; and in the process of reconciliation, concomitant and graver breaches of orthodoxy inevitably develop. Milton's mortalism, for example, might be regarded as a minor or merely eccentric quarrel with received opinion; but, as his mortalism is a logical extension of that materialism which posits matter *ex deo* rather than *ex nihilo*, it leads him into a denial of the absolute spirituality of God himself, and no more radical defection from established Christian doctrine than this can be conceived. Actually, the degree to which Milton's opinions are heretical may be determined with comparative ease once they are clearly understood and once a dogmatic position from which to evaluate them has been agreed upon. I will attempt such an evaluation in connection with my synopsis of Milton's theological system.

It is, I think, partly the failure to recognize the pervasively heretical character of Milton's doctrinal concepts which has encouraged critics to attribute individual aspects of the theology of *Paradise Lost* to discrete sources, often contemporary. G. L. Mosse and George Williamson suggest that Milton's mortalism was an outgrowth of

---

[8] John Milton, *Of True Religion*, in *The Prose Works of John Milton*, ed. J. A. St. John (London, Henry G. Bohn, 1848–53), II, 511. Future reference to Milton's prose will be to *Bohn* by volume and page number. I also cite the Columbia Edition by volume and page number: *CE*, VI, 168.

theories revitalized in the seventeenth century.[9] Nathaniel H. Henry points out as significant the mortalist views of Hobbes, the Socinians, and the Baptists.[10] Walter Clyde Curry follows Saurat in the conjecture that Milton's ideas on the creation were inspired by the work of an obscure seventeenth-century physicist, Robert Fludd.[11] Leon Howard argues that Milton's concept of God's retraction in the creation may stem from his knowledge of Ramean logic.[12]

None of these scholars, and for good reason, is willing to go beyond the demonstration of coincidence between the poet's treatment of specific theological details and their appearance in precedent works. To imply that Milton adopted his beliefs in their entirety from any single source (other than the Bible) is far from the purpose of most Miltonists; but it is also unsound to imply that the poet's theological system is a collage of ideas extracted from the utterances of writers distant in time and disparate in fundamental philosophical positions — and this implication inescapably accompanies the search for the origin of an isolated Miltonic tenet.

The number of sources proposed for the theological details which inform *Paradise Lost* has grown so formidable since Greenlaw in 1917 first argued Spenser's influence on Milton's thought that I shall not attempt to assess them individually nor even to offer a comprehensive survey. Analogues for bits of theological lore have been adduced in recent times from the writings of the Church Fathers, from the hexameral literature, from Boethius, Calvin, Servetus, the seventeenth-century Arminians, Chaucer, the Fletchers, and the Cambridge Platonists. Saurat confidently traces "the whole of Milton's philosophy" to the cabala (the esoteric Jewish doctrine), to Robert Fludd, and to the Zohar, a thirteenth-century repository of nonorthodox Jewish traditions.[13] H. F. Fletcher urges Milton's in-

---

[9] George L. Mosse, "Puritan Radicalism and the Enlightenment," *Church History*, XXIX (1960), 424–39; George Williamson, *Seventeenth Century Contexts* (London, 1960).

[10] Nathaniel H. Henry, "Milton and Hobbes: Mortalism and the Intermediate State," *SP*, XLVIII (1951) 234–49. Henry, Mosse, and Williamson link Milton's mortalism with writers and sects contemporaneous with the poet — Overton, the Ranters, Baptists, Mennonites, and Socinians. Henry notes (p. 244) that Bishop Hall had traced the mortalist belief back to Origen.

[11] Walter Clyde Curry, *Milton's Ontology, Cosmogony, and Physics* (Lexington, Va., 1957). See the notes to Chapter II and *passim*. Future reference will be to *Curry*.

[12] Leon Howard, " 'The Invention' of Milton's 'Great Argument': A Study of the Logic of 'God's Ways to Men,' " *HLQ*, IX (1945), 149–73.

[13] Denis Saurat, *Milton: Man and Thinker* (London, 1946), p. 231. Future reference will be to *Saurat*.

debtedness to Hebraic writers — Levi ben Gerson, Rashi, Ibn Ezra, and Yosippon.[14] Grant McColley is persuaded that Milton's ideas are so similar to those expressed in the Book of Enoch that Milton must have had access to this work, despite rather substantial evidence to the contrary.[15] In his *The Common Expositor* and in several articles Arnold Williams contends that aspects of the theology of *Paradise Lost* are derived from the Renaissance commentaries upon Genesis.[16] W. C. Curry relates a number of Milton's central ideological concepts to Plotinus and the later neo-Platonists.[17]

To be sure, Milton's unparalleled erudition, the omnivorous character of his reading, and his linguistic accomplishments frustrate any attempts to narrow the sphere of possible influences upon the formulation of his thought, while strengthening automatically the legitimacy of arguments for the significance of analogous passages. At the same time, it is well to heed the warning of Robert Adams in his *Ikon*:

For if we suppose that Milton was capable of only a given amount of reading in the thirty years of adult life before he lost his eyesight, that quantum — however generously we estimate it after discounting sleep, "gawdy days," domestic life and duties, labor in a vocation, and other necessary activities — is pretty well taken care of by the readings and rereadings of which he has left evidence. The total of those speculative readings which he "may well have undertaken" should not exceed the leisure time available to an already heavily overtaxed pair of eyes. After a while, the more little guesses we put forward the less probable any of them look.[18]

Since the appearance of Professor George Taylor's *Milton's Use of Du Bartas* (Cambridge, Mass., 1934), the conviction has increased that many details in *Paradise Lost* are "theological commonplaces." Taylor's brief for the influence of Sylvester's translation of *La Semaine* certainly deserved a favorable hearing; but the orthodoxy of Du Bartas' Christian doctrine restricts Milton's alleged use of the compendium to particulars quite incidental or at best peripheral to his serious dogmatic beliefs. It seems to me, also, that the assump-

---

[14] Harris Francis Fletcher, "Milton and Yosippon," *SP*, XXI (1924), 496–501; *Milton's Semitic Studies and Some Manifestations of Them in His Poetry* (Chicago, 1926); *Milton's Rabbinical Readings* (Urbana, Ill., 1930).

[15] Grant McColley, "The Book of Enoch and *Paradise Lost*," *Harvard Theological Review*, XXXI (1938), 21–39.

[16] Arnold Williams, "Milton and the Renaissance Commentaries on Genesis," *MP*, XXXVII (1939–40), 263–78; "Renaissance Commentaries on 'Genesis' and Some Elements of the Theology of *Paradise Lost*," *PMLA*, LVI (1941), 151–64.

[17] *Curry*, pp. 22, 41, 50–58, and *passim*.

[18] Robert Adams, *Ikon: John Milton and the Modern Critics* (Ithaca, N.Y., 1955), p. 129.

tion of Milton's discovery in Du Bartas even of indisputably traditional lore may be somewhat impulsive; a reader of Milton's
antiquarian bent might find much of Du Bartas quite familiar.
Moreover, in any effort to analyze Milton's religious thought, the
distinction between "theological commonplaces" and matters of philosophic principle should be maintained whenever possible. Milton's
debt to Du Bartas for hexameral details of a descriptive as opposed
to doctrinal nature may have been considerable. That Milton, the
last great hexameral writer, borrowed eclectically to embellish his
religious history from the mass of imaginative Christian literature
extending from Basil through Raleigh goes without saying. That
Milton's central theological beliefs were derived from such material,
however, is a supposition completely untenable.

Such a supposition is at variance with Milton's character, with his
attitude toward source material, and with the fact that *The Christian
Doctrine* was written. Neither Milton's pride in his intellectual abilities, nor his profound concern with religious truth, nor the conviction, intensified by his blindness, that he was God-illumined would
have allowed him to shape the primarily theological action of his epic
on the basis of ideas taken at random from the entire store of religious and secular literature. In questions of faith, only the Bible
could be the arbiter for Milton, who, always impatient with secondary sources, treated the Apocrypha, the Church Fathers, and all other
"authorities" with a skepticism in inverse proportion to their proximity to the fountainhead of truth.[19] Milton's reliance upon the
Bible to the exclusion of all other sources is obvious to anyone acquainted with *The Christian Doctrine*, which is very largely composed of Biblical proof texts. The heterodox portions of the treatise
are as fully documented as the orthodox. The existence of *The Christian Doctrine* means to any student of *Paradise Lost* that, as Kelley
maintains, a decisive aid in interpreting the epic is at hand.[20] There
are, of course, some who remain unconvinced by Kelley's thesis. But
the contention that the dogma of the epic differs in any important
respect from that of the treatise rests upon one of two assumptions:
that the poet changed his mind between the composition of the
works, or that he espoused a set of views for public approbation

---

[19] Grant McColley, "Milton's Technique of Source Adaptation," *SP*, XXXV
(1938), 61–110.
[20] Maurice Kelley, *This Great Argument* (Princeton, N.J., 1941), p. 7. Future
reference will be to *Kelley*.

which he privately despised. So little time (if any)[21] elapsed between the writing of the *De Doctrina* and *Paradise Lost* that the first assumption would justify a charge of vacillation or indifference of conviction, while the second would brand him a coward or cynic. It is far more plausible to conjecture that *The Christian Doctrine* was written in part as a kind of preliminary exercise to the composition of *Paradise Lost,* just as, perhaps, the *History of Britain* was compiled as a compendium of background material suitable for use in the national epic he at one time planned to write.

In his study of *The Christian Doctrine,* Professor George N. Conklin concludes that Milton was influenced in the formulation of his views only by the Bible and, working through his own spirit, by the Word of God. He disagrees with Kelley, who attributes to the early seventeenth-century divines Wolleb and Ames a part in the shaping of the poet's theology; Conklin admits the likelihood of their contributing to the form of the treatise, but he believes that they "would have deplored its contents." [22] I think that Conklin is more right than wrong when he insists that personal Biblical exegesis is responsible for the theological dicta of the *De Doctrina,* both heretical and orthodox. Yet Conklin's thesis seems to me an oversimplification. No one approaches an intellectual problem unaffected by experience, and Milton's interest in doctrinal questions began in his early youth. He read extensively in patristic and later theological writings. He cites hundreds of authors; he argues with them and from them; he is always aware of his own doctrinal position in relation to theirs. With the works of Catholic, Protestant, and Jew he was familiar; he knew Augustine, Calvin, and Josephus. His linguistic accomplishments enabled him to read Hebrew, Latin, and Greek. He studied the orthodox and he studied the heretical. When he set for himself the task of interpreting the Bible, did he make no use of this arduous preparation? I cannot believe it.

Though I can agree in part with Conklin that Milton's heresies in the *De Doctrina* "derive largely from his method of Biblical criticism," I do not agree that either the method itself or the heresies are unique with Milton. I do not agree because, as this study is committed to showing, Milton's way of reading the Bible and the

---

[21] Kelley considers the *De Doctrina* and *Paradise Lost* to be "apparently synchronous works" (p. 192).

[22] George N. Conklin, *Biblical Criticism and Heresy in Milton* (New York, 1949), p. 39.

theological system which resulted from it are markedly similar to those of Origen Adamantius. And though my familiarity with other primitive Christians is by no means as thorough as that which several years of concentration allow me to claim with the works of Origen, I nevertheless most confidently state that Milton's system as a whole is in accord with the thought of the ante-Nicene Fathers, that his views are far more often coincidental with theirs than with the views of Augustine and all who follow him. I shall try in the following chapter to present the climate of opinion in which Origen wrote. It is this climate of opinion which, I think, more than any other, stimulated the mind of Milton during his search for religious truth.

I was led to examine the writings of the primitive Church by the opening sentence of the Dedication to *The Christian Doctrine*:

Since the commencement of the last century, when religion began to be restored from the corruptions of more than thirteen hundred years to something of its original purity, many treatises of theology have been published, conducted according to sounder principles, wherein the chief heads of Christian doctrine are set forth sometimes briefly, sometimes in a more enlarged and methodical order.

.What Milton hoped to recover in his treatise, as he tells us in the first part of this topic sentence, was religion in its original purity, uncluttered by more than thirteen hundred years of theological corruption. Recent theological writers, he believed, had been on the right track — they had begun to restore religion "to something of its original purity" — but, evidently, they had not achieved the goal of complete restoration. Milton describes his preparation for the writing of the treatise:

I entered upon an assiduous course of study in my youth, beginning with the books of the Old and New Testaments in their original languages, and going diligently through a few of the shorter systems of the divines, in imitation of whom I was in the habit of classing under certain heads whatever passages of Scripture occurred for extraction, to be made use of hereafter as occasion might require.[23]

From this it is clear that the form of *The Christian Doctrine* derives from "the shorter systems of the divines"; it is also clear that they exerted no further influence. His reading in the standard theologians (unspecified but surely including Augustine and Aquinas) which followed this initial preparation, according to his own account, rather quickly left him disillusioned.

At length I resorted with increased confidence to some of the more copious theological treatises, and to the examination of the arguments advanced

---

[23] *Bohn, A Treatise on Christian Doctrine*, IV, 2–3; *CE*, XIV, 5.

by the conflicting parties respecting certain disputed points of faith. But, to speak the truth with freedom as well as candour, I was concerned to discover in many instances adverse reasonings either evaded by wretched shifts, or attempted to be refuted, rather speciously than with solidity, by an affected display of formal sophisms, or by a constant recourse to the quibbles of the grammarians; while what was most pertinaciously espoused as the true doctrine, seemed often defended, with more vehemence than strength of argument, by misconstructions of Scripture, or by the hasty deduction of erroneous inferences. Owing to these causes, the truth was sometimes as strenuously opposed as if it had been an error or a heresy — while errors and heresies were substituted for the truth, and valued rather from deference to custom and the spirit of party than from the authority of Scripture.[24]

Milton denies learning anything from the "more copious theological treatises"; but this period of reading must have been of vital importance, if only in a negative way, to the fashioning of his own theology. He became cognizant, for example, of "certain disputed points of faith" and of the arguments advanced by theologians upon them. If he disagreed with the "wretched shifts," the "adverse reasonings," the "formal sophisms" (surely Aquinas), the "quibbles of the grammarians," the "misconstructions of Scripture," and the "erroneous inferences" of the theologians, he nevertheless thoroughly acquainted himself with the problems which faced the writer of doctrine.

He found, too, that the ideas which he espoused were not orthodox. Several paragraphs in the preface to his treatise demonstrate his complete awareness of the fact.

But I do not expect from candid and judicious readers a conduct so unworthy of them, — that like certain unjust and foolish men, they should stamp with the invidious name of heretic or heresy whatever appears to them to differ from the received opinions, without trying the doctrine by a comparison with Scripture testimonies.[25]

Milton was not afraid of heresy. He was far more afraid of blindly following the doctrines developed by men and accepted simply because they were ancient and traditional. Always he worked backward toward the sources of Christianity; and, as Conklin and McColley ably argue, the Bible was his ultimate and only undisputed authority. But he discovered much in the writings of the earliest theologians with which he could be in accord.

I had not even read any of the works of heretics, so called, when the mistakes of those who are reckoned for orthodox, and their incautious han-

---

[24] *Bohn*, IV, 3; *CE*, XIV, 5–6.
[25] *Bohn*, IV, 7; *CE*, XIV, 13.

dling of Scripture first taught me to agree with their opponents whenever those opponents agreed with Scripture.[26]

Though Milton in the *De Doctrina* declares his readiness to credit the "heretics, so called" of post-Apostolic times with an understanding of the Word of God, in *Of Reformation* he succinctly notes his grounds for regarding their utterances with the same mistrust which he feels later orthodox theologians deserve: "1. The best times were spreadingly infected. 2. The best men of those times were foully tainted. 3. The best writings of those men were dangerously adulterated."[27] No one could be more caustic than Milton when, as a polemicist, it served his purpose to belittle the authority of the Fathers: "Who is ignorant of the foul errors, the ridiculous wresting of Scripture, the heresies, the vanities thick sown through the volumes of Justin Martyr, Clemens, Origen, Tertullian, and others of eldest time?"[28] In his elaboration of this rhetorical question Milton singles out with scorn Justin Martyr's preachment that the devils resulted from the union of angels with women, and he excoriates Tertullian for presuming to condemn St. Paul when the Bible upholds him. Yet, and this seems to me significant, Milton offers what amounts to an apology for Origen, blaming the flaws in his works upon the adulterations of others: ". . . who knows not how many superstitious works are ingraffed into the legitimate writings of the fathers? And of those books that pass for authentic, who knows what hath been tampered withal, what hath been razed out, what hath been inserted? . . . that which Sulpitius writes concerning Origen's books gives us cause vehemently to suspect there hath been packing of old."[29]

In *The Reason of Church Government*, Milton speaks of how unwillingly he has been forced by circumstances to

leave a calm and pleasing solitariness, fed with cheerful and confident thoughts, to embark in a troubled sea of noises and hoarse disputes, put from beholding the bright countenance of truth in the quiet and still air of delightful studies, to come into the dim reflection of hollow antiquities sold by the seeming bulk, and there be fain to club quotations with men whose learning and belief lies in marginal stuffings, who, when they have, like good sumpters, laid ye down their horse-loads of citations and fathers at your door, with a rhapsody of who and who were bishops here or there, yet may take off their packsaddles, their day's work is done.[30]

---

[26] *Bohn*, IV, 8–9; *CE*, XIV, 15.
[27] *Bohn, Of Reformation in England*, II, 378; *CE*, III$_1$, 20.
[28] *Bohn*, II, 379; *CE*, III$_1$, 21.
[29] *Bohn*, II, 380; *CE*, III$_1$, 22.
[30] *Bohn, The Reason of Church Government*, II, 481; *CE*, III$_1$, 241–42.

Here, of course, Milton's anger is directed at contemporary theological disputants; yet the scathing "horse-loads of citations and fathers"
reflects a judgment not infrequently encountered in his writings.
Sheer bulk of testimony, no matter how venerable the witnesses, did
not for Milton insure the determination of truth.

Milton's attitude toward the Fathers, however, is often favorable,
particularly when they happen to agree with the view he is trying
to buttress. The time of Constantine "was an age of the church, both
ancient and cried up still for the most flourishing in knowledge and
pious government since the apostles." [31] The age of Justin Martyr
he calls "those pure and next to apostolic times." [32] And when he
wishes to make a point upon which he is in accord with the Fathers, as
he does in *Tetrachordon*, he carefully smoothes the way for a pro-
pitious reception of his ancient authories.

This opinion which I bring, hath been favoured, and by some of those
affirmed, who in their time were able to carry what they taught, had they
urged it, through all Christendom; or to have left it such a credit with
all good men, as they who could not boldly use the opinion, would have
feared to censure it. But since by his appointment on whom the times and
seasons wait, every point of doctrine is not fatal to be thoroughly sifted out
in every age, it will be enough for me to find, that the thoughts of wisest
heads heretofore, and hearts no less reverenced for devotion, have tended
this way, and contributed their lot in some good measure towards this
which hath here been attained.[33]

A passage from *Of Prelatical Episcopacy* offers, I think, the most
reliable index to the use Milton makes of the primitive Christians
and to the value which he places upon their authority.

He that thinks it the part of a well-learned man to have read diligently the
ancient stories of the church, and to be no stranger in the volumes of the
fathers, shall have all judicious men consenting with him; not hereby to
control and new fangle the scripture, God forbid! but to . . . gather up
wherever we find the remaining sparks of original truth, wherewith to stop
the mouths of our adversaries, and to bridle them with their own curb,
who willingly pass by that which is orthodoxal in them, and studiously cull
out that which is commentitious, and best for their turns, not weighing
the fathers in the balance of scripture, but scripture in the balance of
the fathers.[34]

What "sparks of original truth" which remain valid when the Fathers are weighed "in the balance of scripture" did Milton discover
in his study of those who wrote before religion needed "to be re-

---

[31] *Bohn, Tetrachordon*, III, 421; *CE*, IV, 215.

[32] *Bohn*, III, 416; *CE*, IV, 208.

[33] *Bohn*, III, 415; *CE*, IV, 206–7.

[34] *Bohn, Of Prelatical Episcopacy*, II, 435; *CE*, III$_1$, 101.

stored from the corruptions of more than thirteen hundred years"? This question must remain unanswered, though by "mouse-hunting" through indices (to use Milton's term of opprobrium) it is easy enough to come up with an impressive number of religious tenets common to the ante-Nicene Fathers and to Milton. But no final proof of Milton's indebtedness can be put forward, and refutation of claims would follow swiftly, since other works of different times and places are sure to yield to the continuing search an abundance of analogues. Still, Milton leaves us in no doubt that the post-Apostolic era, being the freest from corruption, was the most congenial to his mind. When we resist the temptation to compare the fragments of Milton's thought with ideas similarly parted from their contexts, when we look for a theological system which is a coherent and logically independent whole, Milton's own words encourage us to begin our investigation with works uncluttered by centuries of interpolation.

It will be the business of the following chapter to demonstrate the general tenor of ante-Nicene Christianity and to argue that Origen is its fittest representative.

In this monograph, no system other than Origen's will be studied as a whole, and no views but his will be compared in detail with those of Milton. If it can be shown, as I believe it can, that in its orthodox parts, in its heterodox parts, and in what were to become theological commonplaces, the doctrine of Origen in its entirety differs in few major respects from the doctrine of Milton, then, at least, the partisans of sources more remote from the times in which the New Testament came into being can be challenged to produce a resemblance equally complete.

CHAPTER TWO

ANTE-NICENE CHRISTIANITY, ORIGEN, AND HERESY

Milton's anti-Trinitarianism makes it reasonable to suppose that he thought of the Council of Nicea in A.D. 325 as a terminal date for the golden age of "original purity" in religion. In the brief survey of early Christianity contained in this chapter, no writer whose works are still extant is knowingly excluded from mention, provided that his utterances are doctrinal in nature and that his influence was mainly felt before this date.[1]

Christian dogma may profitably be traced back to the teachings of the Hellenistic Jews in Alexandria. These men, cultivated and sophisticated, from whose ranks Philo (b. c. 20–10 B.C.) may be taken as representative, lived in a time which allowed great intellectual freedom, and in a place where members of many races, cultures, and religions mingled in comparative amity. They were the guiding force behind a new religious thought which has been called by Harnack "Cosmopolitanism." In this system, which was composed very largely of elements drawn from Judaism and combined with others from the philosophies of Plato, Pythagoras, and the Stoics, the ancient ceremonial laws of Judaism were generally unimportant, while the worship of a single God and the belief in a future existence were

---

[1] The works of a number of the ante-Nicene Fathers have been lost: Quadratus, Aristo of Pella, Miltiades, Apollinaris of Hierapolis, Pantaenus, Ammonius of Alexandria, Firmilian of Caesarea, Lucian of Antioch. Another group, so far as I have been able to ascertain, made no statement upon matters which fall within the scope of this monograph: Ignatius of Antioch, Polycarp of Smyrna, Aristides of Athens, the unknown author of the "Epistle to Diognetes," Hegesippus, Dionysius of Alexandria, Hesychius, Cyprian, and Peter of Alexandria. I have not looked into what remains of early heretical writings, nor into the papal and episcopal defenses of the second century against heresies and schisms.

essential. Yet the Old Testament, especially the Pentateuch, was held to be the source of all true knowledge of God.[2]

Basing his thought upon this neo-Judaism, Philo, one of the greatest figures in the field of theological speculation, developed a philosophy which has had much to do with the final shape of Western Christianity. He began with a fundamentally Platonic idea, the dualism of God and the world, of spirit and matter. In order that God might affect matter, Philo, following a concept originally stoic, posited a secondary deity, the Logos, who was granted the intelligence of God and who was able to operate with God's power. Philo regarded the Logos as that aspect of God which is intelligible, which turns toward the world. The Logos is that which bridges the primal dualism. He is the first creature, the Viceroy of God, a power and a person, an active and divine being. He is also the principle of the world, the spirit of the world, even, perhaps, the world itself. Man, the inhabitant of the world, resembles the Logos; for man comprehends within himself both spirit and matter. His spirit is divine; but it is fettered to a material body. By freeing himself of his material body through habitual contemplation of the divine spirit glimpsed in the world, man may draw closer to the Logos and through him to an eternity with God.[3]

Upon the earliest Christians the Philonic teachings apparently made no impression; but by the beginning of the second century, their influence began to be felt. At the end of the century Philo's ideas pervaded the entire Christian world.[4] Logos Christianity was permanently established among the ante-Nicene Fathers. It was natural that Philo's system should appeal to them. They had been born pagans, most of them, and converted to Christianity as adults. They were well-educated men, readers of secular literature, often students of the Greek philosophers. By these early followers of Christ, Philo, whose thought drew very largely upon the teachings of Plato, was welcomed almost as an old acquaintance. The merging of the satisfying new religion which they had discovered with the intellectual and aesthetic virtues of the Greek learning they had long known brought them the best of two worlds.

The major Philonic elements which were early assimilated by Christian writers are as follows:

---

[2] Adolph Harnack, *History of Dogma*, tr. Neil Buchanan (Boston, 1895), I, 107–35. Future reference to this edition will be to *Harnack* by volume and page number.

[3] *Ibid.*, pp. 10–11.

[4] *Ibid.*, pp. 113–14.

1. A belief in an Absolute God, bare of all quality and hence beyond comprehension and incapable of creation.

2. The idea of a creating agent, the manifested reason emanating from God's Wisdom and as a result of God's free and unnecessitated will. The agent is variously styled by Philo as the firstborn, the Son, Reason, Logos, the Word of God; but, of course, he is not linked directly with Christ. The Logos is a subordinate God, a distinct person or entity.

3. The Logos is the creator of the world and the inspirer of all wise men, whatever their religious beliefs. Philo bridges the chasm between the Old Testament prophets and the Greeks, who, he thought, had borrowed their ideas from Moses.

4. The gods of nonbelievers are really either angels or demons.[5]

Among the earliest of extant Christian documents, written before A.D. 138 and undoubtedly affected by the precepts of Philo, is the anonymous "Epistle of Barnabas." Its author proclaims the pre-existence of Christ, placing him with God at the creation of the world and identifying him as the one to whom were spoken the words "Let us make man after our image and likeness." God is invisible and incomprehensible; man can know him only through the incarnate Christ. "For if he had not come in the flesh how could men have been saved by beholding Him? Since looking upon the Sun which is to cease to exist, and is the work of His hands, their eyes are not able to bear his rays." The parable of the sun and its beams is characteristic of Alexandrian theology. "Barnabas" is a follower of chiliasm, a sect whose main tenet is that the six days of creation typify six thousand years, after which the world will come to judgment and Christ's thousand-year reign upon earth will begin.[6]

"The Shepherd of Hermas," written before A.D. 150, presents a dualistic system in which there are two divine persons, the Father and the Holy Spirit, related as father and son. This Holy Spirit is the creator of all things; it came to men in the flesh; incarnate, it rose to a place of habitation with God. Thus "The Shepherd" treats of two divine persons, one of whom is an adoptionist Saviour. In both "The Shepherd" and "Barnabas" the second person is a subordinate deity.[7]

Another early chiliast was Papias of Hierapolis (fl. A.D. 130):

---

[5] *Ibid.*, pp. 107–35.

[6] *Ante-Nicene Christian Library*, ed. Alexander Roberts and James Donaldson (Edinburgh, various dates), I, iii, 108–9, 127–28. Future reference will be to *ANCL* by volume and page number.

[7] *Ibid.*, pp. 386–87.

". . . there will be a millennium after the resurrection from the dead, when the personal reign of Christ will be established on this earth." [8]

Justin Martyr, who died in A.D. 165, conceived an Absolute God, comprehensible only through a Logos who was originally an attribute of God and who was generated by an act of his will. The Logos is equated with reason in man. Justin, like Philo, thinks that the Greek philosophers, instructed by the Logos, borrowed their ideas from Moses. The angels of God, according to Justin, have bodies and take nourishment. He, also, is a chiliast: "But I and others are right-minded Christians in all points and are assured that there will be a resurrection of the dead and a thousand years in Jerusalem which will then be built, adorned, and enlarged." [9] Justin admits, however, that not all good Christians hold this view. Concerning his anti-Trinitarianism and his subordinationist ideas there can be no doubt.

There is another God and Lord under the Creator of the universe, who is also called Angel, because he announces to men what the Creator of the universe — above whom there is no other God — wishes to declare. . . . He who is said to have appeared to Abraham, to Jacob, and to Moses, and is called God, is other than the God who made all things. I say, in number, but not in will; for he never did anything except what the Creator of the universe — over whom there is no other God — willed him to do and say.[10]

Tatian (fl. A.D. 176) was a disciple of Justin; it is therefore not remarkable that his language is similar to that of his master. He thinks of God's power as the beginning of the Logos. Before the world was created, all things were with God. The Logos existed potentially in him. By a simple act of God's will, the "Logos springs forth; and . . . becomes the first-begotten work of the Father." The Logos is an inferior person.[11]

Athenagoras of Athens (fl. A.D. 170) argues the impossibility of more than one infinite God:

If there were from the beginning two or more gods, they were either in one and the same place, or each of them separately in his own. In one and the same place they could not be. For, if they are gods, they are not alike; but because they are uncreated they are unlike: for created things are like their patterns; but the uncreated are unlike, being neither produced from anyone, nor formed after the pattern of anyone. . . . But if, on the contrary, each of them exists separately, since he that made the world is above

---

[8] *Ibid.*, p. 445.
[9] Justin Martyr, *Dialogue with Trypho*, in *The Fathers of the Church*, ed. Ludwig Schopp *et al.* (New York, 1948), VI, 277.
[10] *Ibid.*, pp. 233-34.
[11] *ANCL*, III, 9.

the things created, and about the things he has made and set in order, where can the other or the rest be?[12]

Theophilus of Antioch (fl. A.D. 180) speaks of God as supreme, without beginning, invisible, unbegotten, immutable, and incapable of being comprehended in space. The Logos is originally in him as an attribute, wisdom. "God, when about to make those things he had designed, begot this Logos; producing, or throwing him out, the first born of every creature." [13] The Logos was a real and separate person used by God to create the world. Theophilus was the first to use the term "trinity"; but by the word he meant no equality of persons; his trinity is made up of God, the Logos, and Wisdom. As far as I can ascertain, Theophilus was the first writer to distinguish between the internal Word immanent in God and the external Logos. Of the origin of the Logos he says: "'God, then having his own Word internal, within his own bowels begot him, emitting him along with wisdom before all things. He had this Word as a helper in the things that were created by him, and by him he made all things." [14] It was the Logos who spoke to Adam in Eden.[15]

Melito of Sardis (fl. A.D. 175) also taught the pre-existence of Christ as the Logos.

> This [Christ] is the firstborn of God
> who was begotten before the morning stars
> who made the light to rise
> who made the day bright
> who parted the darkness
> who fixed the first mark for creation
> who hung the earth in its place
> who dried up the abyss
> who spread out the firmament
> who brought order to the world.[16]

Irenaeus of Lyons (b. A.D. 150) emphasized in his teaching that there was only one true God, the creator of the world, the God of the Old Testament, the Father of the Logos; and one Son, the Logos, Christ, Jesus, Saviour, and Lord. He denies that anyone can understand the generation of the Son:

If anyone says to us "how then was the Son produced by the Father?" we reply to him, that no man understands that production or generation

---

[12] Johannes Quasten, *Patrology* (Westminster, Md., 1950–60), I, 232. Future reference will be to *Quasten* by volume and page number.

[13] *ANCL*, III, 88.

[14] *Ibid.*, p. 75.

[15] *Ibid.*, p. 88.

[16] *Quasten*, I, 245.

or calling or by whatever name one may describe his generation, which is
in fact altogether indescribable . . . but the Father only who begot and
the Son who was begotten. Since, therefore, his generation is unspeakable,
those who strive to set forth generations and productions cannot be right
in their mind, inasmuch as they undertake to describe things which are
indescribable.[17]

Yet, for Irenaeus, the Son was not equal with the Father. The Father
sends, the Son is sent; the Father commands, the Son obeys; the
Father knows all things, the Son's knowledge is incomplete; the Son
describes his powers and authority as the gift of the Father. Irenaeus
is famous for his theory of recapitulation, according to which Christ
is the second Adam who renovates and restores mankind: "When he
became incarnate and was made man, he recapitulated in himself
the long history of man, summing up and giving us salvation in order
that we might receive again in Christ Jesus what we had lost in
Adam, that is, the image and likeness of God." [18] The recapitulatory
theory becomes for Irenaeus one of the proofs of the pre-existence of
Christ as the creating Logos: "Now the Lord would not have recapitulated in himself that ancient and primary enmity against the
serpent, fulfilling the promise of the creator, if he had come from
another Father. But as he is one and the same who formed us at the
beginning and sent his Son at the end, the Lord did perform his
command, being made of a woman, by both destroying our adversary
and perfecting man after the image and likeness of God." [19]

Clement of Alexandria (c. A.D. 150–215) is justly called the father of
speculative theology. His system is very like St. Justin's, but it goes
far beyond it in fertility and daring. For Clement the Logos doctrine
is central. The Word is the creator of the universe, the manifesting
agent of God in the Old Testament, the inspiring spirit behind
Greek philosophy and the Christian faith. God, otherwise unsearchable, can be known only through the Logos, who, though greater
than any other being in creation, is still a creature. Clement speaks
of the Logos always as inferior to and dependent upon God. The Son
is said to be "next to the only omnipotent Father"; his power is
granted by the will of the Father; he is the "first created of God,"
the image of God just as man is the image of man.[20] The most outstanding pupil of Clement was Origen, whose beliefs will be examined later in this chapter and in subsequent chapters.

---

[17] *Ibid.*, p. 295.
[18] *Ibid.*, p. 296.
[19] *ANCL*, IX, iii.
[20] Alvan Lamson, *The Church of the First Three Centuries* (Boston, 1860),
p. 89.

The pseudo-Clementine *Recognitions* and *Homilies,* once attributed to Clement of Rome (d. A.D. 101), can be shown by internal
evidence to have been written, at least in part, after A.D. 211. Origen
quotes from them in his *Commentary on Genesis,* which was completed by A.D. 231. The *Recognitions* introduces a concept not found
elsewhere in the works of the early Fathers and one especially interesting to me since I believe that Milton also held it. This is that the
"only begotten Son of God" was "ineffably self-originated." [21] In
the *Homilies* the distinction is made not only between the unbegotten Father and the self-begotten Son but also between the self-
begotten Son and begotten man.[22] The author of the *Homilies*
argues that the Son of God, like man, is of the substance of God but
not of his essence.[23]

Tertullian (A.D. 155–220) differs from most of the early Fathers in
his contention that Christianity and Greek philosophy have little in
common. "What indeed has Athens to do with Jerusalem?" he asks.
"What concord is there between the Academy and the Church?" [24]
Nevertheless, aspects of his theology are very like those of the Fathers
who make use of the ancient Greek writings. Wisdom and Word for
him are both names for the second person; yet he distinguishes between Wisdom who existed with God before the creation and the
Logos who was manifested in a perfect birth at the moment of creation. Of his subordinationist tendencies there can be no doubt:
"There was a time when the Son was not," he asserts. "Before all
things, God was alone, himself a world and place, and all things to
himself." [25] Nothing existed without or beyond God. "Yet he was
not alone; for he had his own reason, which was in himself, with
him. For God is rational." [26] Like most of the other Fathers, Tertullian shared the chiliastic view of the thousand-year reign of Christ
on earth in the New Jerusalem.[27]

Hippolytus of Rome, who died in A.D. 237, left us perhaps the
most thoroughly articulated account of Logos Christianity. He distinguishes, as did Theophilus, the Logos immanent within God from
the external or emitted Word. He describes the generation of the

[21] *ANCL,* III, 188.
[22] *Ibid.,* XVII, 253.
[23] *Ibid.,* pp. 252–53.
[24] *Ibid.,* XV, 9.
[25] *Ibid.,* p. 341.
[26] *Ibid.*
[27] *Ibid.,* VII, 170.

Logos as a tripartite development, teaching that the Word became a person long after his generation.

God, subsisting alone, and having nothing contemporaneous with Himself, determined to create the world. And conceiving the world in mind, and willing and uttering the Word, He made it; and straightway it appeared, formed as it had pleased Him. For us, then, it is sufficient simply to know that there was nothing contemporaneous with God. Beside Him there was nothing; but He, while existing alone, yet existed in plurality. For He was neither without reason, nor wisdom, nor power, nor counsel. All things were in Him, and He was the All. When He willed, and as He willed, He manifested His Word in the times determined by Him, and by Him He made all things. When He wills He does; and when He thinks, He executes; and when He speaks, He manifests; when He fashions, He contrives in wisdom. For all things that are made He forms by reason and wisdom — creating them in reason, and arranging them in wisdom. He made them, then, as He pleased, for He was God. And as the Author, the fellow-Counsellor, and Framer of the things that are in formation, He begot the Word; and as He bears this Word in Himself, and that, too as yet invisible to the world which is created, He makes Him visible; and uttering the voice first, and begetting him as Light of Light, He sent Him forth to the world as its Lord, and His own mind; and whereas He was visible formerly to Himself alone, and invisible to the world which is made, He makes Him visible in order that the world might see Him in His manifestation, and be capable of being saved.

And thus there appeared another beside Himself. But when I say another, I do not mean that there are two Gods, but that it is only light from light, or as water from a fountain, or as a ray from the sun. For there is but one power, which is from the All, from whom cometh this Power, the Word. And this is the mind which came forth into the world, and was manifested as the Son of God. All things, then, are by Him and He alone is of the Father. Who then adduces a multitude of Gods brought in, time after time? For all are shut up, however unwillingly, to admit this fact, that the All runs up into one.[28]

Three phases of the evolution of the Logos are here treated. First, the Word is immanent in God as an attribute. Second, he is produced by God as an invisible agent, who bridges the gap between the unknowable Father and the cognizable Son. Third, he is made visible as the Son. A fourth phase comes into being at the incarnation:

What Son of His own, then, did God send through the flesh but the Word, Whom He addressed as Son because He was to become such (or be begotten) in the future? And He takes the common name for tender affection among men in being called the Son. For neither was the Lord, prior to the incarnation and when by Himself, yet perfect Son, although He was perfect Word, only begotten. Nor could the flesh subsist by itself apart

---

[28] *Ibid.*, IX, 60–62.

from the Word, because it has its subsistence in the Word. Thus, then, one perfect Son of God was manifested.[29]

For Hippolytus, the Word is clearly a created being, existing as the result of a free act of God: "Man is neither God nor angel; make no mistake. If He had willed to make thee God He could have done so; but willing to make thee man, He made thee thus." [30]

Novatian (fl. A.D. 250) argues that since the Logos was begotten before time began, he is eternal; yet, since he has a father, he must have had a beginning.

The Son, then, since He is begotten of the Father, is always in the Father. When I say "always", I do not maintain that He is unborn, but that He is born. Yet He Who is born before all time must be said to have always existed in the Father; for a date in time cannot be fixed for Him Who is before all time. He is eternally in the Father; otherwise the Father were not always Father. At the same time, the Father is antecedent to Him, for the Father must be of necessity before the Son, as Father, inasmuch as He Who knows not an origin must of necessity exist before Him Who has an origin.[31]

Novatian contends that although the Son wields all power, it is power "as delivered, as granted, as by the Father Himself permitted to Him." [32] So concerned is Novatian with maintaining the unity of God that he makes the Son merely the chief of the angels.[33] But fearing the charge that he worships two Gods, he provides for the return of the Son to his original status in God. "The Son is shown to be God, since Divinity is manifestly delivered and granted to Him; yet none the less, the Father is proved to be the One God, while step by step that same Majesty and Divinity, like a billow returning upon itself, sent forth again from the Son Himself, returns and finds its way back to the Father who gave it." [34] Just as the Son is less than the Father, so the Spirit is less than the Son. Novatian is a consistent subordinationist.[35]

Origen's most devoted and also most famous pupil, Gregory Thaumaturgus (A.D. 213–75?), advocates the doctrine of materialism. In answer to the question "Is the soul substantial?" he offers the following Aristotelian reasoning: ". . . if the body is a substance, the soul must also be a substance. For it cannot be, that what only has life

---

[29] Ibid., p. 66.
[30] Quasten, II, 200.
[31] Ibid., p. 227.
[32] ANCL, XIII, 364.
[33] Ibid., p. 381.
[34] Quasten, II, 229–30.
[35] Ibid.

imparted should be a substance, and that what imparts the life should be no substance: unless one should assert that the non-existent is the cause of the existent. . . ." [36]

Commodianus (fl. A.D. 250) suggests lust as the motive for the angelic fall.[37] He is a millenarian and a materialist: "This has pleased Christ, that the dead should rise again, yea, with their bodies; and those, too, whom in this world the fire has burned, when six thousand years are completed, and the world has come to an end. The heaven in the meantime is changed with an altered course, for then the wicked are burnt up with divine fire." Even the wicked, according to Commodianus, take part in the glorious reign of Christ in the latter day: ". . . living again in the world for a thousand years, indeed, that they may serve the saints, and the High One, under a servile yoke. . . ." [38]

Lactantius (fl. A.D. 285) is the originator of a curious dualistic system quite unlike anything in the other Fathers. Before the creation of the world, according to his theory, God produced a Son like himself endowed with perfection. He then generated a second spirit, who, though created good, envied the elder and fell of his own free will into evil. Cast from Heaven, he makes his abode on earth, ruling the north and the west, while God rules the south and the east. According to Lactantius, God created man a microcosmos consisting of two warring elements, soul and body; the soul belongs to God, the body to Satan. Upon the outcome of the war in his own nature depends the salvation or damnation of man. Good cannot exist without evil; man is left by God to choose between them. In this system there is no room for the Holy Spirit. Lactantius was a chiliast, and he believed that only two hundred of the six thousand years which the world had been designed to endure were left. Then the Son would preside at the final doom and begin his thousand-year reign of bliss. At the end of this glorious period, however, the devil would once again rise in power, only to be smitten by the just wrath of God in a fierce three days of destruction, while good men took shelter in the caves of the earth.

Then the righteous shall go forth from their hiding places, and shall find all things covered with carcasses and with bones. . . . But when the thousand years shall be completed, the world shall be renewed by God, and the heavens shall be folded together, and the earth shall be changed, and God

---

[36] *ANCL*, XX, 113–14.
[37] *Ibid.*, XVIII, 435.
[38] *Ibid.*, p. 434.

shall transform men into the similitude of angels. . . . At the same time shall take place that second and public resurrection of all, in which the unrighteous shall be raised to everlasting punishment.[39]

Victorinus of Pettau (d. A.D. 304), also a millenarian, was, according to Quasten, a follower of Origen; only the commentary "On the Apocalypse of John" survives of the works of Victorinus. In this appears an interpretation of Rev. xiii, 3–4: "And his tail drew the third part of the stars of heaven, and cast them upon the earth." Like Milton (cf. *P.L.*, ii, 692), Victorinus equates "the stars of heaven" with the fallen angels. "Now . . . this may be taken in two ways. For many think that he may be able to seduce the third part of the men who believe. But it should be more truly understood of the angels that were subject to him, since he was still a prince when he descended from his estate, he seduced the third part. . . ."[40]

This interpretation is disputed by Methodius (d. A.D. 311), who identifies the "third part of the stars" as heretical men.[41] The extant work of Methodius contains very little which is germane to the theological ideas examined in the present study (he is mainly concerned with virginity, asceticism, and the exegesis of minor prophets). He does, however, declare himself a millenarian.[42]

Though unanimity on particular points of doctrine is not found among the ante-Nicene Fathers, their views as a whole constitute a climate of opinion alien to that considered orthodox in the seventeenth century. The majority of the Fathers were subordinationists. They posited a time when God was alone; some argued that he existed plurally because he was ever accompanied by his attributes, wisdom and power. As a personification of God's wisdom and power, the Logos was thought by several to have developed within the Father (by the psuedo-Clementines the Logos was held to be self-generated); and the Son was consistently regarded as a secondary deity. Invisible at the time of his production, the Logos became manifest, many of the Fathers taught, shortly before or concurrent with the visible creation of the world. By all the Fathers the Logos was called the Son of God, though some, verging upon adoptionism, denied him perfect Sonship until his incarnation as Jesus. He was deemed the immediate creator of all things, exercising in the creation the power of the Father. They reasoned that if the Logos was manifest in

[39] *Ibid.*, XXI, 482.
[40] *Ibid.*, XVIII, 422.
[41] *Ibid.*, XIV, 76–77.
[42] *Ibid.*, pp. 93–94.

Christ, Christ must have existed before the world began. Finally, most were adherents of chiliastic eschatology.

The ante-Nicene Fathers were the spokesmen and the shapers of the primitive Church and in their day the judges of orthodoxy. In the absence of established dogma, religious speculation was encouraged; yet as the result of untrammeled theorizing, and as a reaction to it, the solidification of doctrinal positions originally arbitrary began. The desire for authority brought about the great councils of the Church; it accounts for the formulation of the major creeds.

The ideas which underlie the theological framework of *Paradise Lost* and *The Christian Doctrine* are far closer to those which were current among the ante-Nicene Fathers than to the orthodox conclusions of later ages. That Milton was familiar with the works of many of the Fathers is easy enough to prove. He mentions "The Shepherd of Hermas," Dionysius of Alexandria, Papias, Athenagoras, and Theophilus once each; but he refers many times to "Barnabas," Clement of Rome, Justin, Clement of Alexandria, Origen, Irenaeus, Tertullian, and Lactantius. Hippolytus he cannot have known, for the works of that most interesting writer have all been discovered since the seventeenth century. These, in fact, when they first came to light, were attributed to Origen; some of them were printed in his name, so similar were the views of the two men.[43]

My choice of Origen as representative of the primitive Church and as one best calculated to engage the attention of Milton in his

---

[43] In a most important article, "Milton's Arianism Reconsidered," *Harvard Theological Review*, LII (1959), 9–35, Professor William B. Hunter argues as I have here that the ante-Nicene Fathers exert a strong influence upon Milton's theology. Hunter touches upon the trinities of Plotinus, of Hermes Trismegistus, and of Macrobius; and he shows also the importance to the early Fathers of the system of Philo. "Indeed Wolfson finds the influence of Philo from Justin Martyr to Clement of Alexandria and Lactantius, all of whom seem to have identified the Johannine and Philonic Logos and interpreted the former in terms of the latter" (p. 21). Hunter further mentions Tertullian, Hippolytus, Tatian, and Theophilus as having been in some degree affected by the Philonic disciplines. Hunter concludes: "Thus the various 'Arian' passages in *The Christian Doctrine* and *Paradise Lost* fall into place as revelations of a tradition which antedates even the Council of Nicea." Hunter's articles, and this one in particular, are the best things that have been written upon Milton's theology in recent years.

J. H. Adamson, in "Milton's Arianism," *Harvard Theological Review*, LIII (1960), 276, likewise traces Milton's theological sources to the ante-Nicene Fathers: "While the ultimate source of Milton's trinitarian thought may lie in Neoplatonic writers, I think that neither he nor his contemporaries thought of themselves as having derived their thought from such sources. They seem, rather, to have believed that they had rediscovered in the early Greek Fathers the original and therefore 'true' doctrine of the Trinity. Neo Platonism was thought of as a support, not a source."

search for religious truth was dictated by many considerations. It was arrived at during the course of my preliminary survey of the Fathers as a group. Some of them, like "The Shepherd" and "Barnabas," patently lack the scope of theological speculation for which I was looking. Others, because of some inherent incompatibility with Milton's outlook, were tentatively excluded. Tertullian's somber and legalistic way of reasoning, his scorn for the Greeks ("Quid simile philosophus et Christianus? Graeciae discipulus et coeli?"), and his preoccupation with Christ's death, rather than with the resurrection and the work of redemption, would probably have alienated Milton. The system of Lactantius differs radically from the poet's in respect to its equation of matter with evil, which leads to the hypothesis that God possesses man's soul and the devil his body. This view and Lactantius' treatment of Satan as God's second son verge upon Manichaeanism. As Kathleen Hartwell plausibly concludes in her study, *Lactantius and Milton*, some minor influence may be presumed, especially in matters of style. Lactantius, however, tends to derive the particulars of his theology from his own imagination rather than from the Bible; and Milton was seeking purity in religion, not romance. Clement's work is unsystematic. His questions are subtle and penetrating, but his writings resemble a commonplace book of theological inferences. His title *Stromata* means "carpet," and indeed one is reminded of a richly patterned oriental rug in which no two parts are alike and in which total design is not the aim of the weaver. Clement records his intention of submitting his materials to a proper arrangement, but this ambition was not realized. A failure to give order to their thought is the common flaw among early Christian writers. Often, it is true, they were concerned with other aims — Irenaeus, for example, was bent only on a defense of Christianity against the Gnostics. It remained for Origen to create the first organized dogmatic theology.

The *De Principiis* and the *Contra Celsum*, upon which I shall draw heavily in my subsequent presentation of Origen's ideas, are particularly admirable in the coherence of their organization. The *Contra Celsum* takes its form from the now lost works of Celsus, whose attacks upon Christianity Origen took upon himself to refute. But the form which Origen invented for the *De Principiis* charted an area of speculation which, according to Harnack, later theologians did not appreciably increase. One is struck by the brilliance of Origen's reasoning, even in the often pedestrian translations of Rufinus (A.D. 340–410). Erasmus said that he "learned more Christian philosophy from a single page of Origen than from ten of Augustine";[44] and Cardinal Newman averred that he loved the name of Origen.[45]

The charges of heresy made posthumously against Origen would not have lowered him in Milton's esteem. He calls the Alexandrian Father "erroneous Origen"; but his strictures upon the darlings of orthodoxy are frequently more vehement than is this mild epithet. One who erred was no heretic for Milton, who so testifies in *Of True Religion*: "Heresy is in the will and choice professedly against scripture; error is against the will, in misunderstanding the scripture after all sincere endeavors to understand it rightly; hence it was said well by one of the ancients, 'Err I may, but a heretic I will not be.' It is a human frailty to err, and no man is infallible here on earth." [46]

From his own time to the present Origen has had the respect of outstanding theologians. His pupils, among them Dionysius of Alexandria, who later headed the famous catechetical school so well served by his illustrious teacher, and Gregory the Wonder Worker, who wrote the *Panegyric to Origen*, revered and loved their famous elder. In his youth the learned St. Jerome thought highly of him; even after the later diatribes against Origen's heresies, Jerome venerated his intelligence. Gregory of Nyssa speaks warmly of him. Augustine and Aquinas cite him often, and usually with approval. Ambrose and St. Bernard were attracted by the keenness of his mind. The Venerable Bede admired him. Duns Scotus made use of his teachings. Erasmus edited his works.

Origen was admired by at least two of Milton's contemporaries whose reputations for theology or humanistic scholarship were deserved. Henry More, the Cambridge Platonist, said that Origen "was surely the greatest Light and Bulwark, that ancient Christianity had. . . ." Alexander Gill, once Milton's schoolmaster, asks rhetorically: "Ah, blessed Origen! hath thy too much charity been blamed so long?" [47]

The writings of Origen were readily available to Milton. The *Homilies* had been published as early as 1475. In 1481 the *Contra Celsum* was printed in Rome by Persana. Collected editions appeared in 1512, 1519, 1522, and 1530 in Paris. Erasmus' edition was

---

[44] Quoted in William Fairweather, *Origen and Greek Patristic Theology* (New York, 1901), p. 259.

[45] *Ibid.*, p. v.

[46] *Bohn*, II, 511; *CE*, VI, 168.

[47] I am indebted to Adamson, *op. cit.*, for the substance of this paragraph.

finished by Beatus Rhenanus and issued at Basel in 1536, 1557, and 1571. Gilbertus Genebrardus published a two-volume folio edition at Paris in 1574, in 1604, and again in 1619. Hoeschel published the treatise against Celsus at Augsburg in 1605.[48]

For many reasons Milton might have been drawn to Origen's thought. Both men were deeply religious and both strove in their respective ages to rediscover an earlier and purer religion. Each had an encyclopedic knowledge of the Bible. Each had been a student of classic literature; and each believed that the great poems, myths, and philosophies of antiquity owed their inspiration to God's Word and accordingly were the handmaidens of religion. Each urged the importance of individual exegesis and the freedom of religious opinion. Though each thought the Bible simple in its essence, since it was accommodated to limited human intelligence through the wisdom of God, each further held that God's Word could be resolved for the individual only by patient and prayerful study.

Origen lived at a time (A.D. 185–253) which falls within the period indicated by Milton as embodying the original purity of the Church; he wrote well before the Trinitarian controversy culminated in the Council of Nicea, and yet late enough that he was able to incorporate into his own system the teachings of influential early Fathers. More is known of the life of Origen than is known of almost any other figure in the primitive Church. Alexandria, the city of his birth, was exceeded in importance only by imperial Rome. Indeed, it was perhaps a greater center of culture than Rome. As the empire's outstanding grain port, it was the gateway both to Egypt and to the East. Its strategic location brought wealth; and the authorities, whose main concern was the uninterrupted flow of grain to Rome, only occasionally curtailed civil liberties, although the Christian community in the second century A.D. suffered the usual sporadic persecutions. Wealth and comparative peace attracted men from many nations. Greek, Arab, Jew, and Roman lived together in Alexandria, attended the same philosophical schools, listened to the same able teachers, and competed amicably on the whole for a share of the vast trade which daily passed through the port. Here were located the greatest of libraries and the most famous schools in the world; to this city scholars naturally gravitated. It was in Alexandria that the Hebrew Scriptures were translated into Greek at different times and by different persons. In the process of translation, elements of Greek

---

[48] *ANCL*, XXIII, xxxvii–viii.

thought entered into the Septuagint, which, of course, Origen used. Philo Judaeus was an Alexandrian and so was Plotinus, under whom the highest development of the neo-Platonic school was reached.

Origen was educated in the classics and taught the Christian faith by his father, Leonidas, who, according to Suidas, was a bishop, but who more probably was a teacher of literature. The father took great pride in his son, thinking he saw the mark of the Holy Spirit upon him. Origen was remarkable for his quick mind. He early absorbed the Greek science; daily he memorized a portion of the Bible; his eagerness for study had to be restrained. According to one of his biographers, "as a child, he deliberately made choice of the Word, and knowledge and love of the Word were always what counted most for him, whether 'logos' stood for God's subsistent Word or for his word in Scripture."[48a] As a student in the catechetical school at Alexandria he may have studied under Pantaenus; that he was a pupil of Clement is certain. Much of the work he later accomplished was probably undertaken because Clement had suggested to him the need for an organized system of Christian dogma.

Another most important influence upon the young Origen was the philosophic learning he acquired from Ammonius Saccas, whose lectures gave impetus to the rise of neo-Platonism. Porphyry, the biographer of Plotinus, and Longinus the rhetorician both bear witness that Origen and Plotinus, the father of neo-Platonism, attended together the lectures of Ammonius. Ammonius taught that the world was willed into being by God and that therefore it was not necessary to think of it as derived from a pre-existent matter. "Things are sustained in being by God, who is the demiurge of all organization, apparent or hidden. The artisan of the universe has given it existence without drawing it forth from any matter. An act of his will is enough to cause beings to subsist."[49] Ammonius further believed that body is subordinate to spirit and that everything according to the law of God has its fixed position in a great chain of being, extending from insensate matter upward to God. He held that the soul, even when embodied, is imperishable, incorporeal, and divine. Only God, he taught, can exist without a body. Evil is from within; it comes about when one forgets his divine nature.[50]

The philosophical ideas of Ammonius were utilized by his two

[48a] Jean Danielou, *Origen*, tr. Walter Mitchell (London and New York, 1955), p. 5.

[49] René Cadiou, *Origen, His Life at Alexandria*, tr. John A. Southwell (St. Louis and London, 1944), Chapter IX. Future reference will be to *Cadiou*.

[50] *Ibid.*

great pupils, Origen, the father of Christian dogma, and Plotinus, the founder of neo-Platonism. An interesting anecdote is recounted by Porphyry in his biography of Plotinus, demonstrating the thoroughness of Origen's knowledge of early neo-Platonism: "One day the master [Plotinus] blushed and wished to rise from his seat when he perceived that Origen was in the audience. When Origen besought him to proceed with the lecture, he replied that he no longer had a mind to do so since he was sure of addressing people who already understood what he was about to say. After a few brief observations the master rose from his chair and left the gathering."[51]

Origen's father was martyred in the persecution of Septimus Severus, which took place in 201. Origen wished to join his father but was prevented when his mother hid his clothes. All his life he seems genuinely to have longed for martyrdom; indeed, he apparently made no attempt to avoid the attention of the authorities. Because continuing persecution drove the Christian teachers of Alexandria into hiding, Demetrius, the bishop of the city, appointed the eighteen-year-old Origen head of the famous catechetical school. The position offered prestige as well as risk, but, we may suppose, no remuneration, as Origen was forced to sell a fine secular library for a daily pension of four obols (about twenty cents). Upon this meager allowance he lived and taught. He wore no shoes, had but one change of clothing, and slept on the bare ground. This ascetic life was of his own choosing, for he did not then nor ever lack friends of wealth and influence. He was fearless in advising and comforting the martyrs of the time, many of them his own catechumens. It was at about this time that Origen committed in an excess of zeal an act of self-mutilation which Milton sneeringly suggested that his opponents in the divorce controversy might profitably emulate;[52] but during his own lifetime the great Alexandrian seems to have been forgiven his rashness by most of his contemporaries, though the fact that he was a eunuch may have retarded his advancement in the Church. He later came to regret his gross error.

---

[51] *Ibid.*, p. 188. Émile Bréhier, in *The Philosophy of Plotinus*, tr. Joseph Thomas (Chicago, 1958), p. 17, remarks: ". . . in certain respects the system of Plotinus may be placed in the same line of thought as the theological speculations of Origen. Both are marked by a relative sobriety of imagination and a certain tendency to react against excessive fancies, such as those of the second century Neoplatonists or the Gnostics. The third century was, on the whole, of a rationalist turn of mind, and it had not yet given itself over to theurgy and to the magical practices to which the last Neoplatonists were to descend."

[52] *Bohn, The Doctrine and Discipline of Divorce*, III, 255; *CE*, III₂, 486.

In 216 Origen left for Palestine, where, as a layman, he preached
before Alexander, Bishop of Jerusalem, and Theoktistus, Bishop of
Caesarea, with such success that he aroused the jealousy of Demetrius, who called him home. Milton refers to this event in Origen's
life to argue his own right and responsibility as a layman to uphold
and spread the Christian faith and not to leave this duty to the
"ignorance and pride" of usurping prelates. St. Peter, he says, granted
the title of clergy to all Christians, a title which remained theirs
until it was wrested away by Pope Hyginus and appropriated by the
priesthood. "Although these usurpers could not so presently over-
master the liberties and lawful titles of God's freeborn church; but
that Origen, being yet a layman, expounded the scriptures publicly,
and was therein defended by Alexander of Jerusalem, and Theoktistus of Caesarea, producing in his behalf divers examples, that the
privilege of teaching was anciently permitted to many worthy lay-
men. . . ."[53] In 228, Origen again left his native city to travel in
Greece. On his way he was ordained presbyter by the Bishop of
Caesarea. This action of Theoktistus aroused the wrath of Demetrius,
who instigated a largely successful attempt to excommunicate Origen
from the Church. The bishops of Jerusalem and Caesarea, as might
have been expected, however, upheld his cause; to Caesarea he removed in 231, where he again established a school. It was here that
Gregory the Wonder Worker was his pupil; and here he taught and
wrote until the persecution of Decius (A.D. 249–51). At this time the
aged Origen was tortured; his feet were for many days kept in the
stocks "at the second hole." He died soon after in 254.

Such a man as Origen, it seems to me, by the very sweetness of
his personality and by the very purity of his life, would have immediately engaged the sympathies of Milton, whose own standards
of personal conduct and dedication to the highest ideals are well
known. The accounts of Origen's childhood, which, like other details of his life, were all available to Milton in the works of Gregory
the Wonder Worker, Eusebius, Epiphanius, Methodius, Jerome, and
Rufinus, may bring to mind the lines spoken by Christ in *Paradise
Regained*:

> When I was yet a child, no childish play
> To me was pleasing, all my mind was set
> Serious to learn and know, and thence to do
> What might be publick good; my self I thought
> Born to that end, born to promote all truth,

---

[53] *Bohn, The Reason of Church Government*, II, 493; *CE*, III₁, 258.

All righteous things: therefore above my years,
The Law of God I red, and found it sweet,

                                        i, 201–7

Origen's persecution by the Bishop of Alexandria and his intrepidity
when his life was endangered might well have struck a responsive
chord in one whose coolness to bishops and steadfast support of un-
popular causes need no comment. Milton's conviction that only a
good man was capable of true eloquence [54] would also prejudice him
in Origen's favor. Reading the various biographies of this Alexandrian Father, we see a man singularly free from the faults of his fel-
lows. There is nothing of the maneuvering for position in the
hierarchy of the Church such as that which marred the life of Jerome,
nothing of the fierceness of Tertullian, nothing of the too clever, almost insidious propagandizing associated with men like Rufinus,
nothing of the intolerant self-righteousness which characterized men
like Athanasius, nothing of the sheer skulduggery of a Tatian, nothing of Constantine's vacillation. A steady light, a constant gentleness,
a love of man, an untiring industry, an inquiring and daring men-
tality, a supreme faith, and a habit of graceful acquiescence to the
rebuffs which he received — these were natural to Origen.

Origen's literary output was enormous. While he was still teaching
in Alexandria, he made a convert of a rich man named Ambrose,
who renounced the Valentinian heresy to become one of Origen's
chief supporters. Determined to have Origen write down his teachings, Ambrose paid the wages of seven shorthand secretaries and as
many copyists and girls skilled in calligraphy. From this time forth,
apparently without ceasing, Origen committed his thoughts to writing. Many of his works have been lost; but there still remain a total
of a hundred and ninety-one homilies on Genesis, Exodus, Leviticus,
Joshua, Judges, Psalms, Isaiah, Ezekiel, Jeremiah, and Luke;
parts of commentaries upon the Song of Songs, Matthew, John, and
the Epistle to the Romans; two short pieces, the *Exhortatio ad Mar-
tyrum* and the *De Oratione*; two letters; and two longer works of
great importance, the *De Principiis* and the *Contra Celsum*.[55]

Most of these are preserved only in translations made by Rufinus,
whose redactions have sometimes been adversely criticized by scholars. As he himself admits in his preface to the *De Principiis*, Rufinus
adapted Origen for Latin-speaking readers who were not ordinarily
interested in philosophical subtleties but who sometimes needed ex-

---

[54] *Bohn, An Apology for Smectymnuus*, III, 100; *CE*, III$_1$, 287.
[55] *ANCL*, XXIII, xxxiii–xxxvii.

planations for ideas which to them might have seemed esoteric. An uninspired theologian but a sound one, Rufinus often brought Origen's thought into closer harmony with orthodoxy; and some of Origen's more audacious conjectures were undoubtedly modified in the process. Those few texts which are available both in the original Greek and in Rufinus' Latin translation, when compared, give an idea of the extent and nature of the modification. Cadiou, who has made such a comparison, thus summarizes his findings:

> It has not been proved, however, that Rufinus ever substituted his own theories for the doctrine of Origen. His main preoccupation seems to have been the watering-down of the more rash expressions or theories, either by the simple process of passing them over in silence or by an effort to forestall possible objections. Wherever a passage was unlikely to offend the Christian reader, the translation is as exact as was permitted by the usage of his contemporaries, who were far from observing the stricter standards of modern criticism. Thus he reproduced the less coherent of the theories, regarding them as old and of secondary importance. Other parts of the work were too well known, too daring or too important, to justify any temptation he may have had to suppress them; and since Origen himself had taken care to present them as conjectures, Rufinus preserved them in their original setting. The one exception to this method of procedure was Origen's doctrine on the Trinity, for it might have given advantage to the Arians of the time. The prudent and comprehensive way these speculations were advanced makes their authenticity the more certain, for this was always Origen's method of discussing free questions, as can be seen from the study of his other works. Rufinus is not to be held responsible for the mingled irresoluteness and subtlety of all such passages, for he usually considered it simpler to suppress what puzzled him. On the contrary, they were natural to a theologian whose rashness in speculation was always tempered by his respect for the foundations of Christian belief.[56]

Whatever toning-down Origen's works may have received at the hands of the translator, enough originality and daring are left to intrigue a student of primitive Christianity like Milton, who was not afraid of heretical dogma and who sought only the truth. And, after all, much of Origen's speculative theology has come through. Cadiou says further:

> Rash theories, and even theories that run directly counter to the tradition of the Church, are not lacking to Rufinus' version. The timidity of the man's own theology and his loyalty to Origen's memory are a sufficient guaranty that he did not invent them. Indeed he is not even suspected of having done the slightest violence to them.[57]

Whatever ideas may have been suggested to Milton by Origen must have been transmitted to him largely through the translations

---

[56] *Cadiou*, p. 210.
[57] *Ibid.*, p. 212.

of Rufinus, for the sources available to us today are the only ones which Milton could have used.

One man, St. Jerome (A.D. 340–420), is largely responsible for the centuries of disrepute which the theology of Origen has suffered.[58] And Jerome's hostile utterances upon the writings of the Alexandrian Father stemmed from his long and increasingly bitter quarrel with Rufinus. Had someone other than Rufinus translated Origen's works, it is quite possible that Jerome would have been less prone to condemn Origen's thought as heretical.

Both the historian and the theologian owe a debt to St. Jerome. His writings are a major source for knowledge of events which took place during a most melancholy time in the history of Western Europe, the last age of the Greco-Roman civilization and the beginning in darkness of a new world. Jerome lived in the reigns of Julian, Valens, Valentinian, Gratian, Theodosius, and the sons of Theodosius; and he witnessed the results of the sack of Rome by Alaric in 410. He helped to bring about the establishment of orthodox Christianity in the Roman Empire. He was a contemporary of some of the greatest Fathers of the Church, several of whom he knew. Of St. Ambrose he often speaks in his letters; with Augustine he carried on a prolonged correspondence; he studied under Gregory of Nazianzus; he was a friend of Gregory of Nyssa; his early friendship with Rufinus of Aquileia, as has been mentioned, turned into enmity. Ranked as one of the four Doctors of the Latin Church, he is among the few men sainted for services to the Church rather than for holiness of life. Perhaps more than any other he was responsible for the introduction into Western Europe of asceticism. His writings vividly portray the secular as well as the ecclesiastical life of his day. He was asked by Pope Damasus, who had heard of his abilities as scholar and translator, to revise the "Old Latin" translation of the Bible. With the help of three rabbis who came to him secretly, he translated the Hebrew Bible into Latin; and his translation, with the New Testament from Greek sources, became the Vulgate, the Bible of Western Christendom till the Reformation.

Jerome's fondness for relics and sacred places and his reverence for episcopal authority, especially for that of the Roman pontiff, must have impressed Milton unfavorably; yet the poet, in his prose works,

---

[58] The details of Jerome's life and works here presented come from the admirably thorough introduction to *Letters and Select Works of St. Jerome*, tr. W. H. Fremantle, in *A Select Library of Nicene and Post-Nicene Fathers of the Christian Church*, 2nd ser., ed. Philip Schaff and Henry Wace (New York, Oxford, and London, 1893), VI, xi–xxxv.

cites him several times. In *The Reason of Church Government*, calling him "the learnedest of the fathers," Milton quotes with approval Jerome's teaching that "custom only . . . was the maker of
prelaty. . . ." In the *Areopagitica*, with ponderous humor, Milton
tells the story of the devil's having whipped Jerome for reading
Cicero. In *The Judgment of Martin Bucer Concerning Divorce*, Milton relates Jerome's spirited defense of Fabiola, a Roman matron
who divorced one husband to marry another. The Columbia Index
lists more than a dozen quotations from Jerome in the prose works.
Though these quotations support arguments Milton is making, it is
always my feeling that he is using Jerome to impress others while remaining unimpressed himself.

One cannot read very deeply in Jerome before becoming aware of
the ambivalence of his attitude toward Origen. In a letter written
about 384, Jerome favorably compares the literary industry of Origen
with that of the Roman Varro and the Greek "man of brass," Didy-
mus, who is reported by Athanaeus to have written 3,500 books.
Calling Origen "our Christian man of adamant," he lists the works
of the Alexandrian and then remarks:

> So you see, the labors of this one man have surpassed those of all pre-
> vious writers, Greek and Latin. Who has ever managed to read all that he
> has written? Yet what reward have his exertions brought him? He stands
> condemned by his bishop, Demetrius, only the bishops of Palestine, Arabia,
> Phenicia, and Achaia dissenting. Imperial Rome consents to his condem-
> nation, and even convenes a senate to censure him, not — as the rabid
> hounds who now pursue him cry — because of the novelty or heterodoxy of
> his doctrines, but because men could not tolerate the incomparable elo-
> quence and knowledge which, when once he opened his lips, made others
> seem dumb.[59]

Later Jerome defends himself against the charge of having praised
Origen. By 401 he triumphantly writes: "Demetrius expelled Origen
from the city of Alexander; but he is now thanks to Theophilus
outlawed from the whole world. . . . Where now is that heresy
which crawled hissing through the world and boasted that both the
bishop Theophilus and I were partisans of its error?" [60] This drastic
change in attitude was brought about by circumstances most complex. In brief, this is the story. In the preface to his translation of
the *De Principiis*, Rufinus linked Jerome's name with Origen's at a
time when the latter's opinions were receiving hostile review. Friends
brought this to the attention of Jerome, urging him, for the sake of

[59] *Ibid.*, p. 46.
[60] *Ibid.*, p. 187.

his reputation, to deny sympathy with the Alexandrian's heretical views. Anxious to escape guilt by association, Jerome penned a mild remonstrance to Rufinus, pointing out that while he admired Origen's mind, he deplored his deviations from orthodoxy; but the letter was deliberately withheld from Rufinus by self-seeking prelates. Rufinus' failure to explain or retract his implications outraged Jerome, whose nature was choleric; and the breach between the two churchmen became irreparable. One version of the whole sorry tale can be discovered in Jerome's letters; and, as so often happens in quarrels, all the participants including Jerome himself suffered a considerable loss of dignity.[61] Jerome's fulminations did not cease even with the death of Rufinus. The result was that Origen's reputation was blemished and the power of his theology, taken as a systematic whole, was destroyed, though parts of his exegesis were incorporated into the expositions of influential theologians, including Augustine, Aquinas, and Duns Scotus.

During the height of the controversy, St. Jerome, in a letter to a correspondent whose name, Avitus, is all that is known of him, listed the heresies of Origen.[62] It is an impressive collection. The letter itself is far too long to quote. In the following précis, the ordering of the "heresies" is my own; the phraseology is largely Jerome's; I have numbered the heresies to facilitate subsequent discussion.

1. There is nothing increate except the Father.

2. God is by nature invisible — invisible even to the Son.

3. The Father and the Son are compared to two statues, a large one and a small — the first filling the world and being somehow invisible through its size, the second cognizable by the eyes of men.

4. Compared with God, the Son who is his invisible likeness is not the truth, is not glorious, is but a minute brightness, is not good.

5. The Son was made the Son, not born.

6. The Holy Spirit is third in dignity and honor.

7. The Holy Spirit is a creature.

8. All reasonable beings, that is, the Father, the Son, and the Holy Ghost, angels, powers, dominations, and virtues, and even man by reason of his soul's dignity, are of one and the same essence. God and his only begotten Son and the Holy Spirit are conscious of an intellectual and reasonable nature. But so also are the angels, the

---

[61] *Ibid.*, p. xxii, and the letters by Jerome cited in this part of Fremantle's introduction.

[62] *Ibid.*, pp. 238–44.

powers, and the virtues, as well as the inward man, who is created in the image and after the likeness of God.

9. Rational creatures fell into bodily existence through their sloth and neglect.

10. The fact that souls are made, some tending toward honor, some tending toward dishonor, is to be explained by their previous history, that is, their history before this life.

11. The affairs of the world are so ordered that while some angels fall from Heaven others freely glide down to earth. The former are hurled down against their will; the latter descend from choice alone. The former are forced to continue in a distasteful service for a fixed period; the latter spontaneously embrace the task of lending a hand to those who fall.

12. Demons obtain their positions in the hierarchy of Hell through merit in evil.

13. Demons have special duties assigned to them in particular worlds.

14. While not incapable of virtue, the devil has not yet chosen to be virtuous.

15. What is Hell to some creatures is Heaven to others.

16. Hellfire is not an external punishment, but rather the pangs of guilty consciences.

17. An angel, a human soul, and a demon — all of one nature but of differing wills — as a punishment may be transformed into brutes.

18. One who is now a human being may in another world become a demon; a demon may become a human; an archangel may become a devil or the devil an archangel.

19. There are many worlds: a new one begins as an old one ends.

20. The souls of the sun, moon, and stars existed before the creation.

21. The sun, moon, and constellations are alive.

22. At the consummation of all things, when God will be "all in all," creatures will become disembodied.

23. Bodily substances, at the end of things, will become highly rarified like the ether.

24. "God shall be all in all"; that is to say, all bodily existence shall be made as perfect as possible; it shall be brought into the divine essence, than which there is none better.

The heresies of Origen cataloged in Jerome's letter may be divided into five kinds: (I) those which have to do primarily with the nature of God (1-2, 24); (II) those which treat primarily of the Son and his relationship to the Father (3–5); (III) those which deal with the Holy Spirit (6–7); (IV) those which concern the nature of the sentient creation, of angels, men, and demons (8–18, 22–23); and (V) heresies of a strictly cosmological importance (19–21).

Certain of Origen's beliefs as reported by Jerome deserve special comment. The comparison of Father and Son to two statues — one invisible because of its magnitude, the other cognizable by the senses — which seems so to have outraged Jerome, is not, certainly, a serious part of Origen's dogma. The Alexandrian is simply illustrating his belief in the inferiority of the Son to the Father, a belief which he elsewhere elucidates. But even the Son is not thought always to be capable of apprehension by man's senses; for, in the fourth heresy of the list, the Son is spoken of as "the invisible likeness" of the incomprehensible God.

Jerome's assertion that Origen said the Son was made, not born, cannot be found in Rufinus' translation of Origen, the only one which Milton could have used. In it Christ's divinity is declared in unambiguous language: "Being God he was made man." [63]

Jerome says (8) that Origen believes the Father, Son, Holy Ghost, angels, and men to be one essence. But from Jerome's own statement it is clear that Origen argues merely that the Son, the Spirit, and the sentient creation partake of the divine intelligence and thus are to a certain extent like one another.

How many of the heresies attributed by Jerome to Origen might also be attributed to Milton?

Though Milton does not agree with Origen that as a result of a single fall all sentient creatures simultaneously found their proper positions in the chain of being (this belief underlies the ninth heresy on the list), *Paradise Lost* clearly affirms that negligence played a large part in the fall of man into his mortal state and in the fall of certain angels into their demonic natures. Raphael, for example, tells Adam that angels, like men, must obey God (v, 535–37).

With the idea that some souls, as the result of their choice of good or evil in a previous existence, find places of honor or dishonor as they enter into life here below (10), Milton is not in accord; nor does he anywhere, so far as I know, make poetic use of it.

In *Paradise Lost*, several of the fallen angels express their convic-

---

[63] "Qui cum in omnium conditione Patri ministrasset, per ipsum enim omnia facta sunt, novissimis temporibus seipsum exinaniens *homo factus incarnatus est cum Deus esset*, et homo factus mansit quod erat Deus." Migne, *Patrologia Graeca* (Paris, various dates), XI, 118. Italics mine.

tion that special duties in the world or in the underworld will be assigned to them by God, a concept very close to the thirteenth heresy. Thus Beelzebub suggests that God may employ the devils to work in the fires of Hell, "Or do his errands in the gloomy Deep" (i, 152).

Though Milton does not hold that Satan is capable of salvation (14), in the epic the devil and some of his followers as well are otherwise persuaded. In *The Christian Doctrine*, it seems to me, Milton is upon occasion uneasily aware of the inconsistency of assuming that the demons are destined to undergo eternal punishment, when it is a part of his faith that they are not equally punished. God's becoming "all in all" at the end of time raises a concomitant problem: how can God become One again when adversaries exist externally in Hell?

Origen's fifteenth heresy, that the same place is Hell to one being and Heaven to another, appears when Satan, in prospect of Eden, soliloquizes, "Myself am hell."

The heresy that angels, men, and devils may be turned into brutes (17) was put forward by Origen simply as a conjecture. This Jerome himself admits. The transformation of the demons to serpents after Satan's triumphal return to Hell demonstrates Milton's use of the concept.

The changing of one class of rational beings into another (the eighteenth heresy) occurs in *Paradise Lost*, though it is not a part of Milton's dogma as it is spelled out in the *De Doctrina*. Raphael informs Adam that in time man's nature may be changed to that higher state enjoyed by the angels (v, 496–500).

Like Origen (19) Milton apparently endorses the doctrine of the plurality of worlds (see *P.L.*, iii, 566–71); but Milton thinks of the worlds as existing concurrently rather than sequentially.

Following the account in Genesis, Milton holds that light was created before the sun, the moon, and the stars; but that light may be considered as the soul of the heavenly bodies he nowhere argues. Milton does call the sun the soul of the universe (v, 171). These views are at least similar to those of Origen which Jerome styles heretical (20).

That the starry bodies are alive (21) Milton appears to believe; for Adam's prayer (v, 166–79) asks the planets and stars to join him in praising God.

Without question the remainder of the heresies which Jerome finds in Origen's theology are held by Milton. Actually Milton disagrees entirely with Origen in respect to two particulars of doctrine only, those expressed in the tenth and in the twentieth heresies from Jerome's letter.

To assume that Milton became familiar with Origen's works after his own systematic theology and the great epic had been written is not reasonable. It is far more likely that during the time when he was contemplating the production of a personal belief of his own, when he was studying "some of the more copious theological treatises," when he was reading "the works of heretics, so called" and the works of "those who are reckoned for orthodox," he came upon, or, more probably, was directed by other theological works to the writings of Origen. Surely he would have had to evaluate the thought of Origen in the course of his scholarly research into ante-Nicene times.

If, during his examination of primitive Christianity, Milton had already begun formulating the doctrine which he called his "best and richest possession," he would have found Origen useful in supporting and crystallizing his beliefs. If the poet had not yet begun shaping his credo, Origen must have exerted an influence even more profound. That an influence from Origen upon Milton exists I have no doubt, though its extent, to be sure, can never be ascertained. That there is unquestionable similarity between the approaches, the exegetical methods, the interpretations, the arguments, and the theological systems conceived by Origen and Milton I intend to show.

CHAPTER THREE

AN OUTLINE OF MILTON'S THEOLOGY: ITS HERESIES

Several fine studies have appeared upon Milton's theological beliefs; and to these I am of course indebted.[1] But in them all the system of thought which lies behind the dispassionate phraseology of the *De Doctrina* and informs the argument of *Paradise Lost* seems to me incompletely understood as a philosophic whole. This chapter will present a synopsis of the Miltonic system as I see it, unencumbered by proof or argumentation, in the hope that the short view will clarify the more intensive examination of Milton's theology in juxtaposition with that of Origen which is to follow and which will be fully documented. Further, I shall deal with the heterodoxies inherent in Milton's dogma, and I shall try to explain the logic of their development.

Because *The Christian Doctrine* is so thoroughly interlaced with Biblical proof texts, because the sheer bulk of quotation often tends to obscure a relatively simple concept, it has been, I think, all too readily concluded that the treatise is inconsistent, or illogical, or overly complex, or devoted to minutiae. Despite this judgment, the usefulness of the *De Doctrina* in the interpretation of *Paradise Lost* has been commonly conceded, though, as Kelley points out, only Verity and Hughes among Milton's many editors "have accorded the treatise any real consideration" and until the publication of *This Great Argument* the most conscientious attempt to establish parallels was Bishop Sumner's in 1825.[2] My outline assumes one theological system in the treatise and in the epic. While the articulation of Mil-

---

[1] Though I am particularly indebted to Curry, Kelley, Conklin, Saurat, and Lewis, I have made use of many other studies on aspects of Milton's theology. See bibliography.

[2] Maurice Kelley, *This Great Argument* (Princeton, N.J., 1941), p. 6.

ton's thought derives largely from the *De Doctrina*, the form of the outline is dictated by the real chronology of the action in the poem.

The illustrations which accompany this portion of my study are diagrammatic rather than pictorial. They demonstrate certain vital relationships between the parts of the Miltonic system as a whole; and in their sequence they show something of the development of the cosmos in *Paradise Lost*. From the varying sizes of the circles which constitute the diagrams and from the relationships of these circles one to another nothing more is intended in the elucidation of Milton's cosmos beyond that which I suggest in the text.

I

Milton's cosmos begins with the one incomprehensible God. God is a spirit who fills all space, who is without beginning or end, who

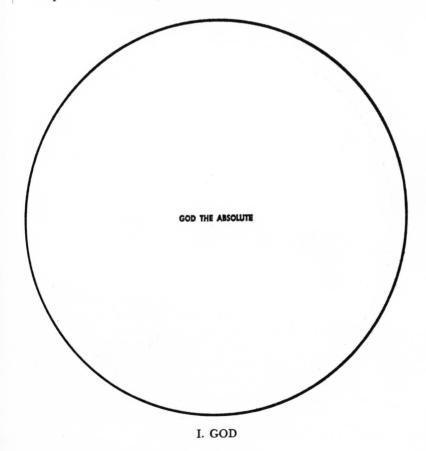

GOD THE ABSOLUTE

I. GOD

is immortal and unchangeable, who is forever invisible and inaudible. He is therefore completely unmanifested and entirely incapable of being understood. He is the Absolute. In the first diagram God is represented by a circle; but the circle must be thought of as having an infinite radius and as existing not in time but in eternity. The Absolute must remain unmanifest forever; for manifestation is limitation, and Milton's God cannot in any way be limited. Yet the creation is a fact — visible, audible, and palpable. Milton's problem was to show the development of the relative from the Absolute. In his thought, the word "create" means to make something of preexistent matter; for example, the cabinetmaker can *create* a chair from wood, but he cannot *make* a chair. So God can *make* matter, but he cannot *create* a visible universe, since by so doing he would become manifest.

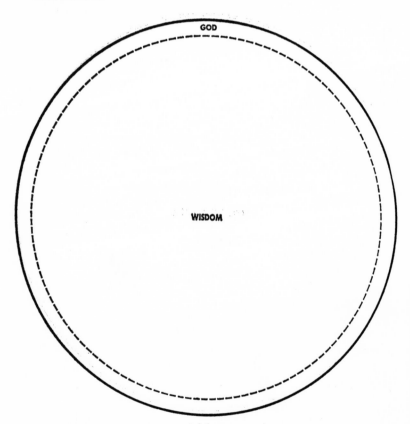

II. INTERNAL EFFICIENCY

II

God, of his own will, unmoved by chance or necessity, decrees the manifestation of his own goodness. The decree is eternal; the plan for the manifestation of God's goodness is eternal. Since God's decrees result from his wisdom, the wisdom of God is likewise eternal; for God was never without wisdom. God's wisdom, however, is not God; it is only one of a multitude of the attributes which are inherent in the Godhead. Diagram II illustrates in an elementary way the relationship between God and his wisdom. To show that wisdom is an integral part of the one Absolute God, the circle of wisdom is described by a dotted line. The two circles should, of course, be superimposed; for, as God is infinite and eternal, so is his wisdom. Although wisdom cannot exist without God, both in the Bible and in Milton's writings Wisdom is sometimes treated as a semipersonified being or entity. Wisdom, even when it is personified, is invisible and inaudible. Like God himself, it is unsearchable; for even the Son knows only what the Father chooses to reveal to him.

III

Matter is made when God withdraws his goodness from a portion of infinity (see Diagram III). Since God fills infinity he is actually freeing a portion of himself from his own control. Matter as it is originally induced is formless and invisible, the substance of God existing uninfluenced by him, differing from the rest of infinity only in respect to its absolute freedom from all control. Of the utmost importance to an understanding of Milton's theology is the freedom of matter. From this fundamental tenet spring most of his heterodoxies. For two reasons primeval matter does not manifest the Absolute: (1) there was no witness to its production; and (2) matter in its original condition differs from God's substance only in that it is free, and freedom cannot be discerned by the senses. Nor does God act in producing matter, which is simply the result of his omnipotent will. Though matter is freed from God's goodness, it is not evil, but rather a neutral substance which can be put to uses good or bad. It is completely insentient and lifeless, whereas evil is the product of intelligence wrongly used. All things in the cosmos are of the same matter, which, by the addition of forms, can become any object of thought. Animal, vegetable, and mineral kingdoms are created of the one matter, as are all etherous or quintessential bodies.

Of itself matter is powerless. But a marvelous potential is inherent in it — the capacity to receive form.

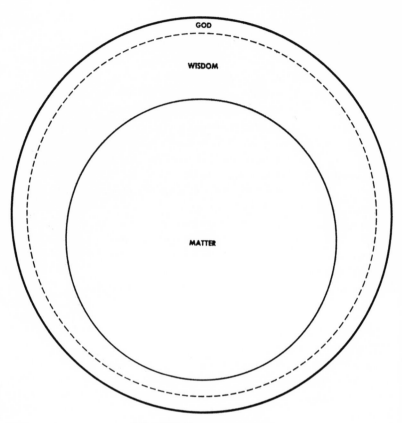

III. THE RETRACTION

IV

With the retraction of his goodness from a portion of the infinite, God's role in the creation ends, though everything which follows results from his plan, wisdom, will, and power. The power to create, however, is given to and exerted by the Logos (see Diagram IV). The Logos or Word passes through three stages. As the Logos he creates the Holy Spirit, Heaven, the angels, and Hell; as the Son he creates the World; as the Christ he redeems mankind from sin and death, and, at his second advent, he judges the quick and the dead. The titles Logos, Son, and Christ designate the same person; yet they are not interchangeable, for each represents a different level of manifestation. The begetting of the Logos marks the beginning of the creation. The Logos is the first of the whole creation, self-created, originating through the will and through the infinite wisdom of God, a separate

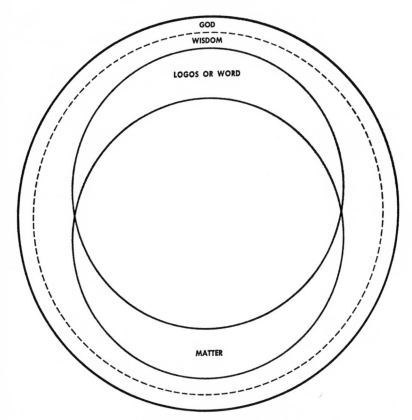

GOD

WISDOM

LOGOS OR WORD

MATTER

IV. THE LITERAL BEGETTING

being, divine, holy, and blessed with the attributes of God, from whom he received them as gifts. But he is not of God's essence; for if he were he would be infinite, and there cannot be two infinite Gods. He is first an invisible though audible Spirit. He is the Word who makes God's Wisdom known. He is the creator of all things in the cosmos which succeed him. Milton asserts that he was produced in time, since the decree of God which allows him to come into being must have antedated him. Because for Milton the Word is material, the circle of the Logos in the diagram intersects the circle of matter. This assumption is based upon the meaning assigned by the poet to the word "create," which is, "to give a new form or character to an already existent substance." In the "beginning," there are in the cosmos only God and the not-God, or matter. Again and again Milton declares that the Logos is not of the essence of God, though he is of

God's substance. Matter is the substance of God, freed from his goodness. Hence the Logos must be material. The Logos does not include
all matter, however, for the creation is extraneous to the creator.

How the Logos comes into being is the greatest mystery in Milton's system. He is created by the external efficiency of God, that is,
by God's creating agent; but he is himself that creating agent. Hence,
by some means beyond human comprehension, it must be assumed
that the Logos, obedient to the will of God and pursuant to his decree in the eternal plan of Wisdom, creates himself.

V

The creation proceeds. Of his own free will, the Logos first produces, from the substance of God, the Holy Spirit (see Diagram V).
As a person, the Holy Spirit in Milton's theology is curiously unim-

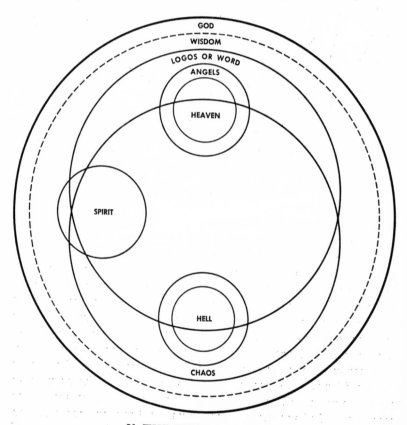

V. THE FIRST CREATION

portant. When Milton uses the word "Spirit," he sometimes refers to the Spirit of God, sometimes to angels who are granted God's Spirit that they may perform his works, sometimes to the Son (as when he identifies the Spirit which broods over the world at the creation as the Son), sometimes as a person or entity created by the Son and unequivocally inferior to him, and sometimes as the gifts of that person in the hearts of men.

Next, out of primal material, the Logos fashions Heaven and its inhabitants the angels, who are free to choose whether to stand or fall because they have been formed of matter already free. The angels, originally created equal, achieve by merit positions high or low in the hierarchy of Heaven. One in particular, Lucifer, is extraordinarily successful.

Hell is then prepared for those spirits who make the wrong choice. During this epoch of cosmic history, Hell is uninhabited and unknown to all save God and the Logos. It must have been created by the invisible Logos, since there is no hint in Milton's writings that it is the work of the visible Son; yet it yawns ready to receive the apostate angels.

What remains of original matter at the end of this tripartite creation is the Chaos of *Paradise Lost*, a vast stock of uncontrolled and undeveloped *materia prima*. During this period the Logos remains invisible. The angels are unaware of his existence; for though he is audible, they take his voice to be the voice of God. Ages pass before any further additions to the cosmos are made.

The diagram locates the Holy Spirit, Heaven, the angels, and Hell within or partially within the circle of matter and also within the circle of the Logos who created them all.

VI

On a day such as Heaven's great year brings forth, the invisible Logos is manifested as the visible Son. He is raised to glory, seated in power at the right hand of God, exalted through his own merit to be the head of the angelic host, and crowned king. Because of his great pride and thwarted ambition to equal the most high, Lucifer envies the Son and rebels against the monarchy of Heaven. He glories in becoming the adversary of God; and he draws with him in his rebellion a third of the angels, who fall of their own choice. Lucifer, now Satan, is cast with his legions into Hell.

Of the freed substance of God, the Son creates the world and, of its dust, man (see Diagram VI). Like all other rational beings, men are free to choose between good or evil; evil, the invention of Satan, is merely a falling away from goodness. God and the Son have had nothing to do with the origination of evil, which results from that freedom of choice necessary to the proper worship of God. Even before mankind is led astray by Satan, the Son offers himself as a sacrifice and assumes the office of mediator. As prophet, the Son inspires those unusual men, pagan as well as Christian, who see into the life of things. As priest, he has interceded for mankind since before the Fall.

In the diagram the shaded portion of the intersecting circles of Logos and matter represents the Son. The world and men lie within this area because they were created by him. The demons come within the Son's influence because he has control over them and be-

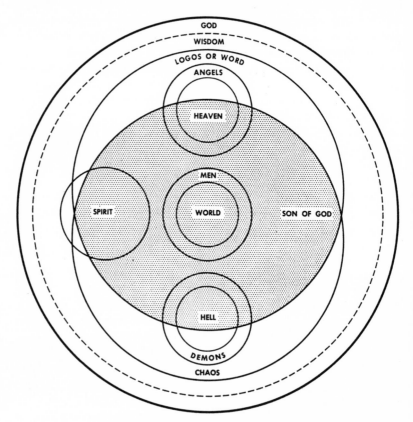

VI. THE METAPHORICAL BEGETTING

cause he permits them to exercise what powers they have. The angels and Heaven belong in this area because he is the king of Heaven and head of the angels. Since the Spirit was produced by the Logos and sent by the Son to the prophets, the circle of the Spirit, too, belongs here.

VII

In the fullness of time, the Son of God appears upon earth among men as Christ. He is the God-man, "the mutual hypostatic union" of God and man, two natures indivisibly one. In performance of his promise, he sacrifices himself to redeem man from sin and death and to elevate man to a state of grace and glory superior even to that which obtained before the Fall. Milton assigns three functions to

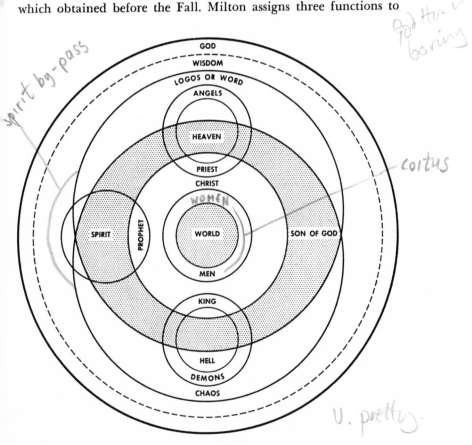

VII. TOTALITY

Christ's office as mediator: he is prophet, priest, and king. His prophetical function consists of two parts, the external, or promulgation of divine truth, and the internal, or the illumination of the understanding. His sacerdotal function resides in his having once offered himself as a sacrifice for sinners and in his continued intercession for mankind. His kingly function is his government and preservation of his church and the conquest of its enemies.

At the crucifixion, Christ dies in his entire nature, both body and spirit. He does not descend into Hell. After three days he triumphs over death, is exalted by the Father to immortality and glory through his own merit and the gift of God. He ascends into Heaven and is enthroned at God's right hand. The risen Christ is not ubiquitous. To Milton the idea of purgatory is repugnant; it is contrary to his concept of Christ's full satisfaction.

Christ will come again, to judge the quick and the dead. When that will be only the Father knows; but the second advent will be sudden, glorious, and terrible. It will be followed by the resurrection, body and soul, of the dead, who, together with the fallen angels, will be judged, the good being admitted into life eternal and the evil being doomed to everlasting punishment in Hell. Almost a thousand years will be taken up by the judgment, during which time and for a short period thereafter Christ will reign on earth. Then will Satan once more rage, but he will be finally overthrown and condemned to everlasting torment. The good will inherit the kingdom of Heaven, and God will again be "all in all." Milton nowhere attempts to explain how God can be "all in all" when Satan, evil angels, and damned men are outside the realm of the blessed. All, however, are not punished in the same degree.

In Diagram VII the circle of Christ contains the world since, (1) the God-man is born into the world; (2) he brings about man's salvation; and (3) he is known on earth before his ascension into Heaven or his final triumph over the demons. Christ is the Son incarnate; consequently the circle of Christ lies totally within that area which represents the visible Son of God. It is within the circle of the Logos because Christ brings the Word of God to men. It is within the circle of matter because Christ is material. The circle of Christ intersects those of the Spirit, Heaven, and Hell respectively because of Christ's threefold function as prophet, priest, and king.

Christ in the Miltonic system is a completely manifested divine being who evolves as the result of the will of his unmanifest and incomprehensible Father. The Father's eternal plan for the cosmos is the unmanifest Wisdom. Wisdom becomes effective through the invisible but audible Logos. The Logos is manifested to the angelic creation as the visible Son. The Son becomes incarnate and is manifested to men as Christ. Thus the Absolute has fulfilled the eternal plan of Wisdom, to make manifest his glory and goodness while remaining himself unmanifested. By the sacrifice of Christ, by the illumination of his teachings, and by the guidance of his Spirit, man is enabled to free himself from Satan's power and to return to God. The end is like the beginning.

This, then, is the full circle of the Miltonic theology. To students of Milton, and perhaps even to those who are just becoming acquainted with his work, the summary I have offered may appear to contain nothing new and nothing exceptionable. Among the familiar concepts, however, are ten which when arbitrarily removed from the integrated system may not so readily be accepted. All but two of these, to my knowledge, have not been put forward before. In the remainder of my essay I hope to prove that with the aid of Origen they may be effectively defended. A list of these concepts follows.

1. That God is the ever unmanifested Absolute — an idea first suggested by Saurat and disputed by Kelley.

2. That the word "create" is consistently used by Milton to mean "to give form to already existent matter" — an idea of Conklin's which deserves widespread attention.

3. That Wisdom as an entity is important in the development of the Logos.

4. That creation results from God's sole action — the retraction of his goodness (only the germ of the idea is Saurat's).

5. That matter is an invisible, intangible, and morally neutral substratum, immanent within God but not manifesting him, not the cause of form (as Saurat argues) but capable of assuming it.

6. That Milton posits a three-stage, divine, self-created Logos, derived from the substance but not of the essence of God.

7. That the Holy Spirit as a being is created by the Son of the substance of God.

8. That the freedom of all rational creatures derives from the nature of matter.

9. That angels were not created in their hierarchies but achieved their positions through merit.

10. That the Son does not become visible until the time of his metaphorical begetting.

From the Dedication to *The Christian Doctrine* and from the "Prefatory Remarks" to Chapter V, "Of the Son of God," it is evident that Milton did not consider himself a heretic; yet it is equally evident that he anticipated a charge of heresy.

Trying Milton's beliefs by the creeds which in the first four centuries of Christian theology served as a true measure of orthodox faith reveals a deviation quite negligible. Milton's system is in complete accord with the Apostles' Creed (second century), with the creed of Eusebius (A.D. 325), with the creed of Jerusalem (A.D. 348), and with the revision of that creed by Cyril of Jerusalem (A.D. 362), except in the portion which deals with the Holy Ghost, and which reads: "We believe . . . in the Holy Ghost, the Lord and Giver of Life, who proceedeth from the Father and the Son, who with the Father and the Son together is worshipped and glorified. . . ."[3]

With the Athanasian Creed (A.D. 420?) Milton unequivocally disagrees. The Athanasian Creed was designed to state definitively the Trinitarian position, and Milton is, of course, anti-Trinitarian. It also includes as doctrine the harrowing of Hell, the tenet that Christ descended into Hell between the time of the crucifixion and that of the resurrection, his mission being to salvage and bring to Heaven the souls of good men there imprisoned. This whole concept is antithetical to Milton's mortalism, according to which souls of men both good and bad are dead until Christ's second advent.

Milton's views are apparently compatible with the various creeds prior to that of Athanasius; but the only safe generalization which can be made is that Milton's heresies, if any, might easily pass through the loosely worded screening of primitive Christian manifestoes. This is not to say that his beliefs would have found acceptance without reservations by the pre-Athanasian formulators of doctrine. The supposition is justified, however, that Milton's theology looks more and more heretical as orthodox doctrine gains definitiveness. In point of fact, whether Milton should be considered heretical, heterodox, or orthodox is a question which can only be resolved when a standard of orthodoxy has been postulated. At the very least this standard should embrace principles of dogma accepted by the majority of professed Christians, regardless of sectarian differences. By comparing the Miltonic system, as it has been outlined in this chapter, with the beliefs of the Eastern Orthodox Church, the Roman Catholic, and with the consensus of Protestant theology, I

---

[3] "Creeds," in *Encyclopaedia Britannica*, 11th ed. (New York, 1910), VII, 392–400.

shall attempt to delineate the poet's heresies. Whatever misgivings I may have in undertaking this task stem not from any ambiguity on Milton's part but from the fact that ecclesiastical doctrines have always been subject to revision. For convenience the parts of the following discussion are numbered to correspond with the sections of the outline.

I

Milton's belief that God is the Absolute is intimately linked with his subordinationism and his materialism. God is substance as well as spirit. He is so far beyond comprehension that he may be neither seen nor heard even by the Son. The Father, the Son, and the Holy Ghost are three different persons and three different essences. These beliefs constitute a major heresy in the eyes of Roman Catholics, Eastern Catholics, and most Protestants. A concomitant heresy is the inability of Milton's God qua God to create.

II

That God and Wisdom are eternally inseparable is a completely orthodox idea.

III

Milton's convictions that God is material, that creation is *ex deo*, that free will derives from freed material, and that angels and men are of the same matter constitute a major heresy judged by Catholic and Protestant doctrine alike.

IV

A. Milton held that the Son is of God's substance, though not of his essence. The first of the Thirty-nine Articles, re-issued both in Latin and in English in 1571, reads, in part: "Et in unitate hujus divinae naturae, tres sunt Personae, ejusdem essentiae. . . ." The English version reads: ". . . three Persons, of one substance"; but commentators point out that "of one essence" more correctly renders the meaning of the phrase.[4]

B. Milton believed that the Son was generated in time.

C. Since God cannot of himself generate or create, the Son creates himself when his generation is willed by God.

By both Catholic churches, by most Protestant churches, these beliefs about the Logos are deemed heretical in the extreme.

---

[4] E. Tyrrell Green, *The Thirty-nine Articles and the Age of the Reformation* (London, 1896), p. 31. Future reference will be to *Green*.

V

Milton asserts that the Logos, of his own free will and from the matter of the Father, creates the Holy Spirit. The Eastern Orthodox Church holds that the Spirit proceeds from the Father; the Roman Catholic Church, that the Spirit proceeds from the Father and the Son; Protestants generally agree with the latter.

VI

Milton accords an unusual emphasis to the concept that the Son offered himself even before the Fall as a mediator between man and God. This concept is quite orthodox; it is included in the present list because Professor Kelley seems to think it original with Milton and one may presume that the error is common. I shall argue elsewhere that there is no essential difference between the *De Doctrina* and *Paradise Lost* on this point of doctrine. Milton does not invent the ordering of events; it is, for instance, subscribed to by the Anglican Church: "The fall was the occasion of the promise of the Deliverer, 'the Seed of the woman,' the incarnate God himself, who should, in time bruise the serpent's head." [5] The Thirty-nine Articles contain the germ of the concept: "Predestination to life, is the everlasting purpose of God, whereby (before the foundations of the world were laid) He hath constantly decreed by His counsel secret to us, to deliver from curse and damnation. . . ." [6]

VII

A. Milton's mortalism, his belief that Christ and men die body and soul, is contrary to the doctrines of both Catholic and Protestant churches, which postulate that Christ dies in his human nature only and that man's soul is immortal. Article XL of the Forty-two Articles of 1553 reads: "The souls of them that depart this life do neither die with the bodies nor sleep idly." This article was omitted from the Thirty-nine Articles of 1563 because the heresy it enunciates had so receded into the background of then current controversies that it was no longer considered worthy of note.

B. The concept of the risen Christ as not ubiquitous, which Milton upholds while admitting its unorthodoxy, is an offshoot of his materialistic ideas; for, since Christ is a *mutual* "hypostatic union" of God and man, and since a man cannot be ubiquitous, the risen Christ can exist in only one place at a time. The Church believes

---

[5] Vernon Staley, *The Catholic Religion: A Manual of Instruction for Members of the Anglican Communion* (London, Oxford, and New York, 1948), p. 162.

[6] *Green*, p. 111 (Article XVII).

in *communicatio idiomatum* but not in any mutual participation of both natures.

C. Milton's literal interpretation of the Bible, combined with his materialism, leads him to the view that a thousand years will be consumed in the last judgment, during which time Christ will reign on earth. This doctrine was specifically condemned in the Articles of 1553: "Thei that goe about to renewe the fable of heretickes called Millenarii, be repugnant to holie Scripture, and caste them selves headlong into a Juishe dotage." [7] The omission of this stricture from the Thirty-nine Articles again was due to the feeling that the belief had only a negligible number of adherents; its heretical nature is unquestionable.

In summary, Milton is in three major respects at odds with the established dogmatics of the Catholic and Protestant churches: he is an anti-Trinitarian; he is a materialist; and he is a mortalist. These major heresies, because he logically develops from them an organized and unified system, necessarily involve him in others. In none of his deviations is he original, though his theology as a whole is. Always, to be sure, the authority upon which he relies is the Bible; but his understanding of Biblical texts is conditioned by his historical knowledge of primitive Christianity. The three major heresies form an integral part of Origen's thought; moreover, in the particulars of doctrine derived from these a further concurrence exists. Milton's millenarianism allies him with the majority of the ante-Nicene Fathers, though not with Origen, who in his opposition to chiliasm is not representative of his contemporaries.

Two transcendent forces govern the shaping of Milton's religious thought. The first is his high regard for liberty, which takes precedence over all other considerations. This great concept illumines his cosmos throughout. If God is free, so are the angels, so are men, and so are the devil and his followers. For Milton creation is liberation; and the result of creation, matter, is left unrestrained to become good or evil according to the power which gives it form. Satan's freedom allows his downfall; Christ's enables him to become king. Man is free to fall and free to rise again. A second force is Milton's equally high regard for reason. Each of his heresies, as I have indicated and as I shall prove more conclusively, is dictated by stern logic; but no less does reason account for those beliefs of his which may be reckoned orthodox.

[7] *Ibid.*, p. 321.

CHAPTER FOUR

ORIGEN AND MILTON

Let us descend now therefore from this top
Of Speculation;

P.L., xii, 588–89

The ancient Fathers of the Church, as we have seen, were influenced strongly by Logos Christianity; they were predominantly anti-Trinitarian in doctrine; because of their familiarity with the philosophy of the Greeks, especially that of Plato, they tended to bring into concord the Jewish and the Greek views of creation and the nature of the universe; and, though they were the champions of a fresh revelation, they used the old and proved dialectic of the pagan thinkers to buttress the tenets of the new religion. Origen summed up much of their thought and presented it in the first organized system of Christian belief, the *De Principiis*. Much of what Origen promulgated is unexceptionally orthodox; still, as I have shown, the treatise was decried by Jerome and by others as heretical and its author's name became anathema.

My presentation of Origen's theology in this chapter will be deliberately limited, for only that which will contribute to the understanding of Milton will be set forth. With the exception of the initial comparison of exegetical methods and the digression on evil which comes in later, my extractions from Origen's integrated system have been chosen to accommodate the structural components of Milton's theology as outlined in the preceding chapter. I am confident, however, that no distortion of the true character of Origen's views results in the process. Indeed, their impact as a unified whole may be experienced by any reader willing to delete for its sake the juxtaposed and sometimes argumentative discussions of the Miltonic doctrine.

Since it is almost exclusively the first book of *The Christian Doctrine* which furnishes the ideological framework of *Paradise Lost*, parallels between Origen's writings and the second book of Milton's treatise have not been sought.

The generous employment of quotation both from Origen and Milton has been made necessary by the nature of my task. A comparison of the thought of these two men should not be made through paraphrase by an author who has a vested interest in proving similarities. There is a sort of compulsion to make X equal Y. Studious to avoid this weakness, I have followed Milton's lead in depending on proof texts:

And whereas the greater part of those who have written most largely on these subjects have been wont to fill whole pages with explanations of their own opinions, thrusting into the margin the texts in support of their doctrine with a summary reference to the chapter and verse, I have chosen, on the contrary, to fill my pages even to redundance with quotations from Scripture, that so as little space as possible might be left for my own words, even when they arise from the context of revelation itself.[1]

Nevertheless, the significant and interesting parts of the *De Doctrina* are those in which Milton speaks for himself. I hope that my own interpretations and the arguments in their support will also prove useful.

EXEGESIS

In the fourth book of the *De Principiis*, Origen adduces rules for the interpretation of Scripture which, however much they have been impugned, are, in fact, the methods adopted by Protestant exegetes. "For as man consists of body, and soul, and spirit, so in the same way does Scripture, which has been arranged to be given by God for the salvation of men . . . there are certain passages of Scripture which do not at all contain the 'corporeal' sense . . . there are also places where we must seek only for the 'soul,' as it were, and 'spirit' of Scripture." [2]

Origen believes that the language of the Bible is unmistakably clear to all men insofar as it relates to what is necessary to salvation; but beyond this fundamental revelation lie meanings less apparent,

---

[1] *The Prose Works of John Milton*, ed. J. A. St. John (London, Henry G. Bohn, 1848–53), IV, 5–6. Future reference will be to *Bohn* by volume and page number. I also cite the Columbia Edition by volume and page number: *CE*, XIV, 11.

[2] *Ante-Nicene Christian Library*, ed. Alexander Roberts and James Donaldson (Edinburgh, various dates), X, 301–3. Future reference will be to *ANCL* by volume and page number.

and these constitute a challenge to the serious and talented searcher into the mysteries of God. Only with the aid of the Holy Spirit may wise men uncover hidden truths.

Now it ought to be known that the holy apostles, in preaching the faith of Christ, delivered themselves with the utmost clearness on certain points which they believed to be necessary to every one, even to those who seemed somewhat dull in the investigation of divine knowledge; leaving, however, the grounds of their statements to be examined into by those who should deserve the excellent gifts of the Spirit, and who, especially by means of the Holy Spirit Himself, should obtain the gift of language, of wisdom, and of knowledge: while on other subjects they merely stated the fact that things were so, keeping silence as to the manner or origin of their existence; clearly in order that the more zealous of their successors, who should be lovers of wisdom, might have a subject of exercise on which to display the fruit of their talents, — those persons, I mean, who should prepare themselves to be fit and worthy receivers of wisdom.[3]

Milton declares that Christian doctrine is discoverable "from the Holy Scriptures alone, under the guidance of the Holy Spirit." [4] He further remarks: "It was also evident to me, that, in religion as in other things, the offers of God were all directed, not to an indolent credulity, but to a constant diligence, and to an unwearied search after truth. . . ." [5] I have elsewhere argued that this is the import of the famous concluding lines of Milton's first sonnet on his blindness.[6] *Paradise Lost*, too, contains this idea, in a passage reminiscent of the digression in *Lycidas* concerning the greed and corruption of the clergy.

> Wolves shall succeed for teachers, grievous Wolves,
> Who all the sacred mysteries of Heav'n
> To thir own vile advantages shall turne
> Of lucre and ambition, and the truth
> With superstitions and traditions taint,
> *Left onely in those writt'n Records pure,*
> *Though not but by the Spirit understood.*
> > xii, 508–14 (italics mine)

Origen believes that the Scriptures are accommodated to the limitations of human intelligence: ". . . the word of God appears to have dealt with the history [that is, the Bible], making the capacity of the hearers, and the benefit which they were to receive, the standard of the appropriateness of its announcements." [7]

---

[3] *Ibid.*, pp. 2–3.
[4] *Bohn*, IV, 11; *CE*, XIV, 19.
[5] *Bohn*, IV, 4; *CE*, XIV, 7–8.
[6] "Milton's First Sonnet on His Blindness," *RES*, n.s., VII (1956), 360–66.
[7] *ANCL*, XXIII, 236.

The Christian Doctrine contains this expression of what has come to be known as the doctrine of accommodation:

For granting that both in the literal and figurative descriptions of God, he is exhibited not as he really is, but in such a manner as may be within the scope of our comprehensions, yet we ought to entertain such a conception of him, as he, in condescending to accommodate himself to our capacities, has shewn that he desires we should conceive. For it is on this very account that he has lowered himself to our level, lest in our flights above the reach of human understanding, and beyond the written word of Scripture, we should be tempted to indulge in vague cogitations and subtleties.[8]

The precept is at work in the epic, also:

> . . . what surmounts the reach
> Of human sense, I shall delineat so,
> By lik'ning spiritual to corporeal forms,
> As may express them best,
>
> v, 571–74

GOD

The following passage will serve to sum up Origen's God: " . . . since all that we know is less than God, there is no absurdity in our also admitting that God possesses none of those things 'of which *we* have knowledge.' For the attributes which belong to God are far superior to all things with which not merely the nature of man is acquainted, but even of those who have risen far above it . . . none of us assert that there is any change in God, either in act or thought."[9]

From the attributes of God as they are derived from Biblical proof texts, Origen, no less than Milton, defines the deity.

The first chapter of the *De Principiis* is largely devoted to a discussion of God as a *spirit*.

The idea of God's *immensity* is developed at some length by Origen as a portion of his argument that God is *incomprehensible*:

For instance, suppose that there were a statue of so enormous a size as to fill the whole world, and which on that account could be seen by no one; and that another statue were formed altogether resembling it in the shape of the limbs, and in the features of the countenance, and in form and material, but without the same immensity of size, so that those who were unable to behold the one of enormous proportions, should, on seeing the latter, acknowledge that they had seen the former, because it preserved all the features of its limbs and countenance, and even the very form and material, so closely, as to be altogether undistinguishable from it; by some such similitude, the Son of God, divesting Himself of His equality with the Father,

---

[8] *Bohn*, IV, 16–17; *CE*, XIV, 31–32. See John E. Parish, "Milton and an Anthropomorphic God," *SP*, LVI (1959), 619–25.

[9] *ANCL*, XXIII, 405.

and showing to us the way to the knowledge of Him, is made the express image of His person.[10]

In the explicit anti-Trinitarianism of this passage St. Jerome found an abhorrent heterodoxy. Led by the same kind of inexorable logic, Milton insists upon the definite inferiority of the Son to the Father.

On the *infinity* of God, Origen quotes approvingly from *The Pastor or Angel of Repentance*, supposedly the work of Hermas, a "prophet" of the third Christian generation. " 'First of all, believe that there is one God who created and arranged all things; who, when nothing formerly existed, caused all things to be; who Himself contains all things, but Himself is contained by none.' " [11]

From God's *eternity* Origen implies the eternity of all creation: ". . . because the nature of Father, and Son, and Holy Spirit, of whose intellectual light alone all created things have a share, is incorruptible and eternal, it is altogether consistent and necessary that every substance which partakes of that eternal nature should last forever, and be incorruptible and eternal, so that the eternity of divine goodness may be understood also in this respect, that they who obtain its benefits are also eternal." [12] To Origen, as to other early theologians, there appeared no obvious fallacy in ascribing eternity to that which had its beginning in time. To later theologians and to Milton, however, under a more rigorous intellectual discipline, that could only be considered eternal which had neither beginning nor end. Yet Milton, too, argues that no created thing can be annihilated; for annihilation is the opposite of creation — and God is unable to contradict himself.

For Origen, following Aristotle, eternity necessitates *incorruptibility*.

Because God is eternal and incorruptible, he must be *immutable*. "We show, accordingly, that the Holy Scriptures represent God as unchangeable, both by such words as 'Thou art the same,' and 'I change not'. . . ." [13] From the same proof texts Milton argues: "The IMMUTABILITY of God has an immediate connection with the last attribute [eternity]." [14] "His INCORRUPTIBILITY is also derived from the fourth attribute." [15] In another place he reasons that God must be immutable because "a being infinitely wise and good would neither

---

[10] *Ibid.,* X, 26–27.
[11] *Ibid.,* p. 35.
[12] *Ibid.,* p. 354.
[13] *Ibid.,* XXIII, 174.
[14] *Bohn,* IV, 24; *CE,* XIV, 47.
[15] *Ibid.*

wish to change an infinitely good state for another, nor would be able to change it without contradicting his own attributes." [16]

Of God's *omnipresence* Origen, in his reply to Celsus, writes: "And we do not ask the question, 'How shall we go to God?' as though we thought that God existed in some place. God is of too excellent a nature for any place: He holds all things in His power, and is Himself not confined by anything whatever." [17]

Origen argues that the creation demonstrates the *omnipotence* of God; for "as no one can be a father without having a son, nor a master without possessing a servant, so even God cannot be called omnipotent unless there exist those over whom He may exercise His power, and therefore, that God may be shown to be almighty, it is necessary that all things should exist." [18] Here he anticipates, though he does not stress, a limitation of God's omnipotence which becomes for Milton a central tenet. This limitation, in Origen's words, is that "God cannot do anything which is contrary to reason, or contrary to Himself." [19] Origen supports the doctrine that God cannot contradict himself by arguments such as this: ". . . as that which by nature possesses the property of sweetening other things through its own inherent sweetness cannot produce bitterness contrary to its own peculiar nature, nor that whose nature it is to produce light through its being light can cause darkness; so neither is God able to commit wickedness, for the power of doing evil is contrary to His deity and its omnipotence." [20] The discussion of omnipotence in the *De Doctrina* closes with the succinct assertion, accompanied by Biblical proof texts, that "the power of God is not exerted in things which imply a contradiction." And *Paradise Lost* contains this passage, in which an identical limitation is placed upon God's omnipotence:

> Can he make deathless Death? that were to make
> Strange contradiction, which to God himself
> Impossible is held, as Argument
> Of weakness, not of Power.
>
> x, 798–801

Origen is most emphatic upon the subject of God's *unity*; and, as we shall see, he holds precisely Milton's view of the subordination of the second and third persons to the first. Furthermore, in postulating *unity* as one of God's attributes, Origen takes care to refute the

[16] *Bohn*, IV, 28; *CE*, XIV, 59.
[17] *ANCL*, XXIII, 456.
[18] *Ibid.*, X, 28.
[19] *Ibid.*, XXIII, 292–93.
[20] *Ibid.*, p. 149.

heresy of Marcion, an early Gnostic (fl. A.D. 144), who maintained the existence of two disparate deities — the God of the Old Testament, just but passionate and revengeful; and the New Testament God of goodness. For Origen, of course, there was no reason to dispute the Trinitarian position, in his day not elevated to the importance of dogma. Milton's argument for the unity of God in *The Christian Doctrine* lays the basis for his subordinationism; the essence of his argument is that if God is one, he cannot be three.

Origen's God is *incomprehensible*, beyond the understanding of man's inadequate intelligence: ". . . according to strict truth, God is incomprehensible, and incapable of being measured. For whatever be the knowledge which we are able to obtain of God, either by perception or reflection, we must of necessity believe that He is by many degrees far better than what we perceive Him to be." [21]

The attributes from which God is defined in the *De Principiis* and in the *De Doctrina* are also those by which God is delineated in *Paradise Lost*:

> Thee Father first they sung Omnipotent,
> Immutable, Immortal, Infinite,
> Eternal King;
>
> iii, 372–74
>
> . . . he also went
> Invisible, yet staid (such priviledge
> Hath Omnipresence). . . .
>
> vii, 588–90
>
> O goodness infinite, goodness immense!
>
> xii, 469
>
> All incorruptible would on his Throne
> Sit unpolluted,
>
> ii, 138–39

As Saurat has argued, it must be inferred from the attributes as Milton derives them that his God is the Absolute. All of the aspects of Milton's theology which seem most daring and unusual, most heretical, are developed consequentially from them. Milton's materialism stems from his belief in the infinity of God; for matter is present in infinity and therefore in God. Milton's anti-Trinitarianism evolves from God's unity and his immutability. Milton's mortalism is dependent upon the condition he attaches to God's omnipotence; for, having once created bodies, God cannot annihilate them — if he did he would create and uncreate and thus contradict himself. Each

---

[21] *Ibid.*, X, 11.

of Milton's lesser divagations from orthodox positions may be traced with equal ease to the attributes which characterize his God.

Once having decided upon the nature of God, Milton is faced with a number of very real difficulties. How may matter be effected from spirit? How can evil exist within a being infinite and pure? How can a cosmos come into being without changing an unchangeable infinity? How can the Absolute suffer change? How, in short, can God create? Milton's obligation as a theologian is to explain away these difficulties, and from this obligation he does not shrink. Professor Kelley, among others, however, accuses the poet of inconsistency: ". . . in the early portion of the *De doctrina*, Milton presents a concept of a Deity so incomprehensible that Saurat identifies it with the Absolute of nineteenth-century philosophy. Later, however, to refute the doctrine that souls are created daily, Milton resorts to an almost literal anthropomorphism — a concept of a God who labors like a man and requires his rest on the seventh day. . . ." [22]

Kelley is, I think, mistaken. Milton has in no way changed his mind about the nature of God. If the passage is almost literally anthropomorphic so is the Biblical text upon which it rests; Milton deals with the problem more than once:

If after the work of six days it be said of God that "he rested and was refreshed" . . . let us believe that it is not beneath the dignity of God . . . to be refreshed in that which refresheth him. . . . For however we may attempt to soften down such expressions by a latitude of interpretation, when applied to the Deity, it comes in the end to precisely the same.[23]

Our safest way is to form in our minds such a conception of God, as shall correspond with his own delineation and representation of himself in the sacred writings.[24]

We may be sure that sufficient care has been taken that the Holy Scriptures should contain nothing unsuitable to the character or dignity of God, and that God should say nothing of himself which could derogate from his own majesty.[25]

Let us require no better authority than God himself for determining what is worthy or unworthy of him.[26]

If therefore we persist in entertaining a different conception of the Deity than that which it is to be presumed he desires should be cherished, inasmuch as he has himself disclosed it to us, we frustrate the purposes of God instead of rendering him submissive obedience. As if, forsooth, we wished

[22] Maurice Kelley, *This Great Argument* (Princeton, N.J., 1941), p. 212n. Future reference will be to *Kelley*.

[23] *Bohn*, IV, 18; *CE*, XIV, 35.

[24] *Bohn*, IV, 16; *CE*, XIV, 31.

[25] *Bohn*, IV, 17; *CE*, XIV, 33.

[26] *Ibid*.

to show that it was not we who had thought too meanly of God, but God who had thought too meanly of us.[27]

Origen anticipates this reasoning of Milton's, warning that man should certainly not be deceived by the anthropomorphic character of individual passages into assumptions unworthy of God's infinite majesty:

. . . in the Old Testament . . . when God is said to be angry or to repent, or when any other human affection or passion is described . . . we have to show . . . that similar statements are found even in the parables of the Gospel. . . . But when we read either in the Old Testament or in the New of the anger of God, we do not take such expressions literally, but seek in them a spiritual meaning, that we may think of God as He deserves to be thought of.[28]

Throughout the writings of Origen, God is the unmanifested Absolute, realized as one spirit, immense, infinite, eternal, unchanging, good, just, omnipotent, omnipresent, incorruptible, incomprehensible — and he is invisible. He is invisible to men, to angels, and even to the Son. "Moreover, John in his Gospel, when asserting that 'no one hath seen God at any time,' manifestly declares to all who are capable of understanding, that there is no nature to which God is visible: not as if He were a being who was visible by nature, and merely escaped or baffled the view of a frailer creature, but because by the *nature* of His being it is impossible for Him to be seen." [29] Origen asserts unequivocally that even the Son is not said in the Scripture to see God, but only to know him: ". . . whatever among bodily creatures is called seeing and being seen, is termed, between the Father and the Son, a knowing and being known, by means of the power of knowledge, not by the frailness of the sense of sight." [30]

In challenging the validity of Saurat's theory that Milton's God is unmanifest, Professor Kelley cites the following from the *De Doctrina*: "'God was made manifest in the flesh': namely, in the Son, his own image; in any other way he is invisible." [31] This passage seems to me not at all a refutation of Saurat's position, which is my own, but rather a strong argument in its favor. Milton insists that God is invisible and that he may only be visualized by means of his image, the Son. Milton says:

. . . to be God, and to be from God, — to be the one invisible God, and to be the only begotten and visible, are things so different that they cannot

---

[27] *Bohn*, IV, 19; *CE*, XIV, 37–39.
[28] *ANCL*, X, 96–97.
[29] *Ibid.*, p. 16.
[30] *Ibid.*, pp. 16–17.
[31] *Kelley*, p. 206.

be predicated of one and the same essence. Besides, considering that his glory even in divine nature before the foundation of the world, was not self derived, but given by the love of the Father, it is plainly demonstrated to be inferior to the Father.[32]

Kelley further contends: "To Milton, moreover, this invisibility of God's did not result from the nature of God, but from the limited and imperfect faculties upon which man depends. . . ."[33] Here Kelley cites from *The Christian Doctrine*:

In this highest heaven seems to be situated the heaven of the blessed; which is sometimes called Paradise . . . where also God permits himself to be seen by the angels and saints (as far as they are capable of enduring his glory), and will unfold himself still more fully to their view at the end of the world.[34]

But the impact of this passage *in vacuo* is obviated by what Milton says immediately preceding and introducing it:

We cannot form any conception of light independent of a luminary; but we do not therefore infer that a luminary is the same as light, or equal in dignity. In the same manner we do not think that what are called *the back parts* of God, Exod. xxxiii. are, properly speaking, God; though we nevertheless consider them to be eternal.[35]

This passage from *The Christian Doctrine* surely was the matrix of one of the most skillfully wrought images in *Paradise Lost*.

> . . . Author of all being,
> Fountain of Light, thy self invisible
> Amidst the glorious brightness where thou sit'st
> Thron'd inaccessible, but when thou shad'st
> The full blaze of thy beams, and through a cloud
> Drawn round about thee like a radiant Shrine,
> Dark with excessive bright thy skirts appeer,
> Yet dazle Heav'n, that brightest Seraphim
> Approach not, but with both wings veil thir eyes.
>
> iii, 374–82

Those who witnessed the explosion of the first atomic bomb in New Mexico were perhaps the first in human history to appreciate fully the phenomenon of light passing beyond brilliance into darkness.

The invisibility of God is frequently declared in both treatise and epic. *The Christian Doctrine* contains, for example, these:

Yet he is not called one with the Father in essence, inasmuch as he was visible to sight. . . .[36]

---

[32] *Bohn*, IV, 143; *CE*, XIV, 337–38.
[33] *Kelley*, p. 207.
[34] *Bohn*, IV, 183–84; *CE*, XV, 31–32.
[35] *Bohn*, IV, 183; *CE*, XV, 31.
[36] *Bohn*, IV, 84; *CE*, XIV, 189.

For the Word . . . is the image, as it were, by which we see God. . . .[37]
. . . for none have seen Jehovah at any time. . . .[38]

And in *Paradise Lost* are found the following:

> . . . th' invisible
> Glory of him that made them,
>
> i, 369–70

> Son in whose face invisible is beheld
> Visibly, what by Deity I am,
>
> vi, 681–82

> Things not reveal'd, which th' invisible King,
> Only omniscient, hath supprest in Night,
>
> vii, 122–23

Origen holds that God, being the Absolute, cannot be heard. When he is said to speak or to command, the anthropomorphism is simply an accommodation to the inferior understanding of man.

Truly, indeed, God can have no voice, if the voice is a concussion of the air, or a stroke on the air, or a species of air, or any other definition which may be given to the voice by those who are skilled in such matters; but what is called the "voice of God" is said to be *seen* as "God's voice" by the people in the passage, "And all the people saw the voice of God;" the word "saw" being taken, agreeably to the custom of Scripture, in a spiritual sense.[39]

In *The Christian Doctrine* God is declared to be inaudible:

It follows therefore that whoever was heard or seen, it was not God; not even where mention is made of God, nay even of Jehovah himself, and of the angels in the same sentence.[40]

For even if he [Esaias] had been of the same essence, he could no more have seen or heard than the Father himself. . . .[41]

The Word, — therefore the Word, was audible. But God, as he cannot be seen, so neither can he be heard. . . .[42]

For the Word . . . as he is the image, as it were, by which we see God, so he is the word by which we hear him. But if such be his nature, he cannot be essentially one with God, whom no one can see or hear.[43]

In *Paradise Lost* God either speaks or appears to speak. Dramatic necessity we may presume accounts for this deviation from Miltonic doctrine. God, though he does not act in the poem, and though he remains otherwise completely unmanifest, is yet most vital in Milton's

[37] *Bohn*, IV, 168; *CE*, XIV, 401.
[38] *Bohn*, IV, 127; *CE*, XIV, 299.
[39] *ANCL*, XXIII, 404.
[40] *Bohn*, IV, 108; *CE*, XIV, 251.
[41] *Bohn*, IV, 108–9; *CE*, XIV, 251.
[42] *Bohn*, IV, 109; *CE*, XIV, 253.
[43] *Bohn*, IV, 168; *CE*, XIV, 401.

scheme. He is the grand center from which all else radiates. The most detailed and abstruse parts of Milton's theology, those most necessary to the true faith, are to be discovered in God's speeches. Milton's real conviction, however, was that God was in every way incomprehensible; this is the dogma of treatise and epic. In allowing God to speak the poet in no way violates orthodoxy, for God speaks in the Bible, too. His speeches in the epic, like those of the Bible, must be received in the light of the doctrine of accommodation. God's audibility, like his anger, his ironic laughter, his rest after the creation, his place in Heaven, his repentance for having made man, and his accompaniment of the Son during the forming of the world, illustrates an ancient theological device through which men may gain a partial glimpse of the unknowable.

It may be argued that God cannot be totally unmanifested or that he cannot be the Absolute because, after all, he *does* have his attributes. But the attributes themselves are absolutes. What limited intelligence can grasp totality in any form? Who can know infinity, omniscience, omnipotence, eternality, or incorruptibility? And how can a God, one of whose very attributes is incomprehensibility, be comprehended by any being other than himself?

The God of *The Christian Doctrine* and of *Paradise Lost* is totality. He fills all space and all time. He has no place because he *is* place; he has no past or future because he *is*; he has no thoughts because a thought, as Milton says, is the expression of an opinion; and God, being omniscient, can have no opinions — he knows. He is "through all numbers absolute, though One" (*P.L.*, viii, 421).

Saurat curiously complains that Milton does not allow God his own attributes, suggesting that God is deprived of them that they may be bestowed upon the Son: ". . . Milton takes all attributes away from God with a zeal which must seem excessive to the right-minded. Justice seems the only attribute he leaves Him, and even then he is careful to show us that justice always takes its course naturally, that it flows from the very constitution of man, without God's interference." [44] As I shall demonstrate, however, Milton insists that the Son's attributes, though they originate from the Father, are to be understood only as partial and derived. To say that Saurat is mistaken here, as I think he surely is, should not obscure the tremendous importance of ideas we owe to him. Of these none is more

---

[44] Denis Saurat, *Milton: Man and Thinker* (London, 1946), p. 170. Future reference will be to *Saurat*.

central to Milton's religious thought than the conception of God as the Absolute.

WISDOM

How may an infinite God produce a finite universe, an eternal God introduce time, the measure of motion, how may a changeless God design a mutable cosmos? In short, how may the relative be generated by the Absolute? This impasse, as Saurat points out, defeated the post-Kantian German philosophers and led Schelling to found the metaphysics of the irrational, which posits an unbridgeable chasm between God and Nature. The difficulty was perceived, however, long before Kant. Plato saw it; and in the *Timaeus* he solves it by having the one unmanifest God make use of the demigods, the gods of Greek mythology, who serve him as agents in the creation. Plato refuses to attempt a serious explanation of the remaining problem: in what manner did the agents themselves come into being? "To know or tell the origin of the other divinities is beyond us, and we must accept the traditions of the men of old time who affirm themselves to be the offspring of the gods — that is what they say — and they must surely have known their own ancestors." [45] When God had given instructions to his agents concerning the creation of man, he remained "in his own accustomed nature, and his children heard and were obedient to their father's word." [46] The neo-Platonists further develop the idea of separation between the One and the many. Their God gradually reveals himself in a variety of emanations. The nous is a second god; the logoi are lesser deities included in the nous; and the process continues with each manifestation becoming less Godlike until the separation is almost complete. Thus Proclus maintains that a hierarchy of five successively descending orders of gods exists between the Absolute and the mundane agencies responsible for the phenomena of our world; below the lowest order is Nature, a spirit subordinate even to these. [47]

In Origen's theology, generation begins with Wisdom, one of the attributes of the Absolute.

And who that is capable of entertaining reverential thoughts or feelings

[45] *The Dialogues of Plato*, tr. B. Jowett (New York, 1937), II, 22.
[46] *Ibid.*, p. 24.
[47] Walter Clyde Curry, *Milton's Ontology, Cosmogony, and Physics* (Lexington, Va., 1957), Chapters I and III. These provide an able summary of neo-Platonic thought upon the creation. Curry's detailed notes are most useful.

regarding God, can suppose or believe that God the Father ever existed, even for a moment of time, without having generated this Wisdom? For in that case he must say either that God was unable to generate Wisdom before He produced her, so that He afterwards called her into being who formerly did not exist, or that He possessed the power indeed, but — what cannot be said of God without impiety — was unwilling to use it; both of which suppositions, it is patent to all, are alike absurd and impious: for they amount to this, either that God advanced from a condition of inability to one of ability, or that, although possessed of the power, He concealed it, and delayed the generation of Wisdom.[48]

It should be noted that Origen thinks of Wisdom as a kind of rational, bodiless, feminine being, and as somehow apart from God. He derives this view, of course, from the words of Solomon in Prov. viii, 22–25, texts which he cites again and again. Wisdom is the great architect's plan for total creation; from it stem all future actions.

Whoever is able to conceive a bodiless existence of manifold speculations which extend to the rationale of all existing things, living and, as it were, ensouled, he will see how well the Wisdom of God which is above every creature speaks of herself, when she says: "God created me in the beginning of His ways, for His works." By this creating act the whole creation was enabled to exist, not being unreceptive of that divine wisdom according to which it was brought into being; for God, according to the prophet David, made all things in wisdom.[49]

In another passage Origen explains the nature of the creative act involved in the generation of Wisdom.

And since all the creative power of the coming creation was included in this very existence of Wisdom (whether of those things which have an original or of those which have a derived existence), having been formed beforehand and arranged by the power of foreknowledge; on account of these very creatures which had been described, as it were, and prefigured in Wisdom herself, does Wisdom say, in the words of Solomon, that she was created in the beginning of the ways of God, inasmuch as she contained within herself either the beginnings, or forms, or species of all creation.[50]

Wisdom in Origen's thought is a personified abstraction, unmanifested as the Absolute himself, "a bodiless existence of manifold speculations," existing simply as Idea within God, yet separate from him. Wisdom and foreknowledge are linked.

The correspondence between Origen's and Milton's conceptions of Wisdom seems to me most striking. In his discussion of God's

[48] *ANCL*, X, 19.

[49] *Origen's Commentaries on John* . . . , in *The Ante-Nicene Fathers*, ed. and tr. Allan Menzies (New York, 1906), IX, 39. Future reference will be to *Comm. John.*

[50] *ANCL*, X, 19.

general decree in *The Christian Doctrine,* Milton first defines his
terms:

The DECREES OF GOD are GENERAL or SPECIAL. GOD'S GENERAL DECREE is that
WHEREBY HE HAS DECREED FROM ALL ETERNITY OF HIS OWN MOST FREE AND
WISE AND HOLY PURPOSE, WHATEVER HE HIMSELF WILLED, OR WAS ABOUT TO DO.

He then explains the component phrases of the definition, among
them:

MOST WISE — ; that is, according to his perfect foreknowledge of all things
that were to be created.

.   .   .   .

Hence it is absurd to separate the decrees or will of the Deity from his
eternal counsel and foreknowledge, or to give them priority of order. *For
the foreknowledge of God is nothing but the wisdom of God, under another
name, or that idea of every thing, which he had in his mind, to use the
language of men, before he decreed anything.*[51]

In other words, Wisdom precedes God's decree; and the decree precedes its execution. The working out of God's plan for the cosmos, in
Milton's view, does not change God. The universe, though given
form within the limits of time, has existed from eternity as Idea in
the intelligence of God. In *Paradise Lost,* God's Wisdom is eternal:

Thou with Eternal wisdom didst converse,
vii, 9

It is personified once as a feminine being.

Wisdom thy Sister. . . .
vii, 10

It is instrumental in the creation.

. . . whose wisdom had ordaind
Good out of evil to create, in stead
Of Spirits maligne a better Race to bring
Into thir vacant room, and thence diffuse
His good to Worlds and Ages infinite.
vii, 187–91

And in the following passage there is perhaps a hint of that time
before the measurement of time when God was utterly alone and
Wisdom had not yet been called into existence as an entity:

So Ev'n and Morn accomplishd the Sixt Day:
Yet not till the Creator from his work
Desisting, though unwearied, up returnd,
Up to the Heav'n of Heav'ns his high abode,
Thence to behold this new created World
Th' addition of his Empire, how it shewd

---

[51] *Bohn,* IV, 30–31; *CE,* XIV, 65. Italics mine.

In prospect from his Throne, how good, how faire,
Answering his great Idea.

vii, 550–57 (italics mine)

MATTER

The nature of matter and where it came from are problems which
lie at the core of doctrinal utterances on the creation. The orthodox
belief has from earliest times been that God created matter *ex nihilo*;
this belief is dictated by the need to preserve the absolute spirituality
of God. A second theory, which never received support from influential theologians, is that God discovered in the void the material from
which the universe was created. This theory supposes that the creation was a cosmic accident. Differing radically from these, the position of both Origen and Milton is that matter was created *ex deo.*
Fundamental to Origen's argument is his definition of the word
"incorporeal." The term, he maintains,

is disused and unknown, not only in many other writings, but also in our
own Scriptures. And if any one should quote it to us out of the little treatise
entitled *The Doctrine of Peter,* in which the Saviour seems to say to His
disciples, "I am not an incorporeal demon," I have to reply . . . that that
work is not included among ecclesiastical books. . . . But even if the point
were to be conceded, the word incorporeal there does not convey the same
meaning as is intended by Greek and Gentile authors when incorporeal nature is discussed by philosophers. For in the little treatise referred to he
used the phrase "incorporeal demon" to denote that that form or outline
of demoniacal body, whatever it is, does not resemble this gross and visible
body of ours; but agreeably to the intention of the author of the treatise,
it must be understood to mean that He had not such a body as demons have,
which is naturally fine, and thin as if formed of air (and for this reason is
either considered or called by many incorporeal), but that He had a solid
and palpable body. Now, according to human custom, everything which is
not of that nature is called by the simple or ignorant incorporeal; as if one
were to say that the air which we breathe was incorporeal, because it is not
a body of such a nature as can be grasped and held, or can offer resistance
to pressure.[52]

Origen here advances the idea that the bodies of demons, termed
incorporeal by the unlearned, are really bodies of such tenuousness
that the gross senses of human beings are incapable of apprehending
them. (Milton's spirits, angelic and demonic, at times in *Paradise
Lost* are corporeal in just this sense.) Origen is working toward a
conclusion with which few theologians have ever concurred: "We
shall inquire, however, whether the thing which Greek philosophers

---

[52] *ANCL,* X, 5–6.

call . . . 'incorporeal,' is found in holy Scripture under another name. For it is also to be a subject of investigation how God himself is to be understood, — whether as corporeal, and formed according to some shape, or of a different nature from bodies, — a point which is not clearly indicated in our teaching." [53]

Origen's opinion that God, though a spirit, is yet in some sense material must be understood in the light of his concept of matter. This concept is very largely Aristotelian, though it contains elements drawn from other Greek philosophers. He believes, first, in a substratum or *materia prima*, which is invisible and formless in its essence. This is never found upon earth in its purest state; for it is always accompanied by, or combined with, four qualities: hot, cold, moist, and dry. Aristotle says that these qualities are paired in all possible ways except that direct opposites cannot unite (for example, moist and dry will not mix). Thus, the qualities moist and cold, together with the underlying *materia prima*, combine to make "pure" water, or what Aristotle terms the "like water," which, deteriorating, becomes water as we know it on earth. In similar fashion, moist and hot, with the substratum, make air, dry and cold make earth, and dry and hot make fire. Any element may be transmuted into any other by the gradual replacement of a quality by its opposite: for example, earth (cold and dry) can be changed into either fire (hot and dry) or water (cold and moist) in one step, and into air (hot and moist) in two. Origen is surely following this Aristotelian concept of matter when he writes:

By matter, therefore, we understand that which is placed under bodies, viz. that by which, through the bestowing and implanting of qualities, bodies exist; and we mention four qualities — heat, cold, dryness, humidity. These four qualities being implanted in . . . matter (for matter is found to exist in its own nature without those qualities before mentioned), produce the different kinds of bodies. Although this matter is, as we have said above, according to its own proper nature without qualities, it is never found to exist without a quality.[54]

In Milton's description of Chaos, the stockpile of unused matter left over from the creation of the cosmos, principles of Aristotelian physics are recognizable.

> For hot, cold, moist, and dry, four Champions fierce
> Strive here for Maistrie, and to Battel bring
> Thir embryon Atoms; they around the flag
> Of each his Faction, in thir several Clanns,

---

[53] *Ibid.*, pp. 6–7.
[54] *Ibid.*, pp. 75–76.

> Light-armd or heavy, sharp, smooth, swift or slow,
> Swarm populous,
>
> *P.L.*, ii, 898–903

Pure matter, the *materia prima*, is invisible, formless, and without qualities. It is, in Origen's terminology, "incorporeal." God, too, is incorporeal; and the final, venturous linkage of matter with God is but one step farther in Origen's thought. Answering the pagan Celsus, he writes:

But "God does not partake even of substance." For He is partaken of [by others] rather than Himself partakes of them. . . . A discussion about "substance" would be protracted and difficult, and especially if it were a question whether that which is permanent and immaterial be "substance" properly so called, so that it would be found that God is *beyond* "substance," communicating of His "substance," by means of office and power, to those to whom He communicates Himself by His Word . . . or even if He *is* "substance," yet He is said to be in His nature "invisible," in those words respecting our Saviour, who is said to be "the image of the *invisible* God," while from the term "invisible" it is indicated that He is "immaterial." It is also a question for investigation, whether the "only-begotten" and "first-born of every creature," is to be called "substance of substances," while above all there is His Father and God.[55]

In this passage it seems to me that Origen (or perhaps Rufinus, for his own sake, in an attempt to protect Origen from a charge of heresy) deliberately takes refuge in abstruseness in order to postulate the material nature of God. From what Origen says, however, these inferences are inescapable: (1) God includes all matter; (2) God *is* matter, but matter so pure, so tenuous, so formless, as to be completely beyond apprehension by the senses and capable only of being conceived by the most enlightened intelligence; (3) not the Word but God is the "substance of substances"; (4) the impermanence which Plato attributes to matter is not attributable to the *materia prima*.

Origen's contention that matter is developed from the "incorporeal" substance of God derives from his understanding of God's nature. Matter cannot come *ex nihilo* because God is infinite, filling all space and obviating the possibility of nothingness. For matter to have existed apart from God and to have been discovered accidentally by God is precluded by God's infinity and omniscience. Since God is totality, matter cannot even emanate from him, for there would be no *place* to receive it. Matter comes into existence

---

[55] *Ibid.*, XXIII, 406–7.

when, at the time of the creation, the freed substance of God is given form through the addition of the Aristotelian qualities.

Milton's belief that original matter is *ex deo* has been noted by readers since 1825; it is held by almost every critic to be one of the poet's boldest heresies.[56] Conklin goes so far as to declare that the principle is Milton's. "No precise parallel can, in fact, be found between Milton's conception of the creation and that of any other. To examine the hexaemeral literature is of no avail here for the simple reason that Milton did not believe in the orthodox creation *ex nihilo* but a creation from a preexistent matter which proceeded somewhere in time out of God Himself." [57]

Milton admits only two possibilities: either matter existed independently from eternity or it must have been originated by God at some particular time. The attributes of God prohibit the eternal existence of matter; for God alone is eternal and infinite. Milton reasons: "If on the contrary it did not exist from all eternity, it is difficult to understand from whence it derives its origin. There remains, therefore, but one solution of the difficulty, for which moreover we have the authority of Scripture, namely, that all things are of God." [58] Since God is infinite and omnipresent, since he is totality, matter is of necessity formed of and within him. "Nor, lastly, can it be understood in what sense God can properly be called infinite, if he be capable of receiving any accession whatever; which would be the case if anything could exist in the nature of things, which had not first been of God and in God." [59]

Both Origen and Milton buttress their argument that matter is of God by quoting a verse from the Apocrypha, II Macc. vii, 28: "I beseech thee, my son, look upon the heaven and the earth, and all that is therein, and consider that God made them of things that were not; and so was mankind made likewise." The point of the citation seems to lie in the plural usage of "things"; for as Milton says in connection with Heb. xi, 3, *"Now the things which do not appear are not to be considered as synonymous with nothing (for nothing*

---

[56] For a summary of what was said by the critics upon the occasion of the publication of *The Christian Doctrine* in 1825, see Francis Mineka, "The Critical Reception of Milton's *De Doctrina Christiana," University of Texas Studies in English* (Austin, 1943), pp. 115–47.

[57] George N. Conklin, *Biblical Criticism and Heresy in Milton* (New York, 1949), p. 67.

[58] *Bohn,* IV, 178; *CE,* XV, 21.

[59] *Bohn,* IV, 181; *CE,* XV, 27.

does not admit of a plural, nor can a thing be made and compacted together out of nothing, as out of a number of things), but the meaning is, that they do not appear as they now are. The apocryphal writers, whose authority may be considered as next to that of the Scriptures, speak to the same effect." [60]

Origen argues further that matter, which originates in God, is maintained by his power and returns eventually to him: ". . . Paul declares, that 'Of Him, and through Him, and to Him are all things,' showing that He is the beginning of the substance of all things by the words 'of Him,' and the bond of their subsistence by the expression 'through Him,' and their final end by the terms 'to Him.' " [61] Matter as we know it here on earth, full of impurity and manifested by the admixture of qualities which make it corporeal, cannot return to God. It is, in its essence — in its "incorporeal" state — indestructible. Origen argues: ". . . we know of no incorporeal substance that is destructible by fire, nor do we believe that the soul of man, or the substance of 'angels,' or of 'thrones,' or 'dominions,' or 'principalities,' or 'powers,' can be dissolved by fire." [62] A belief in the indestructibility of matter underlies Milton's mortalism. Milton reasons thus: "Since . . . God did not produce everything out of nothing, but out of himself, I proceed to consider the necessary consequence of this doctrine, namely, that if all things are not only from God, but of God, no created thing can finally be annihilated" (Bohn, IV, 181; CE, XV, 27). Fortunately, however, in the thought of both men, matter is alterable in its grosser manifestations — it may be purified until it arrives at that incorporeal state in which it is suited for assimilation into the Heaven of Heavens, and eventually into God. Origen writes: "That the matter which underlies bodies is capable of receiving those qualities which the Creator pleases to bestow, is a point which all of us who accept the doctrine of providence firmly hold; so that, if God so willed, one quality is at the present time implanted in this portion of matter, and afterwards another of a different and better kind." [63] Jerome, who is not interested in softening the heresies of Origen, translates a continuance of this argument thus: "Either we shall always have bodies and in that case must despair of ever being like God; or, if the blessedness of the life of God is

[60] Bohn, IV, 177; CE, XV, 17–19.
[61] ANCL, XXIII, 407.
[62] Ibid., p. 414.
[63] Ibid., p. 224.

really promised to us, the conditions of His life must be conditions of ours." [64]

To Origen matter is holy; it is cognate with reason; and reason is the divine link between God and man. The five senses can operate only upon qualities, while matter must be understood by the sixth and greatest sense, that of mind:

There underlies every bodily sense a certain peculiar sensible substance, on which the bodily sense exerts itself. For example, colours underlie vision; voices, the sense of hearing; odours, that of smell; savours, that of taste; hardness or softness, that of touch. It is manifest to all that the sense of mind is the best. How, then, should it not appear absurd, that under those senses which are inferior, substances should have been placed on which to exert their powers, but that under the sense of mind, nothing at all of the nature of a substance should be placed, but that a power of an intellectual nature should be an accident, or consequent upon bodies? Those who assert this, doubtless do so to the disparagement of that better substance which is within them; nay by so doing, they even do wrong to God Himself, when they imagine He may be understood by means of a bodily nature, so that according to their view He is a body, and that which may be understood or perceived by means of a body; and they are unwilling to have it understood that the mind bears a certain relationship to God, of whom the mind itself is an intellectual image, and that by means of this it may come to some knowledge of the nature of divinity, especially if it be purified and separated from bodily matter.[65]

The Stoics, the Manichees, and even, at times, the neo-Platonists believed that matter is per se evil.[66] In the theologies of both Origen

---

[64] *Letters and Select Works of St. Jerome*, tr. W. H. Fremantle, in *A Select Library of Nicene and Post-Nicene Fathers of the Christian Church*, 2nd ser., ed. Philip Schaff and Henry Wace (New York, Oxford, and London, 1893), VI, 124.
[65] *ANCL*, X, 15.
[66] Émile Bréhier, in *The Philosophy of Plotinus*, tr. Joseph Thomas (Chicago, 1958), quotes Plotinus to demonstrate that the neo-Platonists regarded matter per se as evil: ". . . evil and vice are 'not in any way the suppression of something that the soul possesses, but the addition of an element which is foreign to it, as phlegm or bile in the body' ([*Enneads*] i. 8. 14. 23). The soul is like a bit of pure gold covered with dirt. 'Impure, carried away in one direction then another by the attraction of the objects of sense . . . containing a great deal which is material . . . it is changed through intermingling with what is inferior. It is like a man who is plunged into the mire and no longer displays the beauty which he possessed but only the mud with which he is covered. His ugliness is due to the addition of a foreign element, and to become beautiful again it will be quite an undertaking for him to cleanse himself in order to become what he was' " (pp. 33–34).
Elsewhere Bréhier says: ". . . Plotinus adds the trait, which is almost absent from his two sources [Plato and Aristotle], that matter is the primary evil ([*Enneads*] i. 8. 3), and that it is the cause of evil for the Soul and even for the rational part of the Soul (*ibid.* 4). It is not easy to interpret the thought of Plotinus on this point. We have observed that Plotinus seems to adopt at times, concern

and Milton, matter, as it was produced or created, is pure and holy, without sin or blot. It had to be so; for of it were created rational, intellectual beings — angels and men. Angels and men resemble God by virtue of their intelligence; by virtue of their intelligence men are set apart from the brute creation. Only after it has fallen under the influence of sinful powers does matter lose its pristine goodness. Origen says:

. . . I cannot understand how so many distinguished men have been of opinion that this matter, which is so great, and possesses such properties as to enable it to be sufficient for all the bodies in the world which God willed to exist, and to be the attendant and slave of the Creator for whatever forms and species He wished in all things, receiving into itself whatever qualities He desired to bestow upon it was uncreated, *i.e.* not formed by God Himself, who is the creator of all things, but that its nature and power were the result of chance.[67]

Elsewhere Origen speaks admiringly of "the power and intelligence of uncreated nature," which is of God. And he denies that "matter, dwelling among mortal things, is the cause of evils. . . . For it is the mind of each individual which is the cause of the evil which arises in him, and this is evil in the abstract; while the actions which proceed from it are wicked, and there is, to speak with accuracy, nothing else in our view that is evil." [68]

For Milton, matter as it originated was invisible and without form. It is of God, and as such it cannot be evil:

. . . it is an argument of supreme power and goodness, that such diversified, multiform, and inexhaustible virtue should exist and be *substantially* inherent in God (for that virtue cannot be *accidental* which admits of degrees, and of augmentation or remission, according to his pleasure) and that this diversified and substantial virtue should not remain dormant within the Deity, but should be diffused and propagated and extended as far and in such manner as he himself may will. For the original matter of which we speak, is not to be looked upon as an evil or trivial thing, but as intrinsically good, and the chief productive stock of every subsequent good. It was a substance, and derivable from no other source than from the

---

ing the origin of evil, the thesis of the Stoic theodicy which makes evil an inevitable accompaniment of the cosmic harmony. But here evil, like matter, appears as a sort of absolute opposed to the Good — as darkness, obscure depths, irrationality, opposed to light and reason (vi. 3. 7; ii. 4. 5) — as exhibiting a baneful activity, seeking to arrogate to itself the form which dwells in it, 'to attach to form its own absence of form, to the proportioned being its own excess and lack of measure,' doing its best through its agitation 'to impair the work of the reasons.' Matter appears, as in Manichaeism, as a positive principle of evil, an Ahriman destroyer of the order of Ormuzd" (pp. 179–80).

[67] *ANCL*, X, 76.
[68] *Ibid.*, XXIII, 232.

fountain of every substance, though at first confused and formless, being afterwards adorned and digested into order by the hand of God.[69]

The penultimate sentence in this quotation has, I think, caused Miltonists to go astray. Saurat, for example, derives from it the thesis that everything "has come out of matter by a normal development of its latent powers without any intervention of God."[70] If Saurat were right, a creator would be unnecessary in the Miltonic system; Heaven and earth could have produced themselves; and Chaos would be teeming with self-generated worlds, each containing sentient beings. The words "productive stock," as applied to original matter, are, indeed, misleading. Reference to Milton's Latin will clarify Bishop Sumner's translation. Milton wrote: ". . . neque enim materia illa res mala est, aut vilis existimanda, sed bona, omnisque boni postmodum producendi seminarium. . . ."[71] A literal translation would read: ". . . for that material must not be regarded as an evil thing or a trivial one, but as a good thing, the seed-bed of every good *afterward about to be produced*." It is proper to assume, then, that matter does not itself produce every subsequent good, but that it is the material from which all subsequent good is produced.

Saurat even goes so far as to aver that matter in Milton's theology produces soul: "For matter produces life and all forms, including the soul: 'It is acknowledged by the common consent of almost all philosophers, that every *form*, to which class the human soul must be considered as belonging, is produced by the power of matter.' All this is the normal development of the idea contained in Milton's phrase about matter being the 'productive stock of every subsequent good.' "[72] But the first passage cited by Saurat is immediately preceded in *The Christian Doctrine* by a sentence which clearly indicates that Milton is discussing not the creation of the soul but its propagation. "If the soul be equally diffused throughout any given whole, and throughout every part of that whole, how can the human seed, the noblest and most intimate part of all the body, be imagined destitute and devoid of the soul of the parents, or at least of the father, when communicated to the son by the laws of generation."[73]

Anticipating the objection that matter cannot emanate from spirit, Milton replies, "much less then can body emanate from nothing." For spirit being the more excellent substance, virtually and essentially con-

---

[69] *Bohn*, IV, 179; *CE*, XV, 21–23.
[70] *Saurat*, p. 116.
[71] *CE*, XV, 22.
[72] *Saurat*, p. 118.
[73] *Bohn*, IV, 192–93; *CE*, XV, 47–49.

tains within itself the inferior one; as the spiritual and rational faculty contains the corporeal, that is, the sentient and vegetative faculty. For not even divine virtue and efficiency could produce bodies out of nothing, according to the commonly received opinion, unless there had been some bodily power in the substance of God; since no one can give to another what he does not himself possess.[74]

Origen insists that everything is made of the one holy and pure matter. Angels and men are of the same matter; only in their purity and tenuousness do they differ. All creatures have bodies, though angels and demons do not have bodies of flesh:

. . . that material substance of this world, possessing a nature admitting of all possible transformations, is, when dragged down to beings of a lower order, moulded into the crasser and more solid condition of a body, so as to distinguish those visible and varying forms of the world; but when it becomes the servant of more perfect and more blessed beings; it shines in the splendour of celestial bodies, and adorns either the angels of God or the sons of the resurrection with the clothing of a spiritual body, out of all which will be filled up the diverse and varying state of the one world.[75]

The passage from *Paradise Lost* which best sums up Milton's conception of the indestructibility of matter, of its capacity to assume multitudinous forms, its essential holiness, and its eventual return to God is the following:

> O *Adam*, one Almightie is, from whom
> All things proceed, and up to him return,
> If not deprav'd from good, created all
> Such to perfection, one first matter all,
> Indu'd with various forms, various degrees
> Of substance, and in things that live, of life;
> But more refin'd, more spiritous, and pure,
> As neerer to him plac't or neerer tending
> Each in thir several active Sphears assignd,
> Till body up to spirit work, in bounds
> Proportioned to each kind. So from the root
> Springs lighter the green stalk, from thence the leaves
> More aerie, last the bright consummat floure
> Spirits odorous breathes: flours and thir fruit
> Mans nourishment, by gradual scale sublim'd
> To vital spirits aspire, to animal,
> To intellectual, give both life and sense,
> Fansie and understanding, whence the Soule[76]

---

[74] *Bohn*, IV, 181; *CE*, XV, 25.

[75] *ANCL*, X, 78–79.

[76] The image which likens the gradations of matter to the root, stalk, leaf, flower, and fruit of a plant is several times hinted in Origen; it occurs also in the *De Rerum Principio* of Duns Scotus, himself a disciple of Origen: "Ex his apparet, quod mundus est arbor quaedam pulcherrima, cujus radix et seminarium est materia prima, folia fluentia sunt accidentia; frondas et rami sunt creata

Reason receives, and reason is her being,
Discursive, or Intuitive; discourse
Is oftest yours, the latter most is ours,
Differing but in degree, of kind the same.

. . . .

And from these corporal nutriments perhaps
Your bodies may at last turn all to spirit,
Improv'd by tract of time, and wingd ascend
Ethereal, as wee, or may at choice
Here or in Heav'nly Paradises dwell;

V, 469–500

A significant difference between the theological views of Origen and Milton lies in their conceptions of the interrelationship of matter and free will. Origen, arguing inductively from his observations of change and diversity in the world, holds that rational creatures have achieved their positions in the chain of being through being degraded in various degrees from an original state of equality and purity. Free will, in other words, is bestowed upon the rational creation by God. Origen says:

When He in the beginning created those beings which He desired to create, *i.e.* rational natures, He had no other reason for creating them than on account of Himself, *i.e.* His own goodness. As He Himself, then, was the cause of the existence of those things which were to be created, in which there was neither any variation nor change, nor want of power, He created all whom He made equal and alike, because there was in Himself no reason for producing variety and diversity. But since those rational creatures themselves, as we have frequently shown, and will yet show in the proper place, were endowed with the power of free-will, this freedom of will incited each one either to progress by imitation of God, or reduced him to failure through negligence. And this, as we have already stated, is the cause of the diversity among rational creatures, deriving its origin not from the will or judgment of the Creator, but from the freedom of the individual will.[77]

Milton, on the other hand, contends that the creation is free because it is comprised of matter freed from God's goodness. Upon the freedom of matter rests the poet's defense of the freedom from God's will of both angelic and human beings, who obey or disobey, stand or fall, through their own choice. When they fall away from God, evil enters the cosmos; Satan, leader of the first revolt, is the father of

corruptibilia; flos, rationalis anima; fructus naturae consimiles et perfectionis, natura Angelica." C. R. S. Harris, *Duns Scotus* (Oxford, 1927), II, 84–85n. Further study of the relationship between Scotus and Milton would, I am sure, prove rewarding. Milton, it will be recalled, lists the subtle doctor as a great teacher along with Aquinas, though neither, he maintains, is the equal of the sage and serious Spenser.

[77] *ANCL*, X, 132–33.

evil. Milton's concepts of free will, of the providence of God, of the government of angels and men, and of predestination are based squarely upon the doctrine that matter is divorced from God. In Milton's thought *all* matter is free.

According to Origen's theory of matter, however, only rational creatures (angels, men, and demons) are free — the insentient creation is ruled by necessity. Origen develops this idea at great length. Of things that move, he says, some have the cause of their motion within themselves; others, again, are moved only from without. Wood and stones, for example, are moved from without. Matter in flux or in the process of dissolution, and thus moving, may be ruled out of the discussion. Other things — animals, plants, veins of metals, fire, and springs of water — have the cause of motion within themselves. Some of this class have souls and are alive, while others are alive but without souls. Of creatures with souls there are those, as spiders, bees, even hunting dogs and war horses, which act through natural instinct, following a phantasy leading them to spin, form wax, and perform other specific instinctive functions. Origen says:

The rational animal, however, has, in addition to its phantasial nature, also reason, which judges the phantasies, and disapproves of some and accepts others; in order that the animal may be led according to them. Therefore, since there are in the nature of reason aids towards the contemplation of virtue and vice, by following which, after beholding good and evil, we select the one and avoid the other, we are deserving of praise when we give ourselves to the practice of virtue, and censurable when we do the reverse.[78]

Thus, despite the difference of Origen's approach and despite the distinction which he draws between rational and irrational beings, the construction which he places on the freedom of matter leads him to Milton's conclusion as it is expressed in *Paradise Lost*: "Reason also is choice" (iii, 108).

The *process* by which matter is evolved from the substance of God is not treated by Origen or by Milton in *The Christian Doctrine* except by implication. For an understanding of this process we must turn to *Paradise Lost*. In Book vii, God charges his Son with the creation of the world in these words:

> . . . ride forth and bid the Deep
> Within appointed bounds be Heav'n and Earth,
> Boundless the Deep, because I am who fill
> Infinitude, nor vacuous the space.
> Though I uncircumscrib'd my self retire,
> And put not forth my goodness, which is free

---

[78] *Ibid.*, pp. 159–60.

> To act or not, Necessity and Chance
> Approach not mee, and what I will is Fate.
>
> vii, 166–73

Ever since Saurat drew attention to these lines and based upon them his theory of creation by God's "retraction," they have been the occasion of intense debate among Miltonists. Saurat held that Milton believed in an Absolute God incapable of creation, since creation implies manifestation. Explicating the lines from *Paradise Lost* just quoted, Saurat argues: "According to his eternal plans, God withdraws his will from certain parts of Himself, and delivers them up, so to speak, to obscure latent impulses that remain in them. Through this 'retraction,' matter is created; through this retraction, individual beings are created. The parts of God thus freed from his will become persons." [79] My objections to this explanation are these. First, it is not God's will which is withdrawn from a part of himself, but his goodness. Second, matter thus created by the withdrawal of goodness is insentient; it is incapable of "latent impulses" toward either good or evil. Satan is the father of evil because he freely chooses to set himself against God. Matter in its original state is incapable of further development until creation takes place; then the universe is created from a portion of it. What is left over is Chaos, which must ever remain neutral unless the "Almighty Maker" uses it as "His dark materials to create more Worlds." [80] Matter cannot become persons; it cannot become things; it cannot become even elements until it is brought under control. Bishop Sumner's translation, as I have pointed out, also misled Saurat, who gave the phrase "chief productive stock" an active emphasis which Milton's Latin does not justify.

Saurat is likewise wrong in thinking that matter derives from the Son. "God has created all beings," Saurat says, "not out of nothing, but out of Himself. Since God is entirely non-manifested, this applies to the Son. The Son is thus both Creator and Creation — the spirit or essence that resides in things and is their being, and not a creator that shapes from outside an independent matter." [81] But Milton explicitly denies that matter is made by the Son. "The Father is he *of whom.* . . . The Son is not he *of whom,* but only *by whom.*" [82] The Son is precisely what Saurat has said he is not, "a creator that shapes from outside an independent matter." God has not manifested

---

[79] *Saurat,* pp. 102–3.
[80] *P.L.,* ii, 914–16.
[81] *Saurat,* p. 112.
[82] *Bohn,* IV, 91; *CE,* XIV, 205.

himself in making matter; for matter when originally brought into existence is invisible and without form. That part of himself which God has freed by withdrawing his goodness from it differs from God only in that it is free. Matter becomes manifest when the Son gives it form; it is therefore the Son who is manifested in the creation.

For a number of reasons, some of which seem to me valid and some not, Professor Kelley emphatically rejects Saurat's theory of creation by retraction and proposes instead another more complex. He interprets the lines from *Paradise Lost* upon which Saurat bases his theory thus:

Matter, according to Milton, proceeded directly from God, undigested and unadorned; and God's first encroachment on this chaos was his creation of the invisible universe — an act whereby God put forth his goodness by giving this *materia prima* order and form. After this action, which digested only a limited part of chaos, the Father returned to his natural state of rest and thus left the remainder of matter in its confused, primeval state until he again chose to extend his dormant goodness and create the visible universe. *Paradise Lost* VII, 168–73, accordingly, is God's explanation for the chaotic, uncreated state of the matter from which the Son is to form the terrestrial universe. It is matter because God fills it. It is boundless because God is infinite. It is confused because from it God has chosen to retire — to withdraw into his normal state of rest — rather than to put forth his goodness and give it form and order. And finally this dormancy of God results not from the compulsion of necessity, fate, or chance, but from the will of the Father himself.[83]

In this view, if I understand Professor Kelley, God is normally at rest; but at a certain time he puts forth his goodness and produces matter. He then returns to his normal rest. At the time of the creation of the invisible universe, he again puts forth his goodness and again returns to his rest. Once more, when the visible universe is created, he puts forth his goodness, and once more returns to rest. This is an interesting theory; but it does not properly describe the works of Milton's God, who engages in no such reciprocative activity. According to Adam (who even before his fall was not omniscient), at a time before the creation of the cosmos, God enjoyed a period of "holy Rest."

> . . . what cause
> Mov'd the Creator in his holy Rest
> Through all Eternity so late to build
> In *Chaos*,
>
> vii, 90–93

---

[83] *Kelley*, p. 211. A. S. P. Woodhouse, in his "Notes on Milton's Views on the Creation: The Initial Phase," *PQ*, XXVIII (1949), p. 233, n. 35, is even more vehemently opposed to Saurat's theory, and for about the same reasons.

Adam cannot know whether or not God rested before the creation. Milton himself does not know; for in *The Christian Doctrine* he writes: "As to the actions of God before the foundation of the world, it would be height of folly to inquire into them, and almost equally so to attempt a solution of the question." [84] Raphael cautions Adam,

> . . . nor let thine own inventions hope
> Things not reveal'd, which th' invisible King,
> Only Omniscient, hath supprest in Night,
> vii, 121–23

Should it be granted, however, that Adam was right, and that God's normal state before the creation of the cosmos was one of "holy Rest," there is still no reason to suppose that he quits that rest upon three separate occasions, returning to a dormant state after each such effort; and there are very good reasons for not thinking so. Kelley first argues that "matter, according to Milton, proceeded directly from God, undigested and unadorned." But nothing can proceed from a God who is totality, who already fills the infinite. Whatever takes place must take place *within God*. It is the Son, however, who creates Heaven (which, in *Paradise Lost*, does not seem to be invisible at all, but merely out of man's sight) by giving form to matter already made, but made formless and invisible. Most important, God is never said to put forth his goodness. One of Kelley's objections to Saurat's theory of the retraction begins: "If creation resulted from the retraction of God, creation can hardly be described as a putting forth of God's goodness. . . ." [85] On these lines both Saurat and Kelley base their contentions:

> Though I uncircumscrib'd my self retire,
> And *put not forth my goodness*,
> vii, 170–71 (italics mine)

Kelley further maintains that God must have put forth his goodness, because "both the treatise and epic state that the purpose of the creation was the manifestation of the glory of God's power and goodness." [86] Here he is confusing the purpose of creation with the method of creation — two quite different things, as are the purpose of a pencil and the manufacture of a pencil. Another defect in Kelley's reciprocative creative theory is that the end product appears to be the manifestation of a dormant God. Now one of the indisputable

---

[84] *Bohn*, IV, 169–70; *CE*, XV, 3.
[85] *Kelley*, p. 211.
[86] *Ibid*.

attributes of Milton's God is that he is a living God; in *Paradise Lost* he is declared to be eternally awake.

> . . . for what can scape the Eye
> Of God All-seeing, or deceive his Heart
> Omniscient,
>
> x, 5–7

And in the *De Doctrina* God is asserted to be him who "REGARDS, PRESERVES, AND GOVERNS THE WHOLE OF CREATION WITH INFINITE WISDOM AND HOLINESS ACCORDING TO THE CONDITIONS OF HIS DECREE." [87]

God, however, active or dormant, is not manifested in the creation. The purpose of the creation was the manifestation of God's power and goodness — not the manifestation of God himself, which because of his very nature is impossible.

Twice in *This Great Argument* Kelley offers his own paraphrase of *P.L.*, vii, 168–73, the lines here under discussion. The two paraphrases are in substantial agreement; and I shall consider the longer and later version, which is:

The deep is boundless because I fill infinitude (an assertion of God's infinity), nor is the deep empty (a denial, by implication, of the doctrine of *creatio ex nihilo*). Although uncircumscribed (a statement of God's omnipotence), I retire and do not put forth my goodness (remain at rest and thus set bounds to my goodness by not reducing all matter to form and order), which is free either to act or not (a statement of God's free agency), my dormant state is not contingent on necessity or chance, nor is it compelled by fate, for fate is nothing more than what I myself will.[88]

The second sentence in this paraphrase does violence both to Milton's syntax and to his logic. Milton's lines are, again:

> Though I uncircumscrib'd my self retire,
> And put not forth my goodness,

Kelley has allowed the important words "my self" to drop out of his paraphrase; and he has given to the active verb "retire" the passive sense of "remain at rest," to which he then accords an active, though negative, meaning ("set bounds to my goodness," etc.).

Professor Kelley's assertion that God's dormant state is "not contingent" upon necessity or chance nor "compelled" by fate frustrates Milton's meaning; for it is not a particular state of God but God himself who is uninfluenced by necessity or chance, who is the author of fate. Matter reduced to form and order, according to Kelley, results when God puts forth his goodness. But original matter in Milton's

---

[87] *Bohn*, IV, 196; *CE*, XV, 55.
[88] *Kelley*, p. 211.

thought is neutral; it results when God puts *not* forth his goodness; it is completely without form and order.

Professor Kelley seems in some doubt about his own interpretation, for in a note upon his paraphrase, he admits:

> In the *N.E.D.*, I can find no clear warrant for attaching these broad and general meanings to "retire" and "approach"; but Taylor's criticism of Saurat (*Milton's Use of Du Bartas*, pp. 40–41) seems to justify such liberty by establishing the conventional nature of the ideas contained in his, and my, interpretation: God's natural state of rest, the concept of creation as a putting forth of goodness and as an expanding rather than a contracting process, and God's independence of necessity or chance. I am disposed, therefore, though not without reluctance, to suggest that Milton, as a poet, was struck primarily by the antithesis offered by "retire" and "approach," and that consequently he did not hesitate to use these two words in a fairly extreme and figurative sense.[89]

Kelley concedes that he has attached unsanctioned meanings to words; he calls upon conventional beliefs to help in the explication of a theology acknowledged by its author to be unconventional; and finally he accuses Milton of being so struck by the antithesis of "retire" and "approach" that he employed these words in a sense which his readers might well find baffling. Kelley's interpretation is in want of a less inconclusive defense than this.

As we have seen, Kelley's meanings for "retire" are two: "remain at rest" and "set bounds to my goodness by not reducing all matter to form and order." The first is vaguely cognate with nineteenth-century euphemism, meaning "go to bed" — the *O.E.D.* offers the example "When most of the . . . people had 'retired,' or, in vulgar language 'gone to bed' 1860"; and even this gloss does not lose sight of the verb's action as Kelley's does. I am at a loss to explain how Kelley derives his second meaning.

I propose either of the following denotations for "retire": (1) *intransitive*, to withdraw, go away, remove oneself (from a place, etc.); (2) *transitive*, to remove from the usual sphere of activity; to take off. Milton's line may then be read: "Though I, uncircumscribed myself, retire. . . ." That is, "Though I who am uncircumscribed myself [in contradistinction to that area of the infinite which is shortly to be given "appointed bounds" (line 167)], retire [withdraw or remove myself *from* a place]. . . ."

Milton's line may also be read: "Though I, uncircumscribed, myself retire. . . ." And the meaning, taking the pronoun "myself" as

---

[89] *Ibid.*, pp. 211–12n.

reflexive rather than intensive and as the object of the transitive
verb "retire," becomes: "Though I who am uncircumscribed remove
myself from my usual sphere of activity. . . ."

In either case, Milton's lines picture one action and one only:
God's creation of unformed matter by the withdrawal of himself
from a portion of infinity. The withdrawal is not repeated; by this
single act God has brought into being all the materials subsequently
to be used by the creating Logos in fashioning the universe. God
speaks in the present tense because for him there is no past or future; he lives in an eternal present. Also, the action which he describes still goes on; and it will continue so long as the universe
remains in existence; he "regards, preserves, and governs the whole
of creation."

After commanding his Son to create the world in Chaos, God explains the existence of Chaos:

> Boundless the Deep, because I am who fill
> Infinitude, nor vacuous the space.

"Chaos is, for all practical purposes, unbounded and full of matter.
I fill it because I fill infinity."

> Though I uncircumscrib'd my self retire,
> And put not forth my goodness, which is free
> To act or not,

"Though I who am without the possibility of further extension or
addition, being already infinite, withdraw my goodness from a portion of space which it previously filled and do not exercise it since
I have the option of exerting it or not. . . ."

> . . . Necessity and Chance
> Approach not mee,

"As God I am not moved in whatever action I take by either necessity or chance." [90]

> . . . And what I will is Fate.

"And all of infinity (including the universe) is still absolutely under
my control, should I choose to exercise it." [91]

It is significant that the description of Chaos in *Paradise Lost*

---

[90] See Woodhouse, *op. cit.*, p. 215: "There is no tenet of orthodox belief to
which Milton adheres more tenaciously than the voluntary character of the creative act."

[91] Cf. John Reesing, "The Materiality of God in Milton's *De Doctrina Christiana*," *Harvard Theological Review*, L (1957), 159–73; Ben Gray Lumpkin, "Fate
in *Paradise Lost*," *SP*, XLIV (1947), 56–68; Warner G. Rice, "Fate in *Paradise
Lost*," *Papers of the Michigan Academy of Science, Arts, and Letters*, XXXI (1945),
299–306.

identifies Chance as one of the entities whose operations "govern" the abyss.

> . . . *Chaos* Umpire sits,
> And by decision more imbroils the fray
> By which he Reigns; next him high Arbiter
> *Chance* governs all.
>
> ii, 907–10

Since Chaos is the uncontrolled matter of God, Chance can work in the Deep without in any way approaching God. Chance functions in a freed area. Even Chaos, though, is still subject to God's will; for there the elements

> . . . must ever fight
> *Unless* the Almighty Maker them ordain
> His dark materials to create more Worlds,
>
> ii, 914–16 (italics mine)

Chance and Necessity ("The Tyrant's plea") may both operate in the world; for the world, too, is made of matter no longer under God's control — hence, free.

> . . . what change
> Absents thee, or what chance detains?

asks the creator when Adam comes to be judged after the Fall (x, 107–8). And Adam answers, "strict necessity" (x, 131). God's operations, however, are never governed by chance, nor are they ever necessitated.

The Christian Doctrine contains one interesting comment never before adduced, so far as I can discover, in connection with God's withdrawal as a part of the process of creation. At the close of his argument that the Son is a secondary deity, Milton, apropos of Phil. ii, 5, says:

For if this passage imply his co-equality with the Father, it rather refutes than proves his unity of essence; since equality cannot exist but between two or more essences. Further, the phrases *he did not think it, — he made himself of no reputation,* (literally, *he emptied himself,*) appear inapplicable to the supreme God. For *to think* is nothing else than to entertain an opinion, which cannot be properly said of God. Nor can the infinite God be said to empty himself, any more than to contradict himself; for infinity and emptiness are opposite terms. But since he [Christ] emptied himself of that form of God in which he had previously existed, if the form of God is to be taken for the essence of the Deity itself, it would prove him [Christ] to have emptied himself of that essence, which is impossible.[92]

The Biblical verse which Milton glosses clearly refers to Christ, but Milton's discussion illuminates the natures of both Christ and God.

---

[92] *Bohn,* IV, 145; *CE,* XIV, 343. Italics mine.

Since God cannot empty himself of his essence (infinity and emptiness are antithetical), the Son cannot empty himself of the form of
God *if the form of God be equivalent to the essence of God.* Christ
does, however, empty himself of the form of God when he becomes
incarnate. The implication is that God can empty himself of his
form, though not of his essence; for, were this not so, the whole
argument would be superfluous. When God "retires" himself, he
empties himself of his form. In God's normal state he fills infinity
with goodness; and this is his "holy Rest." His goodness is free to act
or not. When it does not act, when God "retires," the form of God
(but not the essence) is left free (for space cannot be vacuous — the
infinite God fills it) and matter results.

Though I agree with virtually none of Saurat's conclusions, I believe that his theory of the retraction per se is as sound as it is bril-
liant. I do not think that the Zohar was Milton's source for the
idea, as Saurat urges. For it seems to me that Milton must have been
driven to his concept by logic alone.[93] Postulate that matter is of an
infinite God, that it must be free, and what other solution is tenable?
God cannot emanate matter, for there is no place into which matter
can be emanated. A place must be made for matter within God;
and since Milton's God is in some sense material, he need only to
withdraw his control from a portion of himself to leave freed matter
in an area no longer controlled. As God is infinite and omnipresent,
there can be no vacuum in the Miltonic system.

Chaos is filled with God's matter but free of his influence. This
is the matter which *The Christian Doctrine* describes as invisible
and without form; it in no way manifests God. Thus Chaos is de-
picted in the passage which begins:

> Before thir eyes in sudden view appear
> The secrets of the hoary deep, a dark
> Illimitable Ocean without bound,
> Without dimension, where length, breadth, and highth,
> And time and place are lost; where eldest *Night*
> And *Chaos*, Ancestors of Nature, hold
> Eternal Anarchy, amidst the noise
> Of endless wars, and by confusion stand.
>   ii, 890–97 (see also ii, 898–916)

Matter which is boundless, dimensionless, timeless, and without
place is matter invisible and without form. It is ruled by Chaos —

---

[93] Leon Howard argues that the "retraction" may be explained by Milton's
Ramean logic. See " 'The Invention' of Milton's 'Great Argument': A Study of
the Logic of 'God's Ways to Men,' " *HLQ,* IX (1945), 149–73.

that is, it follows no rule — and it is hidden in darkness. Its atoms are embryonic — they have not yet come into being. The Aristotelian qualities, hot, cold, moist, and dry, are present; but none can achieve mastery over the unruled substratum, the prime matter; each rules only a "moment." Matter is present only potentially; for the elements, earth, air, fire, and water, exist only in their pregnant causes. They cannot come into actuality because order is lacking. Yet Chaos is "the womb of nature"; for order alone, that is, God's goodness, his control, is missing. God may choose to make new worlds. If he does, his material stands ready. He need merely to exercise dominion over it; he need merely to put forth his goodness through his agent, the Son, to bring these dark materials into order. But after God withdraws himself, leaving invisible and formless material in the void, he does no more. The Word, as his agent, from this time forward fulfills the great plan of creation.

THE LOGOS

In Origen's system the creation is enabled to exist through Wisdom, the eternal "bodiless existence of manifold speculations" existing as Idea within the Absolute. Wisdom, never manifested, is personified as feminine. A mysterious coalescence takes place when the Logos, the creating Word, comes into being; for Wisdom and Word are, in Origen, at times one and at times two entities.

Now, in the same way in which we have understood that Wisdom was the beginning of the ways of God, and is said to be created, forming beforehand and containing within herself the species and beginnings of all creatures, must we understand her to be the Word of God, because of her disclosing to all other beings, *i.e.* to universal creation, the nature of the mysteries and secrets which are contained within the divine wisdom; and on this account she is called the Word, because she is, as it were, the interpreter of the secrets of the mind. And therefore that language which is found in the *Acts of Paul*, where it is said that "here is the Word a living being," appears to me to be rightly used. John, however, with more sublimity and propriety, says in the beginning of his Gospel, when defining God by a special definition to be the Word, "And God was the Word, and this was in the beginning with God." [94]

In this quotation the Word is a feminine, personified abstraction, a living entity, inexplicably generated within the Wisdom of God. The separation between Wisdom and the Word takes place in time; Wisdom is the beginning, and "In the beginning was the Word." Origen argues it this way: ". . . the testimonies we cited from Proverbs

[94] *ANCL*, X, 20.

led us to place Wisdom first, and to think of Wisdom as preceding the Word which announces her. We must observe, then, that the Logos is in the beginning, that is, in wisdom, always. Its being in wisdom, which is called the beginning, does not prevent it from being with God, and it is not simply with God, but is in the beginning, in wisdom, with God." [95]

Although the Absolute cannot act, since by acting he would manifest himself, yet the creation is a fact and action is prerequisite to its existence. In Chapters III–VII of *The Christian Doctrine*, Milton attempts a solution to this paradox. He begins by defining the efficiency of God as either internal or external. "The INTERNAL EFFICIENCY of God is that which is independent of all extraneous agency. Such are his decrees." [96] From this it may be deduced that God's internal efficiency is Wisdom; for his decrees, Milton says, should not be separated from his foreknowledge, that is, his idea of "every thing, which he had in his mind . . . before he decreed anything"; and his foreknowledge is "nothing but the wisdom of God, under another name." [97] Milton explains God's external efficiency in these words: "His EXTERNAL EFFICIENCY, or the execution of his decrees, whereby he carries into effect by external agency whatever decrees he has purposed within himself, may be comprised under the heads of GENERATION, CREATION, and the GOVERNMENT OF THE UNIVERSE." [98] Milton's dogma is perfectly clear: the execution of God's decrees is carried out by an agent external to himself. But now Milton has brought himself up against a logical impossibility. For how by external agency can God generate the Word who is his external agent? Milton's explanation is somewhat devious. "Generation must be an external efficiency, since the Father and Son are different persons." [99] The Father is "said in Scripture to have begotten the Son in a double sense, the one literal with respect to the production of the Son, the other metaphorical with reference to his exaltation. . . ." [100] In pursuit of this distinction Milton makes several points. It is, he says, impossible to find a single text in all Scripture which proves the external generation of the Son.[101] Many passages (and Milton cites them) establish the existence of the Son before the world was made,

[95] *Comm. John*, p. 321.
[96] *Bohn*, IV, 30; *CE*, XIV, 63.
[97] *Bohn*, IV, 30–31; *CE*, XIV, 65.
[98] *Bohn*, IV, 79; *CE*, XIV, 179.
[99] *Bohn*, IV, 79; *CE*, XIV, 179–81.
[100] *Bohn*, IV, 80; *CE*, XIV, 181.
[101] *Ibid.*

but they conclude nothing respecting his generation from all eternity.[102] Yet it is certain that the Son existed in the beginning, under the name of the Logos or Word, and that he was the first of the whole creation.[103] In Milton's mind, of course, "the beginning" means the beginning of the creation of the cosmos, that is, of all that is not God; eternity has no beginning. In a sense, to be sure, the Logos is eternal, for as a part of the creation he existed in the mind of God as Idea from eternity. Still, in Milton's august point of view, the creation of the cosmos, indeed its entire history, is a very minor incident in the eternal life of God: ". . . it is not imaginable that God should have been wholly occupied from eternity in decreeing that which was to be created in a period of six days, and which, after having been governed in divers manners for a few thousand years, was finally to be received into an immutable state within himself, or to be rejected from his presence for all eternity." [104]

The Son, in Milton's system, comes into being only in time for "the beginning." Nor does his generation result from necessity, for the physical begetting of a coequal would have been tantamount to the Father's denying himself.

According to Milton, all that can be known of the literal generation of the Son is this:

. . . when the Son is said to be *the first born of every creature*, and *the beginning of the creation of God*, nothing can be more evident than that God of his own will created, or generated, or produced the Son before all things, endued with the divine nature, as in the fulness of time he miraculously begat him in his human nature of the Virgin Mary. The generation of the divine nature is described by no one with more sublimity and copiousness than by the apostle to the Hebrews, i. 2, 3. "whom he hath appointed heir of all things, by whom also he made the worlds; who being the brightness of his glory, and the express image of his person," &c. It must be understood from this, that God imparted to the Son as much as he pleased of the divine nature, nay of the divine substance itself, care being taken not to confound the substance with the whole essence, which would imply, that the Father had given to the Son what he retained numerically the same himself; which would be a contradiction of terms instead of a mode of generation. This is the whole that is revealed concerning the generation of the Son of God. Whoever wishes to be wiser than this, becomes foiled in his pursuit after wisdom, entangled in the deceitfulness of vain philosophy, or rather of sophistry, and involved in darkness.[105]

Milton, it is evident, deserts reason and follows faith. How God by

---

[102] *Bohn*, IV, 81; *CE*, XIV, 181–83.
[103] *Bohn*, IV, 80; *CE*, XIV, 181.
[104] *Bohn*, IV, 170; *CE*, XV, 3–5.
[105] *Bohn*, IV, 85–86; *CE*, XIV, 193.

external agency can have created his external agent, the poet is unable to say. The generation of the Logos defies human logic. We are invited to compare the generation of the Logos with the birth of Christ — "as in the fulness of time he miraculously begat him in his human nature of the Virgin Mary." When we look to see what Milton has to say about the Virgin birth, we discover the following eloquent plea for faith:

Since then this mystery is so great, we are admonished by that very consideration not to assert anything respecting it rashly or presumptuously, on mere grounds of philosophical reasoning; not to add to it anything of our own; not even to adduce in its behalf any passage of Scripture of which the purport may be doubtful, but to be contented with the clearest texts, however few in number. . . . What is essential would easily appear, when freed from the perplexities of controversy; what is mysterious would be suffered to remain inviolate, and we should be fearful of overstepping the bounds of propriety in its investigation.[106]

Milton echoes the cry of the chorus in *Samson Agonistes*, "Down, reason, then; at least vain reasonings down." And he agrees with Raphael's advice to Adam:

> Solicit not thy thoughts with matters hid,
> Leave them to God above, him serve and fear;
> viii, 167–68

Milton has followed logic as far as logic will take him; but he must at last rely upon faith. This is his argument in its entirety:

There is but one supreme God. The chosen people, Christ, Paul, the Apostles, and the followers of the Apostles all concur.

Among the attributes of this one God are eternity and infinity.

Since there is but one God, the Son must be a separate and distinct person.

God, being eternal, must have preceded the Son.

God cannot have generated the Son from necessity; for he would then have generated a coequal; and two infinite beings cannot exist.

God, therefore, must have decreed the generation of the Son of his own free will.

God's decrees, "which he hath purposed within himself," and which are "independent of all extraneous agency," exemplify his internal efficiency.

The Son is begotten in consequence of the decree, and therefore within the limits of time, for the decree must have been anterior to the execution of the decree.

---

[106] *Bohn*, IV, 289–90; *CE*, XV, 265.

God's decrees are executed by external agency — for generation does not pertain to God, who stands in no need of propagation.

We are thus led inescapably to the idea that the Son, who is God's agent, is generated by the external agency of God, in other words, by himself.

But this is an impossibility.

We must therefore discard logic and accept through faith the fact of the miraculous self-production of the Son as willed by the incomprehensible God.

Though Milton recognizes the illogicality of his argument, he thinks it less obnoxious to reason than the opinion of orthodox Trinitarians, in opposition to whose thesis *The Christian Doctrine* offers several polemical passages:

All acknowledge that both the essence and the person of the Father are infinite; therefore the essence of the Father cannot be communicated to another person, for otherwise there might be two, or any imaginable number of infinite persons.[107]

Him who was begotten from all eternity the Father cannot have begotten, for what was made from all eternity was never in the act of being made; him whom the Father begat from all eternity he still begets; he whom he still begets is not yet begotten, and therefore is not yet a son; for an action which has no beginning can have no completion.[108]

If he was originally in the Father, but now exists separately, he has undergone a certain change at some time or other, and is therefore mutable. If he always existed separately from, and independently of, the Father, how is he from the Father, how begotten, how the Son, how separate in subsistence, unless he be also separate in essence?[109]

Undoubtedly, Milton's arguments against Trinitarianism excel at least in clarity his contentions that God is unipersonal and that the Logos is self-generated. In these particulars he must fall back upon faith; he again finds reason inadequate when he comes to explain the generation of Christ as the mutual hypostatic union of God and man.

That Wisdom and the Logos are intimately linked in Milton's system as in Origen's may not yet be clear. I believe that this is a fair summation of Milton's doctrine: God's everlasting Wisdom, or foreknowledge, or idea of what he is about to do becomes manifest in the beginning (of creation) with the generation of the Logos. In

---

[107] *Bohn*, IV, 97; *CE*, **XIV**, 223.

[108] *Bohn*, IV, 131–32; *CE*, **XIV**, 309. See also the argument on p. 133 (*CE*, **XIV**, 311) beginning, "Now as the effect of generation. . . ." There are, of course, others.

[109] *Bohn*, IV, 132; *CE*, **XIV**, 309.

other terms, God's internal efficiency is disclosed by his external efficiency. His decrees are materialized when the Logos is brought into being, when the Logos creates the cosmos, and when thereafter he governs it (external efficiency equals generation plus creation plus government of the universe). The external efficiency of God (the Logos) and the internal efficiency of God (Wisdom) are mutually dependent; the external efficiency must follow the internal; yet unless God's decrees are executed, they remain incomprehensible in the realm of the Absolute and do not really exist, since their existence can be proved only when they are embodied in action. Thus in Milton's system Wisdom and Word are one, in the sense that together they comprise God's Efficiency. They are also clearly two. While Origen gives to this esoteric concept a harder outline by virtue of the personification of Wisdom and Word, Milton's treatment of it is the more intellectual and the more specific.[110]

According to Origen, the Logos is the invisible image of the invisible God: ". . . as He is Himself invisible by nature, He also begat an image that was invisible. For the Son is the Word, and therefore we are not to understand that anything in Him is cognizable by the senses. He is wisdom, and in wisdom there can be no suspicion of anything corporeal." [111] In his own nature, that is, and not because he is beyond the view of men or angels, the Logos or Son is invisible. It should be observed that he becomes masculine at the moment of his miraculous generation or separation from Wisdom.

Milton declares that the Son was begotten in a dual sense, "the one literal, with reference to the production of the Son, the other metaphorical, with reference to his exaltation." [112] I believe that Milton held the Son to be invisible during his first stage, which endures until his metaphorical begetting; and in my discussion of the Son I shall present my case for this conviction in full. Though Milton uses the titles Word, Son, and Christ interchangeably, there is a distinction, and not an arbitrary one, which it is proper and useful to bear in mind. While all three titles comprehend the nature of the

---

[110] Professor George W. Whiting, in "The Father to the Son," *MLN*, LXV (1950), 191–93, reaches a conclusion very similar to that which I argue here. "Milton's idea of the Trinity seems to approach those comparatively early stages in the evolution of the dogma when the Son, partly defined as the Logos of Greek philosophy, was regarded as inferior to the Father, though sharing his essence" (p. 193). Milton, however, is very careful to say that God's essence is incommunicable. The Son, in Milton's thought, partakes of God's substance, but not of his essence. This is also the view of the early Fathers.

[111] *ANCL*, X, 24.

[112] *Bohn*, IV, 80; *CE*, XIV, 181.

second person, the Logos or Word best identifies him from the time
of his generation until he was metaphorically begotten. By implication in the *De Doctrina* and, as I shall later show, by inference in
Paradise Lost, the second person as Logos is not visible. Milton says:
"John i. 1. 'in the beginning was the Word, and the Word was with
God, and the Word was God.' It is not said, from everlasting, but
in the beginning. The Word, — therefore the Word was audible.
But God, as he cannot be seen, so neither can he be heard; John
v. 37." [113] Here Milton contends that God and the Word are not of
the same essence. Had the Word been visible, the argument would
have been unnecessary; for, since God is invisible always, any visible
being could not have been mistaken for God. The Word is referred
to as "audible"; his title, according to Milton, so signifies. Pursuing
the same course of reasoning, we must infer that a "word" is *not*
visible though it *is* audible. This is the burden of the passage: "in
the beginning" a word was audible which apparently proceeded from
the invisible God; since God is inaudible, the word must have proceeded from the Logos, at this particular period likewise invisible.
In the chapter on the Son, Milton says: "Certain however it is . . .
that the Son existed in the beginning under the name of the logos
or word, and was the first of the whole creation, by whom afterwards
all other things were made both in heaven and in earth." [114]

The aspect of the creation upon which Origen is the most explicit
is the relationship between God and the Logos as fashioners of the
cosmos.

He [the Logos] was a mighty power, and a God next to the God and Father
of all things. For we assert that it was to him the Father gave the command,
"Let there be light," and "Let there be a firmament," and gave the injunc-
tions with regard to those other creative acts which were performed; and
that to Him also were addressed the words, "Let us make man in our own
image and likeness;" and that the Logos, when commanded, obeyed all the
Father's will. And we make these statements not from our own conjectures,
but because we believe the prophecies circulated among the Jews, in which
it is said of God, and of the works of creation, in express words, as follows:
"He spake, and they were made; He commanded, and they were created."
Now if God gave the command, and the creatures were formed, who, according to the view of the spirit of prophecy, could he be that was able to carry
out such commands of the Father, save Him who, so to speak, is the living
Logos and the Truth? [115]

The function of the Son as God's external agent is defined in this

---

[113] *Bohn*, IV, 110–11; *CE*, XIV, 253.
[114] *Bohn*, IV, 80; *CE*, XIV, 181.
[115] *ANCL*, XXIII, 11–12.

cryptic statement from *The Christian Doctrine*: ". . . the Father is he *of whom*, and *from whom*, and *by whom*, and *for whom are all things*; Rom. xi. 36. Heb. ii. 10. The Son is not he *of whom*, but only *by whom*; and that not without an exception, viz. '*all things* which were made,' John i. 3." [116] It is God, Milton says, who *makes* all things, that is, matter — of matter is the universe; he is "of whom" are all things. The Son is he "by whom" all things are *created*; but things can be created only of *pre-existent* matter. The Son, the creator, gives form to the invisible and formless matter made by God. "It is evident therefore that when it is said 'all things were by him,' it must be understood of a secondary and delegated power; and that when the particle *by* is used in reference to the Father, it denotes the primary cause, as John vi. 57. 'I live by the Father;' when in reference to the Son, the secondary and instrumental cause. . . ." [117] God, it may be said, relates to the Son in much the same way that the architect relates to the builder.

Saurat, as I have indicated, attributed to Milton the belief that matter is produced of the Son, that the entire creation is accomplished in God's generation of the Son. Saurat writes: "'In pursuance of his decree . . . God has begotten His only Son.' 'Only,' and yet all beings are 'sons of God' for Milton, but as parts of this, the 'only Son.' God has done nothing else, and even his title, 'God,' as implying a sort of activity and manifestation, has been passed on to the Son." [118] As no created thing is of the substance of the Son, Saurat is patently wrong. Yet, in a note upon the passage, he raises an interesting problem: "This is naturally the weak point of the system, as of all systems of the Absolute; why has the Absolute become relative? Why has God created the Son? Even that was a creation, hence a limitation, and calls for all the objections that make Milton put the creation to the Son's account and not God's. Milton has done his best to lessen this unavoidable contradiction by setting an abyss between God and the Son." [119] The "abyss" between Father and Son is even greater than Saurat imagines. Milton's system is so ordered that the Father does nothing but *will* the Son's existence and allow him to be free. The Son, in his capacity as God's external agency, then produces himself. To this the self-production of Sin from Satan's head offers a parallel, made the more bizarre by the fact that it is

---

[116] *Bohn*, IV, 91; *CE*, XIV, 205.
[117] *Ibid.*
[118] *Saurat*, pp. 96–97.
[119] *Ibid.*, p. 97n.

Satan's unconscious will which surprises him with the "sudden miserable pain" of her birth.

THE HOLY SPIRIT

The Holy Spirit is not important in the theologies of either Origen or Milton.

Origen admits uncertainty as to whether the Holy Spirit should be regarded "as born or innate, or also as a Son of God or not." These are points which, Origen declares, must be inquired into. At any rate, there is only one Spirit who inspired both the prophets of the Old Testament and the Apostles of the New.[120] Like Milton, Origen sometimes appears to doubt that the Holy Spirit is a person. His clearest discussion of the matter, found in his commentary upon John, is, moreover, expressly anti-Trinitarian.

Now if, as we have seen, all things were made through Him, we have to enquire if the Holy Spirit also was made through Him. It appears to me that those who hold the Holy Spirit to be created, and who also admit that "all things were made through Him," must necessarily assume that the Holy Spirit was made through the Logos, the Logos accordingly being older than He. And he who shrinks from allowing the Holy Spirit to have been made through Christ must, if he admits the truth of the statements of this Gospel, assume the Spirit to be uncreated. There is a third resource besides these two (that of allowing the Spirit to have been made by the Word, and that of regarding it as uncreated), namely, to assert that the Holy Spirit has no essence of His own beyond the Father and the Son. But on further thought one may perhaps see reason to consider that the Son is second beside the Father, He being the same as the Father, while manifestly a distinction is drawn between the Spirit and the Son in the passage, "Whosoever shall speak a word against the Son of Man, it shall be forgiven him, but whosoever shall blaspheme against the Holy Spirit, he shall not have forgiveness, either in this world or in the world to come." We consider, therefore, that there are three hypostases, the Father and the Son and the Holy Spirit; and at the same time we believe nothing to be uncreated but the Father. We therefore, as the more pious and the truer course, admit that all things were made by the Logos, and that the Holy Spirit is the most excellent and the first in order of all that was made by the Father through Christ.[121]

Insofar as the Holy Spirit is a being, it is all but a supernumerary in the Miltonic system. Of its origin Milton writes: ". . . the Holy Spirit, inasmuch as he is a minister of God, and therefore a creature, was created or produced of the substance of God, not by a natural necessity, but by the free will of the agent, probably before the foun-

---

[120] *ANCL*, X, 3–4.
[121] *Comm. John*, p. 328.

dations of the world were laid, but later than the Son, and far inferior to him." [122]

I do not think that the Holy Spirit exists as a *being* in *Paradise Lost*.

In the theologies of Origen and Milton, the Holy Spirit is created by the Word, before the angels, of the substance of God. Its power is greatly inferior to that of the Son. It is sent by the Son to his followers in order that they may understand the ways of God and live righteously.

HEAVEN

Of the "incorporeal" matter of God the Word as agent creates the cosmos — this is an article of doctrine in the theologies of both Origen and Milton. Any comparison of their views on the creation, however, is made somewhat difficult at the outset because Origen's definition of "world" comprehends so much more than Milton's, which includes only the universe contained within the *Primum Mobile*. Furthermore, the chronological ordering of events in the creation, so important to the structure of *Paradise Lost*, did not interest Origen, who wrote, of course, as a pioneer, treating of subjects about which theological battles were subsequently to rage. Milton was obligated to defend or attack many a point which Origen touched upon lightly and many a position which Origen assumed with an innocence unshadowed by centuries of controversy. Some theological questions with which Milton wrestles were not even recognized as disputable until Origen's writings brought them into being; the spiritual versus the material nature of God is a case in point.

Both Origen and Milton conceive of Heaven in four ways: (1) as a real place; (2) as the Platonic world of reality; (3) as an interior psychological Heaven; and (4) as God when he becomes "all in all."

Origen's Heaven should first be seen as a part of his cosmos, which is a curiously syncretic development from Greek philosophy and a sentence by Clement of Rome in the "Epistle to the Corinthians":

. . . the whole universe of existing things, celestial and super-celestial, earthly and infernal, is generally called one perfect world, within which, or by which, other worlds, if any there are, must be supposed to be contained. For which reason he [Clement] wished the globe of the sun or moon, and of the other bodies called planets, to be each termed worlds. Nay, even that preeminent globe itself which they [the Greeks] called the non-wandering [the sphere of the fixed stars], they nevertheless desired to have properly called world . . . above that sphere which they call non-wandering,

---

[122] *Bohn*, IV, 169; *CE*, XIV, 403.

they will have another sphere to exist, which they say, exactly as our heaven contains all things which are under it, comprehends by its immense size and indescribable extent the spaces of all the spheres together within its more magnificent circumference; so that all things are within it, as this earth of ours is under heaven. And this also is believed to be called in the holy Scriptures the good land, and the land of the living, having its own heaven, which is higher, and in which the names of the saints are said to be written . . . by the Savior. . . . When from men all corruption has been shaken off and cleansed away, and when the whole of the space occupied by this world, in which the spheres of the planets are said to be, has been left behind and beneath, then is reached the fixed abode of the pious and the good situated above that sphere, which is called non-wandering . . . these good men after their apprehension and their chastisement for the offences which they have undergone by way of purgation, may, after having fulfilled and discharged every obligation, deserve a habitation in that land; while those who have been obedient to the word of God . . . are said to deserve the kingdom of that heaven. . . . For it is called a descent to this earth, but an exaltation to that which is on high. In this way, therefore, does a sort of road seem to be opened up by the departure of the saints from that earth to those heavens; so that they do not so much appear to abide in that land, as to inhabit it with an intention, viz., to pass on to the inheritance of the kingdom of heaven, when they have reached that degree of perfection also.[123]

The correspondencies are striking indeed between this arrangement of the cosmos and that which is to be inferred from the section of *Paradise Lost*, Book iii, in which Satan explores the newly created world. Both describe one cosmos containing Heaven, Hell, the earth, and all other worlds if any exist (iii, 566–67). Both agree in a system of concentric spheres or heavens (iii, 481–83), with one above the fixed stars pictured as firm and opaque, dividing the luminous interior spheres from their surroundings (iii, 418–20). Both make the convexity of this orb a Limbo midway between earth and Heaven (iii, headnote, 440–500, 494–96). Both depict disembodied souls passing through the lower spheres to Limbo, intending to proceed upward into Heaven (iii, 481–86), and both allow the saints to bypass Limbo and enter Heaven directly (iii, 519–22). In both, a specific road or passage connecting Heaven with earth and Limbo is mentioned (iii, 501–15). The astronomical details in both accounts are incidental to the central subject, Heaven, and each system makes use of descriptive rather than scientific astronomy.

There are, to be sure, differences between Origen's conception and Milton's, and these differences are the more interesting because they demonstrate how Milton transmutes the material of a doctrine

---

[123] *ANCL*, X, 87–91.

distasteful to him. It has long been recognized that Satan's explora-
tory journey on the outside of the world constitutes an anti-Catholic
digression as full of invective as the equally unexpected diatribe
against a worldly clergy in *Lycidas*. Origen's purgatory is trenchantly
satirized in the Miltonic passage, which was expressly designed to
denigrate what the poet considered a religion of "painful Supersti-
tion and blind Zeal." Whereas Origen's Limbo is a land of peace,
protected and illuminated by the empyrean Heaven, a place in which
the spirits of good men undergo their final preparation for entrance
into the blessed Heaven above, Milton's Limbo is dark, starless,
waste, wild, threatened by Chaos and Night, racked by windy storms,
and inhabited by friars, giants, and monsters. It is a place where
vanities and vain men are hopelessly and eternally lost.[124]

The development of Milton's cosmos perhaps came about like this.
Beginning with a general world system similar to that outlined by
Origen in the *De Principiis*, Milton brought it into accord with later
theological descriptive astronomy by the addition of the crystalline
sphere and the unmoved mover. Because he was militantly Protestant, he changed the "good men" who inhabit Origen's Limbo into
the "vain men" who fill his own Paradise of Fools, satirizing by this
alteration the Catholic purgatory. Origen's orbicular highest heaven,
which contained, it will be remembered, "the whole universe of existing things," and which was the home of the saints, was flattened out
and opened up so that it allowed room for Chaos and Hell, and it
became Milton's Heaven of Heavens. Minor touches from many
sources were then incorporated into the whole — the golden chain
linking Heaven and the world from Plato, the golden stair and the
waters above from Genesis, and the methods by which souls enter
Heaven from Luke and II Kings.

Heaven is certainly a real place in *Paradise Lost*. The *Christian
Doctrine* affirms its reality by Milton's assigning it a position outside
the universe where it is invisible to men though not invisible in its
nature (*Bohn*, IV, 182; *CE*, XV, 29); where it is the site of the angelic war (*Bohn*, IV, 217; *CE*, XV, 105); where the Son of God, not
ubiquitous, is enthroned (*Bohn*, IV, 308; *CE*, XV, 315). It is also
created by the Logos: ". . . 'by the Word of God the heavens were
of old,' that is . . . by the Son. . . ."[125] Moreover, this real Heaven
is not eternal:

---

[124] The passage describing Limbo in *Paradise Lost* is not really a digression.
See Frank L. Huntley, "A Justification of Milton's 'Paradise of Fools' (*P.L.*, III,
431–499)," *ELH*, XXI (1954), 107–13.

[125] *Bohn*, IV, 171–72; *CE*, XV, 7.

It is improbable that God should have formed to himself such an abode for his majesty only at so recent a period as at the beginning of the world. For if there be any one habitation of God, where he diffuses in an eminent manner the glory and brightness of his majesty, why should it be thought that its foundations are only coeval with the fabric of this world, and not of much more ancient origin? At the same time it does not follow that the heaven should be eternal. . . .[126]

This passage establishes the creation of the real Heaven in Milton's system at a time before the creation of the universe, in which opinion Origen concurs, as I shall show in the following discussion of the angels.[127] Origen in the *De Principiis* and Milton in the *De Doctrina* do not attempt a description of the real Heaven. Origen, moreover, censures the vulgarity of those who "imagine that the earthly city of Jerusalem is to be rebuilt, its foundations laid in precious stones, and its walls constructed of jasper, and its battlements of crystal; that it is to have a wall composed of many precious stones, as jasper, and sapphire, and chalcedony, and emerald, and sardonyx, and onyx, and chrysolite, and chrysoprase, and jacinth, and amethyst." [128] This visualization of Heaven does not, of course, stem from Origen's imagination; for it is taken almost stone for stone from Rev. xxi, 18–21. Assuredly, Milton had all the Biblical proof text he needed had it been his purpose in the *De Doctrina* to make such a nature for the material Heaven a part of his dogma. Since he does not so argue in the treatise, though he often cites Revelation in connection with Heaven, and since his delineation of Heaven in *Paradise Lost* is lavishly embellished with the names of precious minerals, may we not justifiably conclude that he relegated all efforts to specify the character of perfection to the realm of poetry, itself, perhaps, one remove from accommodated truth? For another reason we may suspect that the richly jeweled Heaven of the epic does not represent Milton's approved doctrine. From too much admiration of Heaven's wealth and too little attention to its spiritual excellence, let us remember, Mammon became stoop-shouldered even before his fall (i, 678–84). And Milton directly cautions his readers thus:

---

[126] *Bohn*, IV, 182–83; *CE*, XV, 29–31.

[127] Milton's treatment of angels is the subject of several articles and a book, *Milton and the Angels* (Athens, Ga., 1955), by Robert H. West. In "Milton's Angelological Heresies," *JHI*, XIV (1953), 116–23, West points out that Milton is heretical in his depiction of the angels' power to assimilate food and to love one another *more hominum*. West traces the concept of angels feasting to Aquinas and Tertullian. In *SAMLA Studies in Milton* (Gainesville, Fla., 1953), pp. 20–53, he discusses "The Substance of Milton's Angels."

[128] *ANCL*, X, 146.

> . . . Let none admire
> That riches grow in Hell; that soile may best
> Deserve the precious bane.
>
> i, 690–92

A Heaven real in the Platonic sense is also posited both by Origen and by Milton in *Paradise Lost*. Origen says:

> . . . all things here on earth which are in common use among men, have other things corresponding to them in name which are alone real. Thus, for instance, there is the true light, and *another heaven beyond the firmament*, and a Sun of righteousness other than the sun we see. In a word, to distinguish those things from the objects of sense, which have no true reality, they say of God that "His works are truth"; thus making a distinction between the works of God and the works of God's hands, which latter are of an inferior sort.[129]

God's works, in Origen's thought as in Milton's, are never manifest; accordingly a palpable Heaven must be understood as the work of God's hands or the Logos.

Raphael, after explaining to Adam how truth is accommodated to man's limited intelligence, says parenthetically:

> . . . what if Earth
> Be but the shaddow of Heav'n, and things therein
> Each to other like, more then on Earth is thought?
>
> v, 574–76

Though these lines may appear at first to affirm the existence of a material Heaven, this is not, in fact, their import. For the true reality of Heaven is conceived here as casting a shadow which is the evanescent materiality of earth.

Origen treats Heaven most fully as a state in which the intellect attains complete satisfaction. His utterances concerning this conviction are so diffuse as to make direct quotation unfeasible. Scorning the innocence of those who expect to gratify their earthly appetites in Heaven, Origen traces man's ascension to God through gradations of mental achievement which are likened to the spheres of Greek astronomy and the heavens envisaged by Paul, until at last "the rational nature, growing by each individual step . . . is raised as a mind already perfect to perfect knowledge." [130]

Milton, too, in one place in *Paradise Lost*, indicates a belief in a psychological Heaven. The context in which this belief is expressed offers an interesting opportunity for a comparison with Origen's concept of man's intellectual journey toward perfection. Near the

---

[129] *Ibid.*, XXIII, 453.
[130] *Ibid.*, X, 147–53.

close of *Paradise Lost,* Adam exults that he has at last attained wisdom through learning that "to obey is best, and love with feare the onely God." Michael then admonishes him as follows (the numbers are to facilitate the ensuing discussion):

> This having learnt, thou hast attaind the summe
> Of wisdom; hope no higher, [1] though all the Starrs
> Thou knewst by name, and all [2] th' ethereal Powers,
> [3] All secrets of the Deep, [4] all Natures works,
> [5] Or works of God in Heav'n, Air, Earth, or Sea,
> And [6] all the riches of this World enjoydst,
> And [7] all the rule, one Empire; onely add
> Deeds to thy knowledge answerable, add Faith,
> Add Vertue, Patience, Temperance, add Love,
> By name to come calld Charitie, the soul
> Of all the rest: then wilt thou not be loath
> To leave this Paradise, but shalt possess
> A paradise within thee, happier farr.
>
> xii, 575–87

Origen specifically mentions as kinds of knowledge which the soul acquires during its progress toward God: (1) "the nature of the stars," their functions and the positioning of each in the firmament (*ANCL*, X, 152–53); (2) the operations of the Holy Spirit (p. 149) and the nature of the apostate angels (p. 150); (3) those things "which are not seen . . . whose names only we have heard . . . which are invisible" (p. 153. The "Deep" in the quoted passage from *Paradise Lost* must be Chaos since it is apparently outside the universe and since the sea is mentioned in the following line); (4) medicinal and poisonous herbs (p. 150); and (5) "the nature of the soul, and the diversity of animals, whether of those which live in the water, or of birds, or of wild beasts" (p. 150). As can be seen, I have altered Origen's ordering of the facets of learning to correspond with the arrangement of their counterparts in the poem. Milton's denial that the kinds of pure knowledge selected by Origen are necessary to the soul's perfection seems all the more deliberate since Origen himself scoffs at those who identify Heaven as a place where mundane riches will abound (p. 146) and where non-Christians will as slaves serve the elect (p. 146; cf. "riches" in 6, "rule" in 7). Yet, despite Milton's insistence that wisdom without goodness cannot nourish the soul nor enable man to discover paradise within himself, Milton is convinced equally with Origen that reason is our closest link with God.

The fourth and final way in which Origen and Milton depict Heaven is as a state in which all good men and angels achieve unity with God — when God will be "all in all." The idea is a favorite with Origen, who many times returns to it: "When Christ shall have delivered up the kingdom to God even the Father, then also those living things, when they shall have first been made the kingdom of Christ, shall be delivered, along with the whole of that kingdom, to the rule of the Father, that when God shall be all in all, they also, since they are a part of all things, may have God in themselves, as He is in all things." [131] Milton brings the concept twice into *Paradise Lost*. For example, God ends a speech to the Son with these lines:

> Then thou thy regal Scepter shalt lay by,
> For regal Scepter then no more shall need,
> God shall be All in All.
>
> iii, 339–41 (see also vi, 732)

This is the final consummation of God's great Idea. Even the Heaven of Heavens shall pass away; for Milton does not regard it as eternal. At one point in *The Christian Doctrine*, interestingly enough, Milton speaks of a different Heaven, one everlasting, one not made by the Logos but fashioned or rather emanated by God in his own proper person: "For the highest heaven is as it were the supreme citadel and habitation of God . . . where God 'dwelleth in the light which no man can approach unto,' I Tim. vi. 16. Out of this light it appears that pleasures and glories and a *kind of perpetual heaven*, have emanated and subsist." [132]

THE ANGELS

Origen culls from the Bible the names of the orders of angels; but he makes no attempt to arrange them hierarchically:

Now there are, besides the gods of whom God is god, certain others, who are called thrones, and others called dominions, lordships, also, and powers in addition to these.[133]

I might have mentioned, moreover, what is said of those beings which are called seraphim by the Hebrews, and described in Isaiah, who cover the face and the feet of God, and of those called cherubim, whom Ezekiel has described, and the postures of these, and the manner in which God is said to be borne upon the cherubim.[134]

It is hardly surprising that Origen does not arrange the angelic classes according to their traditional ranks, since the first certain dated reference to the writings of the pseudo-Dionysius Areopagiti-

---

[131] *Ibid.*, p. 272.
[132] *Bohn*, IV, 182; *CE*, XV, 29. Italics mine.
[133] *Comm. John*, p. 315.
[134] *ANCL*, XXIII, 357.

cus, in which the whole thing started, is A.D. 533, and even internal evidence precludes any date prior to the fourth century. That Milton pays no more attention to the tradition than Origen is somewhat curious. He certainly was conversant with it.[135] In *The Christian Doctrine* he says of angels that they "are distinguished one from another by offices and degrees."[136] This is, however, as far as he is willing to go in the absence of Biblical sanction for the arrangement of heavenly spirits in order of power or pre-eminence, because "to push our speculations further on this subject, is to incur the apostle's reprehension, Col. ii. 18. 'intruding into those things which he hath not seen, vainly puffed up by his fleshly mind.'"[137] In *Paradise Lost* the names of the angelic hierarchy are treated as sonorous titles which may be interchanged at the demand of metrics (see, for example, v, 840). Milton is especially casual with Satan's rank (calling him "Angel," i, 125; "Arch-Angel," i, 243; "Prince," iv, 871; "King," iv, 821).

It is a serious tenet in the theology of Origen that angelic beings achieve their positions in Heaven through merit.

I am of opinion, then, so far as appears to me, that the preceding discussion has sufficiently proved that it is neither from want of discrimination, nor from any accidental cause, either that the "principalities" hold their dominion, or the other orders of spirits have obtained their respective offices; but that they have received the steps of their rank on account of their merits, although it is not our privilege to know or inquire what those acts of theirs were, by which they earned a place in any particular order.[138]

Though *The Christian Doctrine* contains no hint that Milton holds this view, certain passages in *Paradise Lost*, I am persuaded, strongly suggest that he gave it credence.

Satan, who was motivated to war against God through "sense of injur'd merit" (i, 98), in speaking to the newly fallen angels, defends his pre-eminence thus:

> Mee though just right, and the fixt Laws of Heav'n
> Did first create your Leader, next, free choice,
> With what besides, in Counsel or in Fight,
> Hath bin achievd of merit,
>
> ii, 18–21

Satan's argument is this: it is just and right according to the fixed laws of Heaven that he should lead his companions; subsequent

---

[135] It is commonplace, for example, in Spenser.
[136] *Bohn*, IV, 186; *CE*, XV, 37.
[137] *Bohn*, IV, 186–87; *CE*, XV, 37.
[138] *ANCL*, X, 68–69.

events "in Counsel or in Fight" have augmented his merit. It surely may be inferred from Satan's speech that merit, under the fixed laws of Heaven, is the criterion for advancement. Even though he is the father of lies, we must believe Satan here because he is looking backward to an honor conferred upon him in the past.

When the Son makes his offer to "satisfie for Man," God promises to exalt Christ's human nature equally with his divine to the throne for this reason:

> Because thou hast, though Thron'd in highest bliss
> Equal to God, and equally enjoying
> God-like fruition, quitted all to save
> A World from utter loss, and hast been found
> *By Merit more than Birthright Son of God,*
> Found worthiest to be so by being Good,
> Farr more then Great or High;
> > iii, 305–11 (italics mine)

By birthright Christ is the Son of God; he is not an angel. Yet, God says, such is Christ's merit that even without his birthright he would deserve to be Son of God and head of the angels. Had any angel been willing to offer himself as a sacrifice for man, it is clearly implied, he would have achieved the title "Son of God" through merit. But when God asked his terrible question,

> . . . all the Heav'nly Quire stood mute,
> And silence was in Heav'n;
> > iii, 217–18

One more passage is, I think, relevant; this is a description of the assembled angelic host:

> Ten thousand thousand Ensignes high advanc't,
> Standards, and Gonfalons twixt Van and Reare
> Streame in the Aire, and for distinction serve
> Of Hierarchies, of Orders, and Degrees;
> Or in thir glittering Tissues bear imblaz'd
> Holy Memorials, *acts of Zeale and Love*
> *Recorded eminent.*
> > v, 588–94 (italics mine)

A reasonable assumption, it seems to me, is that there are two kinds of banners borne by the angels — one which indicates rank, and one which records deeds of merit ("acts of Zeale and Love"). The performance of such deeds, I suggest, qualifies the individual angel for membership in a particular order.

In another expression of his belief that angelic spirits are classed in accordance with their goodness, Origen makes it plain that he thinks the creation of angels, and therefore Heaven, antedated the creation of the world: "For we are not to imagine that they obtained these offices otherwise than by their own merits, and by the zeal and excellent qualities which they severally displayed before this world was formed. . . ."[139] Milton, of course, agrees with Origen as to the chronology of events in the cosmic creation. Theirs is an unorthodox view. It is interesting to note in the following excerpt from the *De Doctrina* that Milton, who rarely leans on any authority other than Scripture, here calls upon the primitive Fathers for support:

. . . when it is said . . . that they [the angels] shouted for joy before God at the creation, it proves rather that they were then already in existence, than that they were then first created. Many at least of the Greek, and some of the Latin Fathers, are of the opinion that angels, as being spirits, must have existed long before the material world; and it even seems probable, that the apostasy which caused the expulsion of so many thousands from heaven, took place before the foundations of this world were laid.[140]

Origen declares that men and angels often feast together, an idea not unfamiliar to readers of *Paradise Lost* who remember Raphael, the sociable spirit, and his visit with Adam and Eve. The reader will also recall that Raphael, somewhat to Adam's surprise, consumes food "with keen dispatch/Of real hunger, and concoctive heat." Milton, in fact, uses the occasion to stress a point of doctrine — that all beings are, in a sense, material, and that angels are as capable of assimilating food as men — despite the denials of theologians. If Milton seems intent upon humanizing angels, Origen seems equally anxious to make something spiritual of man's physical requirements; but behind both conceptions of angelic feasting lies a similar conviction of cosmic materiality. Origen says that "they who partake of corn and wine, and the fruits of trees, of water and of air, do not feed with demons, but rather do they feast with divine angels, who are appointed for this purpose, and who are as it were invited to the table of the pious man, who hearkens to the precept of the word, which says, 'whether ye eat or drink, or whatever ye do, do all to the glory of God.' "[141]

Origen's angels are intimately concerned with the affairs of men, accepting it as a duty and pleasure to help good men grow to perfection, and moving between Heaven and earth without impediment: "And these, regarding all as their relations and friends who imitate their piety towards God, and in prayer call upon Him with sincerity, work along with them for their salvation, appear unto them, deem

[139] *Ibid.*, p. 65.
[140] *Bohn*, IV, 185; *CE*, XV, 33–35.
[141] *ANCL*, XXIII, 518.

it their office and duty to attend them, and as if by common agreement they visit with all manner of kindness and deliverance those
who pray to God. . . ." [141a] That the ministry of angels relates especially to believers is one of Milton's many pronouncements in Chapters VII and IX of the first book of the treatise; most of them are
theological commonplaces which find their way into *Paradise Lost*.[142]
Correspondences in the *De Principiis* are easy enough to find but
not, I think, worth reporting.

HELL

Because in the theology of Origen all rational creatures, even the
fallen angels, will eventually see their error and return to God, a
physical or local Hell is really unnecessary. Yet upon occasions he
seems to grant its existence. He includes it among those things
created by the Logos: ". . . the whole universe of existing things,
celestial and super-celestial, earthly and *infernal*, is generally called
one world." [143] Origen several times locates Hell within the earth.
For example, he argues that it was Samuel himself, rather than a
demon, who was called up out of Hell to aid Saul by the witch of
Endor; [144] that Jesus did in fact spend three days in Hades after the
passion (Milton denies it); [145] and that Lazarus returned to life from
the underworld.[146] Origen's interest in the nature of a physical Hell
is negligible; he apparently adopted the Hades of classic mythology
into his Christian system out of indifference.

In the *De Doctrina*, Hell was created before the world, and external to it.

Nor are reasons wanting for this locality; for as the place of the damned
is the same as that prepared for the devil and his angels, Matt. xxv. 41. in
punishment of their apostasy, which occurred before the fall of man, it
does not seem probable that hell should have been prepared within the
limits of this world, in the bowels of the earth, on which the curse had not
as yet passed. This is said to have been the opinion of Chrysostom, as likewise of Luther and some later divines. Besides, if, as has been shown from
various passages of the New Testament, the whole world is to be finally
consumed by fire, it follows that hell, being situated in the centre of the
earth, must share the fate of the surrounding universe, and perish like·

[141a] *Ibid.*, pp. 519–20.
[142] See West, *Milton and the Angels.*
[143] *ANCL*, X, 87. Italics mine.
[144] *Selections from the Commentaries and Homilies of Origen*, tr. R. B. Tollinton (London, 1929), pp. 217–20. Future reference will be to *Tollinton.*
[145] *Ibid.*, pp. 220–22.
[146] *Ibid.*, p. 263.

wise; a consummation more to be desired than expected by the souls in perdition.[147]

In the headnote to Book i of *Paradise Lost*, of course, Hell is likewise located outside the world: ". . . Hell, describ'd here, *not in the Center* (for Heaven and Earth may be suppos'd as yet not made, certainly not yet accurst) *but in a place of utter darkness, fitliest call'd* Chaos. . . ." In Book i, Hell is found

> As farr remov'd from God and light of Heav'n
> As from the Center thrice to th' utmost Pole.
>
> i, 73–74

It is consistent with Origen's view of salvation as ultimately attained by all beings that the flames of Hell are curative rather than punitive, and that the fallen soul is restored to purity when evil is burned away.

Consequently whoever is saved is saved by fire, so that the fire may melt and dissolve any admixture the man has of the leaden element, so that all may become good gold, for it is said that the gold of that land which the saints shall possess is good. . . . The more a man brings there of lead, the more he suffers burning, that the lead may be fully melted, so that even if there be little gold it may still be left in purity. But if a man comes there all of lead, in his case there occurs what is written, He is drowned in the depths, like lead in the mighty waters.[148]

The dark flames in the Hell of *Paradise Lost* are surely penal rather than restorative; punishment is the purpose of Hell, we learn in *The Christian Doctrine*. Milton also asserts in the treatise, however, that punishment "varies according to the degree of guilt."[149]

Though Origen admits the possibility that Hell has its own site and function, he much more frequently expresses his belief in a psychological Hell. I offer two examples:

. . . every sinner kindles for himself the flame of his own fire, and is not plunged into some fire which has been already kindled by another, or was in existence before himself.[150]

But the outer darkness, in my judgment, is to be understood not so much of some dark atmosphere without any light, as of those persons who, being plunged in the darkness of profound ignorance, have been placed beyond the reach of any light of the understanding.[151]

Both in *The Christian Doctrine* and in *Paradise Lost* Hell is also a state of mind. "The second death, or the punishment of the

---

[147] *Bohn*, IV, 490–91; *CE*, XVI, 373–75.
[148] *Tollinton*, p. 202.
[149] *Bohn*, IV, 490; *CE*, XVI, 373.
[150] *ANCL*, X, 140.
[151] *Ibid.*, p. 144.

damned, seems to consist partly in the loss of the chief good, namely, the favour and protection of God, and the beatific vision of his presence, which is commonly called the punishment of loss; and partly in eternal torment, which is called the punishment of sense." [152] Perhaps the most famous expression of the concept in the English language is Satan's speech in the epic, wherein, because he is alone, his anguished self-recognition must be taken for truth.

> Mee miserable! which way shall I flie
> Infinite wrauth, and infinite despaire?
> Which way I flie is Hell; my self am Hell; [153]
> And in the lowest deep a lower deep
> Still threatning to devour me op'ns wide,
> To which the Hell I suffer seems a Heav'n.
>
> iv, 73–78

When Milton depicts Hell as removed from God and Heaven's light by the radius of the universe thrice multiplied, he is treating graphically the theological concept of the punishment of loss.[154] Alienation from God and goodness, from grace and light, is the severest punishment of the damned, of which physical torment is but a type or metaphor — this, though they differ in the degree to which they accept Biblical evidence of a literal Hell, is a firm tenet in the systems of Origen and Milton.

THE SON

It has been shown that the Logos, the first of all creation, is, according to Origen and Milton, the audible but not visible Word of God.

---

[152] *Bohn*, IV, 489; *CE*, XVI, 371. The argument that the physical Hell of *Paradise Lost* is really a metaphor for the interior Hell is presented by J. B. Broadbent in "Milton's Hell," *ELH*, XXI (1954), 161–92. Broadbent has much else of interest to say about Hell in *Some Graver Subject: An Essay on Paradise Lost* (London, 1960). See especially Chapters II, VIII, and the second section of Chapter XI.

[153] Professor Merritt Y. Hughes, in "Myself Am Hell," *MP*, LIV (1956), 80–94, shows that the idea of the interior Hell is a theological commonplace, finding it in Antonio Rusca, Bonaventura, Aquinas, Landino, Ficino, Lucretius, Seneca, Augustine, Henry Greenwood, John Hall, Marlowe, and Thomas Browne. I do not argue Origen as the source of the concept; but he antedated the earliest of the Christians in this list by a century and a half.

[154] Professor B. A. Wright, in "Masson's Diagram of Milton's Spaces (a Note on *Paradise Lost*, I, 73–4)," *RES*, XXI (1945), 42–43, locates Hell "one semidiameter of the Human or Starry Universe" away from the World. He is right. Nevertheless, Satan travels four "semidiameters" from Hell to earth. To get to the top of the World, he travels three "semidiameters" less the distance from the World to Heaven, which is not great, and then one more down through the World to earth. Wright correctly considers *P.L.*, i, 43–44, as intended simply to represent an almost unimaginable distance.

Like Milton, Origen holds that the anointing of the Son marks a second stage in the development of the Logos: "Now it is said in the forty-fourth Psalm, 'Thou hast loved righteousness and hated iniquity, whence Thou art anointed (Christ) above all thy fellows.' His loving righteousness and hating iniquity were thus added claims in Him; His anointing was not contemporary with His being nor inherited by Him from the first." [155] This passage conclusively demonstrates, I believe, that Origen made a distinction very similar to that which Milton posits in the terms "literal" and "metaphorical" begetting; it should be noticed also that just as Milton stresses the Son's *merit*, his goodness, as reason enough for his elevation, so Origen asserts that loving righteousness and hating iniquity were added claims in him.

It is my conviction that in *Paradise Lost*, upon the occasion of the metaphorical begetting, the invisible Logos is manifested as the visible Son. The evidence is circumstantial, but it is nonetheless strong. It is contained in Raphael's account of events in Heaven which lead to the creation of the world. The metaphorical begetting of the Son is announced by the Father to the host of angels assembled before his throne:

> This day I have begot whom I declare
> My only Son, and on this holy Hill
> Him have anointed, *whom ye now behold*
> *At my right hand;*
>
> v, 603–6 (italics mine)

I infer from the word "now" in the context of the italicized words that prior to this time the Son was unknown to the angels, that they had neither seen him at any time in the past or known that he was with God. I infer this also from a number of other places in Raphael's account. That the Son was invisible before his exaltation seems to me the sense of the following passage which immediately precedes the one just quoted:

> . . . the Father infinite,
> By whom in bliss imbosom'd sat the Son,
> Amidst as from a flaming Mount, whose top
> Brightness had made invisible, thus spake.
>
> v, 596–99

The eternal invisibility of God is basic to Milton's doctrine. The word "embosom" has two meanings: (1) *transitive*, to take to, or place in, the bosom; to cherish; to embrace; (2) *transferred*, to enclose, conceal, shelter, in the bosom. I suggest that the Son, embos-

---

[155] *Comm. John*, p. 313.

omed, enclosed, concealed, sheltered in the bosom of the invisible
God, is at this time also invisible.

When God has introduced his son, the elect angels accept him and
rejoice; but one,

> Satan, so call him now, his former name
> Is heard no more in Heav'n; he of the first,
> If not the first Arch-Angel, great in Power,
> In favor and preeminence, yet fraught
> With envy against the Son of God, that day
> Honor'd by his great Father, and proclaim'd
> Messiah King anointed, could not bear
> Through pride that sight, and thought himself impair'd.
>
> v, 658–65

Only two interpretations of this scene are possible — either Satan
has known the Son before this time, or he has not. If the former,
the Son must have existed, until his anointing, as an angel among
angels (so Novatian, differing from other primitive Fathers, held),
and in rank he must have stood not higher than Satan, himself "of
the first,/If not the first Arch-Angel"; for otherwise Satan would
have no reason at all to feel envy or pride and to think himself "impair'd." But Milton rejects the possibility of the Son's having been
an angel, if we are to believe *The Christian Doctrine*: ". . . after
having anointed his King, whence the name of *Christ* is derived, he
says, 'this day have I begotten thee.' Heb. i. 4, 5. 'being made so much
better than the angels, as he hath by inheritance obtained a more
excellent name than they.' No other name can be intended but that
of Son, as the following verse proves: 'for unto which of the angels
said he at any time, Thou art my Son; this day have I begotten
thee?' " [156] Besides, that the Son, the express image of God, could
have remained unrecognized, could have been taken for an equal
by beings he himself created, is hard to believe. Far more credible is
the alternative — that the Son becomes visible when he is metaphorically generated. Is not this interpretation borne out by the fact that
Satan could not bear *that sight*? When the rebel angels have removed
to the quarters of the north, Abdiel rebukes their chief thus:

> Thyself though great and glorious dost thou count,
> Or all Angelic Nature join'd in one,
> Equal to him begotten Son, by whom
> *As by his Word* the mighty Father made
> All things, ev'n thee, and all the Spirits of Heav'n
>
> v, 833–37 (italics mine)

---

[156] *Bohn*, IV, 82; *CE*, XIV, 185.

But Satan peremptorily refuses to accept the doctrine of creation by the Logos:

> That we were form'd then say'st thou? and the work
> Of secondary hands, by task transferr'd
> From Father to his Son? *strange point and new!*
> *Doctrine which we would know whence learnt: who saw*
> *When this creation was?*
>
>   v, 853–57 (italics mine)

All excepting Abdiel agree with Satan ("Hoarse murmur echo'd to his words applause"); and later, during the war in Heaven, one of Satan's followers titles him "Deliverer from new Lords" (vi, 451), from which, again I submit, it must be assumed that the Son, if not a former angel, is *new* upon the scene.

The visibility of the Son, like the invisibility of the Logos, is intimated in *The Christian Doctrine*; for example: "Isai. vi. 1, 2. 'I saw the Lord sitting upon a throne . . . above it stood the seraphim.' I repeat, it was not God himself that he saw, but perhaps one of the angels clothed in some modification of the divine glory, or the son of God himself, the image of the glory of his Father, as John understands the vision, xii, 21." [157]

It is relevant here to take up again the problem of God's apparent audibility in *Paradise Lost*. Although we can account for this inconsistency with his absolute nature by allowing it under the doctrine of accommodation (for God speaks in the Bible, too) and by pleading dramatic necessity, it is still possible to argue that God's audibility in the epic is merely evidence that the invisible Logos, "imbosom'd" within him, serves as interpreter to sentient creatures in Heaven. The case for such an assumption, however, seems to fall apart when, at the time of the metaphorical generation, the Son becomes visible as a separate entity; for the Logos could only be speaking to himself if, after his anointing, he converses with God. Must the assumption, then, be dismissed as a *reductio ad absurdum*, which imputes to the Son a kind of celestial ventriloquism? I think not; for Milton in *The Christian Doctrine* expresses a conviction about the tripartite person of the Son which solves the difficulty:

. . for if the Father has given all things to the Son, even his very being and life, he has also given him to be wherever he is. In this sense is to be understood John i. 48. "before that Philip called thee. . . . I saw thee." For Nathanael inferred nothing more from this than what he professes in the next verse, — "thou art the Son of God," and iii. 13. "the Son of man which is in heaven." These words can never prove that the Son, whether of

---

[157] *Bohn*, IV, 108; *CE*, XIV, 251.

man or of God, is of the same essence with the Father; but only that the Son of man came down from heaven at the period of his conception in the womb of the Virgin, that though he was ministering on earth in the body, his whole spirit and mind, as befitted a great prophet, were in the Father, — or that he, who when made man was endowed with the highest degree of virtue, by reason of that virtue, or of a superior nature given to him in the beginning, is even now *in heaven*; or rather *which was in heaven*, the Greek ὤν having both significations.[158]

Milton expressly declares here that while the Son of man (the incarnate Christ) performed his ministry upon earth, the Son of God (the anointed) was (ὤν) in Heaven, and the Logos ("his whole spirit and mind") was "in the Father." With this conception of the Son's borrowed attribute of omnipresence in mind, it makes sense to think of God's speeches in *Paradise Lost* as utterances of his will through the medium of the audible but invisible Logos within him, even when these speeches are directed to the manifested Son.

Origen, too, asserts the ubiquity of the Son:

. . . and therefore, although the God of the universe should through His own power descend with Jesus into the life of men, and although the Word which was in the beginning with God, which is also God Himself, should come to us, He does not give His place or vacate His own seat, so that one place should be empty of Him, and another which did not formerly contain Him be filled. . . . It is not necessary, then, for the descent of Christ, or for the coming of God to men, that He should abandon a greater seat. . . .[159]

In treating the creation of man, however, both Origen and Milton in *Paradise Lost* apparently go out of their way to make God speak in his own proper person. Arguing that the Son existed before his incarnation, Origen remarks, "for it was to Him that God said regarding the creation of man, 'Let us make man in our image, after our likeness.' "[160] Yet Origen, as we have seen, insists that God cannot be heard — even by the Son. In *Paradise Lost*, throughout the description of the six days' creation, Milton uses simple formulae: "God said," "He nam'd," "he call'd," "th' Almighty spake," etc.; but all these phrases refer unequivocally to the creating Son. When the poet reaches the climactic moment of creation, he seems to accord God an active role:

> . . . therefore th' Omnipotent
> Eternal Father (For where is not hee
> Present) thus to his Son audibly spake.
> vii, 516–18

---

[158] *Bohn*, IV, 134; *CE*, XIV, 315.
[159] *ANCL*, XXIII, 166.
[160] *Ibid.*, p. 308.

This passage may well appear to be a bald refutation of what I have been contending: that the invisible Logos is the voice of God even when God speaks to the Son. Yet I believe that my interpretation is upheld by the *De Doctrina*, in which Milton states: "Previously, however, to the creation of man, as if to intimate the superior importance of the work, the Deity speaks like to a man deliberating." [161] To conclude that "the Deity" here is God would be quite wrong; "the Deity" is the creating Son, as becomes clear from careful retracing of Milton's argument through its topic sentences back to the assertion that the phrase "God said" in Genesis and other similar references to God's speech give to the Son his title of Word.[162] Therefore, when Milton says that the eternal Father audibly spake to the Son, we may assume that the meaning is: the Son as Logos interprets the will of God to the Son as creator, "like to a man deliberating," or speaking to himself. The emphasis is on "the superior importance of the work."

If Origen's commentary on the Son occasionally has Trinitarian overtones, perhaps due to the prudence of Rufinus, the Son is generally portrayed in the *De Principiis* as inferior to God the Father. The powers of the only begotten Son of God are all derived from God. Though the Son can do God's will only, he is still vastly superior to all created beings.

And although we may call Him a "second" God, let men know that by the term "second God" we mean nothing else than a virtue capable of including all other virtues, and a reason capable of containing all reason whatsoever which exists in all things, which have arisen naturally, directly, and for the general advantage, and which "reason," we say, dwelt in the soul of Jesus, and was united to Him in a degree far above all other souls, seeing He alone was enabled completely to receive the highest share in the absolute reason, and the absolute wisdom, and the absolute righteousness.[163]

Thus in Origen's system, the Son, because he receives the "highest share" of the divine virtue, reason, and righteousness, is elevated above the sentient creation; but he is infinitely inferior to the Father; he is a "second" God. In Milton's thought, too, the Son possesses the attributes of God only through derivation. The Son, for example, is not completely omniscient; for there are things which the Father has not revealed even to him. He is not omnipotent; for he "can do nothing of himself, but what he seeth the Father do." In like fashion Milton runs down the complete list of God's attributes to show that they come to the Son only as gifts.[164] *Paradise Lost* offers many illustrations of this view; among them:

> Son of my bosom, Son who art alone
> My Word, my wisdom, and *effectual* might,
>
>   iii, 169–70 (italics mine)

>   . . . all Power
> I give thee, reign for ever, and assume
> Thy Merits;
>
>   iii, 317–19

Origen insists that the Father and the Son are not of the same essence, and that the Son is one with the Father only in their absolute accord. "We worship, therefore, the Father of truth, and the Son, who is the truth; and these, while they are two, considered as persons or subsistences, are one in unity of thought, in harmony and in identity of will." [165] This passage, undeniably anti-Trinitarian, was deplored by Jerome; and the idea, which early won many adherents, was specifically condemned at the Council of Nicea. When he writes thus, Origen may truly be called the spiritual father of Arius. In *The Christian Doctrine*, Milton several times articulates this principle and in language very similar to Origen's:

In the first place, they are one, inasmuch as they speak and act with unanimity. . . .[166]

". . . the words I speak unto you, I speak not of myself, but the Father that dwelleth in me, he doeth the works." Here he [Christ] evidently distinguishes the Father from himself in his whole capacity, but asserts at the same time that the Father remains in him; which does not denote unity of essence, but only intimacy of communion. Secondly, he declares himself to be one with the Father in the same manner as we are one with him, — that is, not in essence, but in love, in communion, in agreement, in charity, in spirit, in glory.[167]

. . . the apostle wished we should principally observe, not that he was in the beginning God, but in the beginning with God; that he might show him to be God only by proximity and love, not in essence; which doctrine is consistent with the subsequent explanations of the evangelist in numberless passages of his gospel.[168]

In *Paradise Lost* Milton succinctly expresses the doctrine that the Father and Son are one not in essence but in accord:

> O Father, O Supream of heav'nly Thrones,
> First, Highest, Holiest, Best, thou always seekst

---

[164] *Bohn*, IV, 133–45; *CE*, XIV, 217–43.
[165] *ANCL*, XXIII, 500.
[166] *Bohn*, IV, 93; *CE*, XIV, 211.
[167] *Bohn*, IV, 93; *CE*, XIV, 211–13.
[168] *Bohn*, IV, 110; *CE*, XIV, 255.

> To glorifie thy Son, I alwayes thee,
> As is most just; this I my Glorie account,
> My exaltation, and my whole delight,
> That thou in mee well pleas'd, declar'st thy will
> Fulfilld, which to fulfill is all my bliss.
> Scepter and Power, thy giving, I assume,
>
>   . . . .
>
> But whom thou hat'st, I hate, and can put on
> Thy terrors, as I put thy mildness on,
> Image of thee in all things;
>
> vi, 723–36

Origen was one of several among the early Church writers who believed that the poets and philosophers of antiquity were unconsciously inspired by the Son and that, accordingly, they wrote better than they knew and were fit to be consulted as arbiters of religious questions. "For no noble deed has ever been performed amongst men, where the Divine Word did not visit the souls of those who were capable, although for a little time, of admitting such operations of the Divine Word." [169] This is to Origen a highly significant point. Because of it he was able to borrow without apology from Greek thought, particularly from that of Plato. Indeed, not only did the philosophical speculations of the Greeks find a place in his theology, but even the gods and demigods of Greek myth were assigned by Origen a peripheral position in his doctrinal beliefs as demons. Milton, of course, also does this; and in *The Christian Doctrine* he does not scruple to buttress theological arguments with quotation from the classics.[170] In *Paradise Lost*, Eve is compared to Proserpine, Adam to Deucalion, and the poet's Christian Muse to the Muses of the pagan Greeks. As a divinely inspired bard, Milton trusts that he may be the equal of his pagan predecessors,

> Blind *Thamyris* and blind *Maeonides*,
> And *Tiresias* and *Phineus* Prophets old.
>
> iii, 35–36

Here, in the same sentence in which Milton characterizes himself as "Smit with the love of sacred Song" and resorting for inspiration to the Muse of Mt. Zion rather than the Muses of Mt. Parnassus, he brings in four great pagan prophets of classic antiquity. That all were blind is, to be sure, not coincidence; nevertheless Milton undoubtedly thought of them as moved by the Word of God.

Origen holds that the Old Testament prophets were visited by

---

[169] *ANCL*, XXIII, 421.

[170] *Bohn*, IV, 77, 107, 258, 259, 278, etc.; *CE*, XIV, 175, 247; XV, 191, 193, 239, etc.

the Word as the Son: "The generality will simply look at what the prophets said, as if that were the Word of the Lord or the Word, that came to them. May it not be, however, that as we say that this person comes to that, so the Son, the Word, of whom we are now theologizing, came to Hosea, sent to him by the Father." [171] That the Son visited, inspired, and directed the Old Testament prophets is a serious article of faith for Milton: "Christ's prophetical functions began with the creation of the world. . . ." [172] In *Paradise Lost*, Book xii, the major prophets — Abraham, Moses, Joshua, David, and Solomon — are pictured as types of Christ, prophesying his future advent.[173]

Before the Fall, according to *The Christian Doctrine*, the Son offers himself as mediator between God and man. This is, as I have hitherto pointed out, an orthodox idea. It appears also in Origen:

But since it was to come to pass that some also should fall away from life, and bring death upon themselves by their declension — for death is nothing else than a departure from life — and as it was not to follow that those beings which had once been created by God for the enjoyment of life should utterly perish, it was necessary that, before death, there should be a resurrection, the type of which was in our Lord and Saviour, and that this resurrection should have its ground in the wisdom and word and life of God.[174]

Professor Kelley insists that *Paradise Lost* differs from the treatise concerning the sacerdotal function of Christ in three respects:

. . . in the *De doctrina*, the person acting is the incarnate Son, Christ; "offer" denotes the actual performance of the sacerdotal work; and the sacrifice takes place in Gospel times. What Milton has done in *Paradise Lost* with his theological material seems primarily this: beginning with the *De doctrina's* concept of the sacerdotal function of Christ, he makes the intercessor not Christ but rather the earlier, not yet incarnate Son, lets "offer" denote rather a declaration of willingness, and thus invents for his epic a feigned scene in which the Son asks for and accepts his sacerdotal duties at a time prior to the actual fall of man.[175]

The scene which Professor Kelley calls "feigned" is presented dramatically but with total fidelity to Milton's doctrinal beliefs. In both epic and treatise, the person acting is Christ, the anointed Son; he is not yet Christ incarnate. In both epic and treatise "offer" denotes a declaration of willingness to become a sacrifice in the fullness of

[171] *Comm. John*, p. 322.
[172] *Bohn*, IV, 300; *CE*, XV, 291.
[173] *P.L.*, xii, 230–44, 310–11, 325–30.
[174] *ANCL*, X, 20–21.
[175] *Kelley*, p. 102.

time and the acceptance of sacerdotal duties prior to man's fall. In *The Christian Doctrine* Milton proclaims:

CHRIST'S SACERDOTAL FUNCTION is that whereby HE ONCE OFFERED HIMSELF TO GOD THE FATHER AS A SACRIFICE FOR SINNERS, AND HAS ALWAYS MADE, AND STILL CONTINUES TO MAKE INTERCESSION FOR US.

ONCE OFFERED; virtually, and as regarded the efficacy of his sacrifice, from the foundation of the world . . . actually, in the fulness of time.[176]

Kelley quotes this very passage to support his contentions; but in his interpretation he is led astray by the word "Christ's," which he takes to mean the *incarnate* Christ's. To Milton the word "Christ" meant only "the anointed," for example, ". . . after having anointed his King, whence the name of *Christ* is derived." [177] Therefore the name can represent either the anointed Son or the God-man. In the context of the quotation "Christ" stands for the Son because the God-man could not have offered himself "virtually, and as regarded the efficacy of his sacrifice, from the foundation of the world," since thousands of years were to elapse before his birth of the Virgin Mary. Kelley's identification of the actor as the incarnate Christ also accounts for his thinking that "offer" is the equivalent of performance of the actual sacrifice. Further, this limits Christ's functions as intercessor to Christian times. Milton plainly says that the anointed Son "HAS ALWAYS MADE" intercession for man. In *Paradise Lost* the poet does not contradict what he has said in the treatise about the Son's sacerdotal role.

Lines 603–6 in Book v of *Paradise Lost* are crucial to the proper interpretation of the poem's theological system:

> This day I have begot whom I declare
> My onely Son, and on this holy Hill
> Him have anointed, whom ye now behold
> At my right hand;

When Kelley discusses these lines, he once more charges Milton with altering his belief to suit the "fable" of his poem by the anachronistic arrangement of "certain dogmatic matters connected with the accession of Christ to the mediatorial office of king" and with the invention of "a new poetic action in which the Father pronounces his only Son ruler over the angelic hierarchies." [178] In a note Kelley adds: "The nearest thing to a sanction for this scene in the epic appears in

---

[176] *Bohn*, IV, 300; *CE*, XV, 291–93. See C. A. Patrides, "Milton and the Protestant Theory of the Atonement," *PMLA*, LXXIV (1959), 7–13. Origen is mentioned in this article as having held views on the atonement similar to those held by Milton.

[177] *Bohn*, IV, 82; *CE*, XIV, 185.

[178] *Kelley*, p. 105.

the following passage from the treatise: 'No one doubts that the Father restored the Son, on his ascent into heaven, to that original place of glory of which he here speaks. That place will be universally acknowledged to be the right hand of God; the same therefore was his place of glory in the beginning, and from which he had descended.' " [179] How much nearer to a "sanction" for the scene should one hope to get? Milton is so positive that there will be no disagreement with what he is saying that he does not bother to argue the point. "No one doubts," he writes, and "will be universally acknowledged." Kelley points out that the Biblical passages that form the basis of *P.L.*, v, 603–6, are proof texts cited by Milton in the *De Doctrina* for the kingship of Christ. These texts are Ps. ii, 6, "I have set my King upon my holy hill"; Ps. cx, 1, quoted by Matt. xxii, 44, "The Lord said unto my Lord, Sit thou on my right hand"; Ps. ii, 7, "Thou art my Son, this day have I begotten thee." Milton might just as well have cited Ps. xvi, 8, cx, 5, cxviii, 15, cxviii, 16, cxxi, 5, or Isa. xlviii, 13. The fact that Milton draws the proof of his doctrine exclusively from the Old Testament patently identifies the king as the Son, the anointed but not the incarnate Christ.

There is, moreover, a clear sanction for *P.L.*, v, 603–6, in Chapter V of *The Christian Doctrine*, "Of the Son of God." It seems to me that this passage alone demonstrates conclusively that the elevation of the Son to kingship before the creation of the world forms an integral part of serious Miltonic doctrine.

Further, it will be apparent from the second Psalm, that God has begotten the Son, that is, has made him a king: v. 6. "yet have I set my King upon my holy hill of Sion;" and then in the next verse, after having anointed his King, whence the name of Christ is derived, he says, "this day have I begotten thee." Heb. i. 4, 5. "being made so much better than the angels, as he hath by inheritance obtained a more excellent name than they." *No other name can be intended but that of Son*, as the following verse proves: "for unto which of the angels said he at any time, Thou art my Son; this day have I begotten thee?" [180]

In both the treatise and the poem, man's redemption, as part of God's unalterable plan, was proposed even before his fall: "Even before man had, properly speaking, confessed his guilt, that is, before he had avowed it ingenuously and in the spirit of repentance, God nevertheless, in pronouncing the punishment of the serpent, previously to passing a sentence on man, promised that he would raise up from the seed of woman one who should bruise the serpent's

---

[179] *Ibid.*, n.
[180] *Bohn*, IV, 82; *CE*, XIV, 185.

head, Gen. iii. 15. and thus anticipated the condemnation of mankind by a gratuitous redemption." [181] *Paradise Lost* supports the doctrine that the Son exists even before the Fall as man's redeemer. The Son speaks:

> Behold mee then, mee for him, life for life
> I offer, on mee let thine anger fall;
> Account mee Man; I for his sake will leave
> Thy bosom, and this glorie next to thee
> Freely put off,
>
> iii, 236–40

EVIL

The discussion of evil, its genesis, purpose, and nature, necessarily forces a departure from the strictly chronological arrangement of Milton's system which I have thus far attempted to follow. The subject lies outside the cosmic chronology — or perhaps it might rather be described as congruent with the whole of it.

In all important respects, the systems of Origen and Milton agree in regard to the concept of evil. How and why evil should exist in a cosmos governed by a God omnipotent, unchangeable, and totally good have long been questions which puzzle the theologian and philosopher. The solution embraced by Origen and Milton has at least the virtues of simplicity and consistency.

Since God is good, evil cannot be in him nor can it proceed from him. Since he is the possessor of eternal wisdom, and since evil is now existent in the cosmos, he must always have had the knowledge of evil. But both Origen and Milton assert that the knowledge of evil does not make God, angel, or man evil unless it is accompanied by an acquiescence of the will. In *Paradise Lost*, Milton makes this quite clear when Adam comforts Eve after her frightening dream foreshadowing the temptation and Fall.

> Evil into the mind of God or Man
> May come and go, so unapprov'd, and leave
> No spot or blame behind:
>
> v, 117–19

It is Kelley's contention that the word "God" in this passage means "angels." [182] Milton, however, when he writes "God" in this line means "God"; for he says the same thing later:

> Th' Almighty thus pronounc'd his sovran Will.
> O Sons, like one of us Man is become

---

[181] *Bohn*, IV, 285; *CE*, XV, 253.
[182] *Kelley*, p. 77.

> To know both Good and Evil, since his taste
> Of that defended Fruit;
>
> xi, 83–86

Of course evil is known to God who is omniscient. If he did not know of it, how could he overcome Satan, how even be aware of him? Knowing everything, God knows evil; being perfectly good, he rejects it; he is not affected by it. And man has the same option, can make the same choice.

According to Origen, all beings were originally created equally good. Being absolutely free, some fell away from their pristine state; and for that fall they were, in various ways, punished. Evil in the cosmos began with those who elected to dispense with virtue. Evil is a state of mind — the negation of goodness; but it remains innocuous until thought becomes action. Origen says:

We are not, however, to imagine that any other result follows from what is suggested to our heart, whether good or bad, save a mental commotion only, and an incitement instigating us either to good or evil. For it is quite within our reach, when a malignant power has begun to incite us to evil, to cast away from us the wicked suggestions, and to resist the vile inducements, and to do nothing that is at all deserving of blame.[183]

In a sense, the diversity which may be remarked among men, indeed among all rational beings — for Origen attributes diversity also to both angels and demons — is directly traceable to that freedom of will which is perhaps the most precious of God's gifts.

For the Creator gave, as an indulgence to the understandings created by Him, the power of free and voluntary action, by which the good that was in them might become their own, being preserved by the exertion of their own will; but slothfulness, and a dislike of labour in preserving what is good, and an aversion to and a neglect of better things, furnished the beginning of a departure from goodness. But to depart from good is nothing else than to be made bad.[184]

In Origen's thought, God is not even remotely responsible for evil, since evil results from a faulty but completely unrestricted choice.

For purposes of his own God may permit the occurrence of evil, though the evil never stems from him. (Of course, God's permission of evil implies his knowledge of it.) Origen argues:

For if God's government extends to sins not only in men, but also in demons and in other spiritual beings who are capable of sin, it is for those who speak in this manner to see how inconvenient is the expression that "all things are ordered by the will of God." For it follows from it that all

---

[183] *ANCL*, X, 231.
[184] *Ibid.*, p. 128.

sins and all their consequences are ordered by the will of God, which is a different thing from saying that they come to pass with God's permission.[185] In *The Christian Doctrine*, Milton declares: "God, however, is concerned in the production of evil only in one of these two ways; either, first he permits its existence by throwing no impediment in the way of natural causes and free agents . . . or, secondly, he causes evil by the infliction of judgments, which is called the evil of punishment." [186] This concept is well illustrated in *Paradise Lost* when Satan rises from the burning lake:

> . . . nor ever thence
> Had ris'n or heav'd his head, but that the will
> And high permission of all-ruling Heaven
> Left him at large to his own dark designs,
> That with reiterated crimes he might
> Heap on himself damnation, while he sought
> Evil to others, and enrag'd might see
> How all his malice serv'd but to bring forth
> Infinite goodness, grace and mercy shewn
> On Man by him seduc't, but on himself
> Treble confusion, wrauth and vengeance pourd.
>
> i, 210–20

The foregoing also illustrates the concomitant idea that God always creates good out of evil; Milton expresses it in the treatise thus: ". . . the end which a sinner has in view is generally something evil and unjust, from which God uniformly educes a good and just result, thus as it were creating light out of darkness." [187]

When the clever pagan Celsus scoffed at Christian redemption, asking why God had not made man good in the first place, Origen had a ready answer: "Where, then, is our free will? and what credit is there in assenting to the truth? or how is the rejecion of what is false praiseworthy? . . . if you take away the spontaneity of virtue, you destroy its essence." [188] This is what Milton is talking about in the justly famous passage from the *Areopagitica*:

As therefore the state of man now is; what wisdom can there be to choose, what continence to forbear, without the knowledge of evil? He that can apprehend and consider vice with all her baits and seeming pleasures, and yet abstain, and yet distinguish, and yet prefer that which is truly better, he is the true warfaring Christian. I cannot praise a fugitive and cloistered virtue unexercised and unbreathed, that never sallies out and seeks her adversary, but slinks out of the race, where that immortal garland

[185] *Ibid.*, XXIII, 488.
[186] *Bohn*, IV, 200; *CE*, XV, 67.
[187] *Bohn*, IV, 204; *CE*, XV, 75.
[188] *ANCL*, XXIII, 164–65.

is to be run for, not without dust and heat. Assuredly we bring not innocence into the world, we bring impurity much rather; that which purifies
us is trial, and trial is by what is contrary.[189]

The sociable angel Raphael is sent by God to teach this precept to
Adam; the angel ably performs his duty.

> God made thee perfet, not immutable;
> And good he made thee, but to persevere
> He left it in thy power, ordaind thy will
> By nature free, not over-rul'd by Fate
> Inextricable, or strict necessity;
> Our voluntarie service he requires,
> Not our necessitated, such with him
> Findes no acceptance, nor can find, for how
> Can hearts, not free, be tri'd whether they serve
> Willing or no, who will but what they must
> By Destinie, and can no other choose?
> My self and all th' Angelic Host that stand
> In sight of God enthron'd, our happie state
> Hold, as you yours, while our obedience holds;
> On other surety none; freely we serve,
> Because we freely love, as in our will
> To love or not; in this we stand or fall:
> And som are fall'n, to disobedience fall'n,
> And so from Heav'n to deepest Hell;
>
> v, 524–42

Thus both Origen and Milton link good and evil with freedom of
will, with choice, with an intellectual act. To understand why this
linkage is necessary, we must go back to the very root of the matter,
back to the time before time began, back to the occasion in eternity
when God in his wisdom, to make known his goodness, willed the
cosmos. He begins, as we have seen, by making primordial matter of
his own substance. Now totality, which is God, includes matter,
which is the not-God. Matter is without form, invisible, and *free*. Of
this freed material are created Heaven and all the hosts thereof,
who are also free. So they must be; for otherwise the goodness of
God could never have been manifested, and the grand design would
have been frustrated at its inception. Only those beings who themselves have wisdom can recognize the wisdom of God. Lewis points
out that Satan is not only the prince of evil; he is the prince of non-
sense. Origen declares: "And if any one were to maintain . . . that
'God exists, and *we* are next to Him,' I would interpret the word
'we,' by using in its stead, 'We who act according to reason,' or rather,
'We *virtuous*, who act according to reason.' For . . . the virtue of

---

[189] *Bohn, Areopagitica*, II, 68; *CE*, IV, 311.

man and God is identical." [190] Right reason is the image of God in
man. Man is created "endu'd / With Sanctitie of Reason," "self-
knowing" and "magnanimous," in order that he may acknowledge
"whence his good descends" and pay homage to God (*P.L.*, vii,
505–16). This is his major function — the reason for his being. But
the homage man pays must be freely paid; it must result from a
willing and free choice. Therefore an alternative choice must be
possible, one which opposes the will of God.

> . . . of the Tree
> Which tasted works knowledge of Good and Evil,
> Thou maist not; in the day thou eat'st, thou di'st;
> > vii, 542–44

Lewis draws out attention to the fact that the forbidden fruit is,
after all, only an apple. No magical virtue is inherent in it. In all
its ramifications, the sin of Eve lies solely in her disobedience of
God's prohibition.

THE ANGELIC FALL

Satan's rebellion, according to Origen, brings evil into the cosmos: "No one, moreover, who has not heard what is related of him
who is called 'devil,' and of his 'angels,' and what he was before he
became a devil, and *how* he became such, and what was the cause
of the simultaneous apostosy of those who are termed his angels,
will be able to ascertain the origin of evils." [191] Before his fall, the
leader of the demons existed as light. Upon his apostasy, even though
he gained this world, and was said to be its prince, his glory was
turned to dust. "In this manner, then, did that being once exist as
light before he went astray, and fell to this place, and had his glory
turned into dust, which is peculiarly the mark of the wicked, as
the prophet also says; whence, too, he was called the prince of this
world. . . ." [192] Before his fall, the leader of the apostate angels
was one of the greatest of the inhabitants of Heaven: ". . . the first
among those that were living a peaceful and happy life to lose his
wings, and to fall from blessedness; he who, according to Ezekiel,
walked faultlessly in all his ways, 'until iniquity was found in him,'
and who being the 'seal of resemblance' and the 'crown of beauty'
in the paradise of God, being filled as it were with good things, fell
into destruction. . . ." [193] Origen holds that the fall of Lucifer was

[190] *ANCL*, XXIII, 190.
[191] *Ibid.*, pp. 231–32.
[192] *Ibid.*, X, 152.
[193] *Ibid.*, XXIII, 385.

brought about by his own pride in his high rank in the heavenly hierarchy. Considering the gifts of God as his own by right, failing to understand that what God gives, he may also take away, he "viewed as his own, and not as given him by God, the primacy which he held at the time when he was unstained; and thus was fulfilled in him the declaration, that 'every one who exalteth himself shall be abased.' "[194] That Satan entered the serpent to tempt Eve, an idea which, of course, is not found in Genesis but which was to become a theological commonplace, Origen asserts: "For the serpent . . . deceived the woman by a promise of divinity and of greater blessings; and her example is said to have been followed also by the man. And, further, who else could the destroying angel mentioned in the Exodus of Moses be, than he who was the author of destruction to them that obeyed him, and did not withstand his wicked deeds, nor struggle against them?"[195]

The Christian Doctrine says nothing of Satan's motive for disobedience, though he is called "the author of all wickedness and the opponent of all good."[196] *Paradise Lost*, of course, suggests envy and pride as the motive for Satan's rebellion (*P.L.*, v, 658–64).[197] Milton's imagery in the following passage suggests that Lucifer in Heaven existed as light:

> At length into the limits of the North
> They came, and *Satan* to his Royal seat
> High on a Hill, farr blazing, as a Mount
> Rais'd on a Mount, with Pyramids and Towrs
> From Diamond Quarries hewn, and Rocks of Gold,
> The Palace of great *Lucifer*, (so call
> That Structure in the Dialect of men
> Interpreted).
>
> v, 755–62

---

[194] *Ibid.*, X, 186.

[195] *Ibid.*, XXIII, 383.

[196] *Bohn*, IV, 219; *CE*, XV, 111.

[197] Arnold Williams, in "The Motivation of Satan's Rebellion in *Paradise Lost*," *SP*, XLII (1945), 253–69, suggests that Satan fell through envy of man, because "God would assume, not the form of angels, but that of the seed of Abraham. He would be made man; he would become the head of the angels. Thus human nature would become exalted over angelic, for no one, angel or man, would be saved except through the grace of Christ." This interpretation seems to me open to objection. The good angels do not need saving in Milton's system; and, once fallen, the evil angels are denied grace. See *P.L.*, iii, 111–32, especially the last four lines. Christ has no need to become man until *after* Satan rebels and tempts man to fall — indeed, Satan's rebellion is, apparently, the cause of the creation of the world and man. Williams' idea, I think, does violence to the chronology of the epic and to the logic of the angelic fall.

Satan's pre-eminence in Heaven is pointed up in the epic:

> *Satan*, so call him now, his former name
> Is heard no more in Heav'n; hee of the first,
> If not the first Arch-Angel,
>
> v, 658–60

The adversary refuses to grant that whatever powers he has are derived from God:

> Who can in reason then or right assume
> Monarchie over such as live by right
> His equals,
>
> v, 794–96

And Abdiel, recognizing the primal sin, thus rebukes him:

> Shalt thou give Law to God, shalt thou dispute
> With him the points of libertie, who made
> Thee what thou art, and formd the Pow'rs of Heav'n
> Such as he pleasd, and circumscrib'd thir being?
>
> v, 822–25

Persisting in foolhardiness, Satan sees his glory turned to dust. The scene in Hell, when the fiend boasts to his legions of his success in tempting Eve, and in which he is answered by the hissing of serpents rather than the applause of angels, is the nadir of Satan's fortunes within the epic. Milton emphasizes the degradation of Satan and his followers when they, turned to reptiles,

> . . . fondly thinking to allay
> Thir appetite with gust, instead of Fruit
> Chewd bitter Ashes, which th' offended taste
> With spattering noise rejected: oft they assayd,
> Hunger and thirst constraining, drugd as oft,
> With hatefullest disrelish writh'd thir jaws
> With soot and cinders filld;
>
> x, 564–70

It is Origen's belief that the fallen angels or demons have deceived men into worshiping them as gods, but Christians do no homage to demons: ". . . it is true of all demons, that they were not demons originally, but they became so in departing from the true way; so that the name 'demons' is given to those beings who have fallen away from God. Accordingly, those who worship God must not serve demons."[198] Milton in the *De Doctrina* explicitly says that the demons were not made by God; for while God made the angels, the angels turned themselves into demons when they sided with Satan against the Father. Origen is not specific about their numbers; in *Paradise Lost* a third of the angels comprise the demonic

---

[198] *ANCL*, XXIII, 489.

horde, which is described as larger than the sum of all human armies (i, 571–87). Milton catalogs as the chief demons the false pagan gods who were occasionally honored by the backsliding Israelites (i, 376–521). After man's fall, according to Origen, the demons dwelt upon earth, each finding a particular place in which to sojourn.[199] The human inhabitants of those areas in which they settled came to worship them as gods, but the Jews and the Christians recognized that "the gods of the nations are demons."[200] In his own day Origen felt the need to dethrone the gods of the Greeks and Romans. He lists specifically as demons Zeus and Apollo,[201] Esculapius,[202] and Bacchus and Hercules.[203] More interestingly, Origen may have been the first to include some who figure as demons also in *Paradise Lost*. Azazel, the scapegoat sent away into the wilderness in Leviticus, is made a demon by Origen; in *Paradise Lost* he becomes Satan's stand-ard-bearer. Belial, a mere abstraction in the Old Testament, acquires demonic identity in the *Contra Celsum*; in the same work, Origen expresses uncertainty whether Mammon is a demon or a generic name for those who worship worldly things, but he allows the per-sonification.[204] Beelzebub figures once parenthetically as "the Prince of demons."[205] Professor Kelley finds that in the *De Doctrina* Satan and Beelzebub are one person, though they are, to be sure, two in the poem.[206] I am inclined to think that separate identities are im-plied in the treatise. Milton designates Beelzebub "Prince" and Satan "leader." Earlier Michael is called "prince," "leader," "captain," and "one who presides over the rest of the good angels." Because of the world "also" in the sentence "The devils also have their prince," I take the meaning to be: "As Michael is the Prince of the good angels and Christ their king, so Beelzebub is the Prince of the evil angels and Satan their leader."

In Origen's system, among demons as among angels a hierarchy exists in which positions are attained through merit. What acts of zeal, love, or hate were performed by individual spirits Origen does not know, but he asserts that

they have received the steps of their rank on account of their merits, al-though it is not our privilege to know or inquire what those acts of theirs

---

[199] *Ibid.*, p. 115.
[200] *Ibid.*, p. 87.
[201] *Ibid.*, p. 119.
[202] *Ibid.*, p. 270.
[203] *Ibid.*, p. 526.
[204] *Ibid.*, p. 383.
[205] *Ibid.*, p. 42.
[206] *Kelley*, p. 138.

were, by which they earned a place in any particular order . . . the same
view is to be entertained of those opposing influences which have given
themselves up to such places and offices, that they derive the property by
which they are made "principalities," or "powers," or rulers of the darkness of the world, or spirits of wickedness, or malignant spirits, or unclean
demons, not from their essential nature, nor from their being so created,
but have obtained these degrees in evil in proportion to their conduct, and
the progress which they made in wickedness.[207]

In *Paradise Lost*, too, the society of the devils is inverted by their
great sin. The hierarchy which they knew in their heavenly condition is maintained in their hellish; the most powerful of the fallen
angels become the lords among the demons.

> Thrones, Dominations, Princedoms, Vertues, Powers
> For in possession such, not onely of right,
> I call ye and declare ye now, returnd
> Successful beyond hope, to lead ye forth
> Triumphant out of this infernal Pit
>
> x, 460–64

Their ranks, like those of the unfallen angels, are achieved through
"merit"; but in Hell to have merit is to be strong in evil.

> High on a Throne of Royal State . . .
>
>   .   .   .   .
>
> Satan exalted sat, by merit rais'd
> To that bad eminence;
>
> ii, 1–6

Demons, Origen says, since they possess "incorporeal" bodies, may
change their shapes at will; they may enter into the bodies of men
or of lesser creatures, particularly animals of the more rapacious
and savage kind.[208] The same tenet obtains in *Paradise Lost*:

> . . . For Spirits when they please
> Can either Sex assume, or both; so soft
> And uncompounded is thir Essence pure;
> Not ti'd or manacl'd with joint or limb,
> Nor founded on the brittle strength of bones,
> Like cumbrous flesh; but in what shape they choose
> Dilated or condenst, bright or obscure,
> Can execute thir aerie purposes,
> And works of love or enmity fulfill.
>
> i, 423–31

During the course of the epic, Satan enters into or takes the form of
cormorant, lion, tiger, toad, and serpent.

Origen grants that the power of demons is great, though, as we
have seen, he does not believe that it can be exerted against men

---

[207] *ANCL*, X, 69.
[208] *Ibid.*, XXIII, 259.

without God's permission. Indeed, he agrees with Milton that God deliberately uses them to tempt and to punish the wicked among mankind:

. . . divine justice employs certain angels to inflict calamities upon man: "He cast upon them the fierceness of His anger, wrath, and indignation, and trouble sent by evil angels." Whether demons ever go beyond this when they are suffered to do what they are ever ready, though through the restraint upon them they are not always able to do, is a question to be solved by that man who can conceive . . . how it accords with divine justice. . . .[209]

Milton says in the treatise that the demons "are sometimes, however, permitted to wander throughout the whole earth, the air, and heaven itself, to execute the judgments of God." [210] Among demons some are stronger than others, Origen avers; but all are alike in having no power over those who "have put on the whole armor of God," though evil spirits "exercise power among the wicked, as a punishment of their wickedness.[211] Milton also believes that malign angels cannot harm good men:

> . . . the Law of Faith
> Working through love, upon thir hearts shall write,
> To guide them in all truth, and also arme
> With spiritual Armour, able to resist
> *Satans* assaults, and quench his fierie darts,
> xii, 488–92

God permits the devils their malefactions, and from them he educes good (see *P.L.*, i, 209–20).

A devil, Origen thinks, may either take complete possession of his victim's mind or by wicked suggestions pervert his intelligence.[212] Ithuriel and Zephon in *Paradise Lost* discover Satan in the garden of Eden,

> Squat like a Toad, close at the eare of *Eve*;
> Assaying by his Devilish art to reach
> The Organs of her Fancie, and with them forge
> Illusions as he list, Fantasms and Dreams,
> iv, 800–803

Demons also, Origen says, are capable of forcing the world of nature to their will; to them belong "famine, blasting of the vine and fruit trees, pestilence among men and beasts." [213] Milton stresses the

---

[209] *Ibid.*, pp. 517–18.
[210] *Bohn*, IV, 218; *CE*, XV, 109.
[211] *ANCL*, XXIII, 260, 520.
[212] *Ibid.*, X, 241–42.
[213] *Ibid.*, XXIII, 517.

terrible power of the fallen angels when he pictures the erection of Pandemonium.

> . . . And here let those
> Who boast in mortal things, and wondring tell
> Of *Babel*, and the works of *Memphian* Kings,
> Learn how thir greatest Monuments of Fame
> And Strength and Art are easily outdone
> By Spirits reprobate, and in an hour
> What in an age they with incessant toil
> And hands innumerable scarce perform.
>
> i, 692–99

Even matter, a substance made intrinsically good by God and then endued with form by the Son, may be perverted through the efforts of Satan and, after the Fall, through those of men. In *The Christian Doctrine* Milton declares: "Strictly speaking indeed it is neither matter nor form that sins; and yet having proceeded from God, and become in the power of another party, what is there to prevent them, inasmuch as they have now become mutable, from contracting taint and contamination through the enticements of the devil, or those which originate in man himself?" [214] In *Paradise Lost*, when Satan turns over the newly won world to Sin and Death and they speed through "thickest Constellations,"

> . . . the blasted Starrs lookd wan,
> And Planets, Planet-strook, real Eclips
> Then sufferd.
>
> x, 412–14

The broad track built from Hell to the world by Sin and Death is probably the most familiar example in the poem of matter fallen into evil hands and put to an unholy use. Another example is Satan's invention of gunpowder and cannon during the heavenly war. At the climax of the epic, matter upon the earth falls with Eve from the pristine state.

> . . . her rash hand in evil hour
> Forth reaching to the Fruit, she pluckd, she eat:
> Earth felt the wound, and Nature from her seat
> Sighing through all her Works gave signs of woe,
> That all was lost.
>
> ix, 780–84

Thus Nature with mankind becomes mortal. No longer will trees blossom and bear fruit all the year round. The rose has now its thorn; and the rank weeds burgeon to stifle the productivity of earth.

---

[214] *Bohn*, IV, 180; *CE*, XV, 25.

Origen says that the demons are ruled by the Son through fear: ". . . they do not yield Him a willing obedience. . . . He rules . . . in the same way that man rules over and subdues lions and beasts of burden." [215] A similar relationship between the fallen angels and the Son is implied in Book ii of *Paradise Lost*; for example:

> . . . the King of Heav'n hath doomd
> This place our dungeon, not our safe retreat
> Beyond his Potent arm, to live exempt
> From Heav'ns high jurisdiction in new League
> Banded against his Throne, but to remaine
> In strictest bondage, though thus farr remov'd
> Under th' inevitable curb, reserv'd
> His captive multitude: For he, be sure,
> In highth or depth, still first and last will Reign
> Sole King, and of his Kingdom loose no part
> By our revolt, but over Hell extend
> His Empire, and with Iron Scepter rule
> Us here,
>
> ii, 316–28

According to Origen, the fallen angels lost much of their power at the coming of Christ: ". . . for they saw that the libations and odours in which they greedily delighted were swept away by the prevalence of the instructions of Jesus." [216] The idea is not touched upon in the *De Doctrina*, nor does it enter into *Paradise Lost*; but it figures prominently in "On the Morning of Christ's Nativity," and it is repeated in *Paradise Regained* (i, 430–59).

One of Origen's more daring heresies is his contention that all rational creatures, including fallen angels, will eventually find salvation and be reunited with God. I know of no other religious writer who supports this tenet; and St. Jerome singled it out as a devastating argument against the followers of Origen. Milton expressly denies it in *Paradise Lost*, in which the almighty Father declares:

> The first sort [angels] by thir own suggestion fell,
> Self-tempted, self-deprav'd: Man falls deceiv'd
> By th' other first: Man therefore shall find Grace,
> The other none:
>
> iii, 129–32

Yet the idea of demonic repentance certainly interested Milton; for several times in the epic the fallen angels seem persuaded that it is possible. In his first speech, Satan patently thinks (or pretends to think) that he may repent and sue for pardon if he chooses.

[215] *ANCL*, XXIII, 504.
[216] *Ibid.*, pp. 110–11.

> . . . To bow and sue for grace
> With suppliant knee, and deifie his power
> Who from the terrour of this Arm so late
> Doubted his Empire; that were low indeed,
>
>   i, 111–16

During the great consultation in Hell, Mammon appears also to believe that the evil angels have the option of pardon and return to
their former condition. Suppose, he asks, God should relent

> And publish Grace to all, on promise made
> Of new Subjection; with what eyes could we
> Stand in his presence humble, and receive
> Strict Laws imposed,
>
>   ii, 238–41

Like Satan, Mammon rejects the course he here suggests. In Book iv,
even as Satan plots the downfall of mankind, and while he is in soliloquy and therefore speaking without guile, he again adverts to the
question:

> O then at last relent: is there no place
> Left for Repentance, none for Pardon left?
> None left but by submission; and that word
> Disdain forbids me, and my dread of shame
>
>   .   .   .   .
>
> But say I could repent and could obtaine
> By Act of Grace my former state; how soon
> Would highth recall high thoughts, how soon unsay
> What feignd submission swore: ease would recant
> Vows made in pain, as violent and void.
>
>   iv, 79–97

As the sole bar to his repentance, Satan sees only his own stiff-necked
refusal; he is not aware that God has decreed for him an eternity of
punishment. These passages bring Milton as close as he comes to
Origen's heretical proposal.

CREATION

Origen believed that all rational beings were created at one time
and that all were equally good. Some, he argues, fell away from
goodness to a greater or lesser degree, thus finding their own positions in a chain of being which extends from Satan, the most evil
being in the cosmos — and the one fallen farthest from his origin —
through the fallen angels, through men evil and good, and through
the heavenly hierarchy to God, who is perfection. An intellectual
being cannot remain stationary; he moves either down the scale to-

ward Satan or up it toward God. He is helped to rise by those above him and to fall by those below; but the upward attraction is stronger than the downward. After many ages of such movement, every soul, including the souls of demons, returns to goodness and to God, who is then said to be "all in all." Origen, however, does not see how such a state of absolute beatitude can long remain; for beings must keep their free will, and some free beings will undoubtedly not continue steadfast in goodness. The process of creation is thus cyclical, renewing itself in sequent worlds throughout eternity.

Milton believed that Heaven and the angels were created long before the making of the world and men. Later, through envy of the Son and pride which made him think himself impaired, Satan, together with a third of the angels, rebelled and was banished from Heaven. To repopulate the celestial regions, Adam and Eve were created as the progenitors of a new kind of rational beings, who were to live in the world until they proved themselves fit to inhabit Heaven. Man's acceptance in the sight of God, like that of the angels, was contingent upon his obedience. Choosing to disobey, he fell.

In their large outlines, the accounts of the two thinkers are very unlike. Origen's depicts a continuing process, the end of which, if in fact it can ever be said to come to a conclusion, is remote in a time long after the dissolution of the world we live in. Even if we consider only the history of the world which we know — one world in a long succession of worlds past and to come — the differences between the conceptions of Origen and Milton look substantial. Origen treats of one fall only: angelic beings created equal and good fall to a greater or lesser degree through the exercise of their free wills, finding their levels as demons, men, or angels. This idea makes of the Biblical Fall in Genesis nothing more than a parable; and indeed the story of Adam and Eve is an embarrassment to Origen, who says little about it. Though his total plan of creation is philosophically interesting, in detail it lacks drama. For Satan becomes in it simply another link upon the great chain of being stretching upward from the abyss to God; man seems hardly worth the battle waged for him between good influences and bad; while saints and angels, evil men and demons have so much in common that they are scarcely distinguishable. From the point of view of any single world, Origen's plan appears optimistic, since the general movement of souls is ever upward toward God and goodness; but from the aspect of the total cycle it is darkly pessimistic, for there is no real chance that the rational creation can achieve perfection — beings rise only to fall again in the next universe to come. In spite of its conceptual majesty, one can easily see why Origen's world view did not achieve popularity.

Milton's creation, far more orthodox than Origen's, is also far more dramatic. Man enjoys a central place in the scheme of things; the world is a battlefield for a vital encounter between good angels and bad for the souls of men, and these are considered a prize worthy of the combat. Satan in this system, a being differing in kind from man and powerful enough to be dangerous as an adversary of the angels, appears darkly magnificent — a figure exciting terror and awe. As a whole the plan retains a subtle balance, full of parallels and parodies, malign forces pitted against beneficent, and the denouement, particularly from the individual's position, is uncertain. If the major plot seems less than cheerful, the fault as well as the remedy is man's.

Yet the two conceptions, in spite of manifold and obvious dissimilarities, have much in common, as I have indicated in earlier sections of this chapter and hope further to demonstrate in this. They are alike in these ways:

1. The Absolute God, who must necessarily remain forever incomprehensible, cannot himself create the world; for if he were to do so he would become manifest.

2. In Wisdom the Logos is brought forth.

3. The Logos exists before the creation as a second God and the immediate creator of the world.

4. Matter is *made* of the substance of God. It is formless and invisible.

5. The role of the Holy Spirit in the creation is negligible.

6. Man is created to manifest the goodness of God. Origen says: "When He in the beginning created those beings which He desired to create, *i.e.* rational natures, He had no other reason for creating them than on account of Himself, *i.e.* His own goodness." [217] (See *P.L.*, iii, 162–66, for one illustration of this indisputably Miltonic tenet.)

7. Man is located upon the great chain of rational being midway between the angels and the demons.

8. The distinction between man as he was originally created and the angels both good and fallen is not great. In Origen's scale of being, as I have already noted, men merge all but imperceptibly on the one hand into angelic nature and on the other into demonic. In

---

[217] *Ibid.*, X, 132–33.

Paradise Lost, Beelzebub (though his judgment may be biased by pride in what he mistakenly deems his own relative eminence) admits the excellent nature of man:

> . . . *Man,* about this time
> To be created like to us, though less
> In power and excellence, but favour'd more
> Of him who rules above;
>
> ii, 348–51

Even Satan, upon the occasion of his first seeing Adam and Eve, admits their worth:

> O Hell; what doe mine eyes with grief behold,
> Into our room of bliss thus high advanc't
> Creatures of other mould, earth-born perhaps,
> Not Spirits, yet to heav'nly Spirits bright
> Little inferior; whom my thoughts persue
> With wonder, and could love, so lively shines
> In them Divine resemblance, and such grace
> The hand that formd them on thir shape hath pourd.
>
> iv, 358–65

9. Man, created of free matter, is endowed at his making with free will. He is therefore responsible for his own destiny.

10. Adam represents all men; his sin is therefore the sin of mankind. Origen writes:

. . . in the Hebrew language Adam signifies man; and that in those parts of the narrative which appear to refer to Adam as an individual, Moses is discoursing upon the nature of man in general. For "in Adam" (as the Scripture says) "all die," and were condemned in the likeness of Adam's transgression, the word of God asserting this not so much of *one particular individual as of the whole human race.*[218]

In *Paradise Lost,* Milton treats it thus:

> . . . thy Saviour, shall recure,
> Not by destroying *Satan,* but his works
> In thee and in thy Seed: nor can this be,
> But by fulfilling that which thou didst want,
> Obedience to the Law of God, impos'd
> On penaltie of death, and suffering death,
> The penaltie to thy transgression due,
> And due to theirs which out of thine will grow:
>
> xii, 393–400

Because he holds that in Adam's fall we sinned all, Milton is a traducianist, one who argues that among men the soul is passed on from father to son according to the laws of propagation: ". . . on what principle of justice can sin be imputed through Adam to that

---

[218] *Ibid.,* XXIII, 206.

soul, which was never either in Adam, or derived from Adam?" [219] Origen admits uncertainty on this point of doctrine: ". . . whether it is derived from the seed by a process of traducianism, so that the reason or substance of it may be considered as placed in the seminal particles of the body themselves, or whether it has any other beginning; and this beginning itself, whether it be by birth or not, or whether bestowed upon the body from without or no, is not distinguished with sufficient clearness in the teaching of the church." [220]

Origen is quite positive, however, that body and soul are indivisible. His reasoning is ingenuous: ". . . the soul which is immaterial and invisible in its nature, exists in no material place, without having a body suited to the nature of that place." [221] He insists, further, that only God, the Son, and the Holy Spirit are capable of existing without bodies.[222] In Milton's thought, too, the soul and body are indivisible:

. . . man is a living being, intrinsically and properly one and individual, not compound or separable, not, according to the common opinion, made up and framed of two distinct and different natures, as of soul and body, — but that the whole man is soul, and the soul man, that is to say, a body, or substance individual, animated, sensitive, and rational; and that the breath of life was neither a part of the divine essence, nor the soul itself, but as it were an inspiration of some divine virtue fitted for the exercise of life and reason, and infused into the organic body; for man himself, the whole man, when finally created, is called in express terms *a living soul*.[223]

This particular doctrine is, obviously, an extension of Milton's views on the production of matter from the substance of God. If man be allowed to partake in any degree of the *essence* of God, then the sins of man involve God in evil. Milton denies that the supreme goodness of God can include evil. Thus the poet's concept of the indivisible nature of man leads him into heretical ideas on the incarnate Christ and on man's resurrection, which ideas will presently be examined.

THE FALL

Oh, Thou, who Man of baser Earth didst make,
And who with Eden didst devise the Snake;
For all the Sin wherewith the Face of Man
Is blacken'd, Man's Forgiveness give — and take!

---

[219] *Bohn*, IV, 192; *CE*, XV, 47.
[220] *ANCL*, X, 5.
[221] *Ibid.*, XXIII, 454.
[222] *Ibid.*, X, 59.
[223] *Bohn*, IV, 188; *CE*, XV, 41.

Both Origen and Milton have an answer to the accusation made in the *Rubaiyat* against a God omniscient and omnipotent who yet allows the defection of angels and men. First, God's foreknowledge in no way influences what is to happen. Origen says: "Celsus imagines that an event predicted through foreknowledge, comes to pass because it was predicted; but we do not grant this, maintaining that he who foretold it was not the cause of its happening, because he foretold it would happen; but the future event itself, which would have taken place though not predicted, afforded the occasion to him who was endowed with foreknowledge, of foretelling its occurrence." [224] In language somewhat more disciplined, Milton presents the same argument:

God of his wisdom determined to create men and angels reasonable beings, and therefore free agents; foreseeing at the same time which way the bias of their will would incline, in the exercise of their own uncontrolled liberty. What then? shall we say that this foresight or foreknowledge on the part of God imposed on them the necessity of acting in any definite way? No more than if the future event had been foreseen by any human being. For whatever any human being has foreseen as certain to happen, will not less certainly happen than what God himself has predicted.[225]

The idea is concisely enunciated in *Paradise Lost*:

> . . . they themselves decreed
> Thir own revolt, not I: If I foreknew,
> Foreknowledge had no influence on thir fault,
> Which had no less prov'd certain unforeknown.
>   iii, 116–19

Second, God cannot be honored by a coerced obedience; rational beings are therefore created free.

Origen, as has been pointed out, practically excludes the story of Adam and Eve from his serious theology. Milton is profoundly concerned with it. He posits two degrees of sin, the *desire* and the *act*. Satan tempts Eve into the desire of sin; when she eats the forbidden fruit, she commits the act of sin by disobeying God. Because of his uxoriousness Adam becomes guilty on both counts.

The fall of man in *Paradise Lost* has received its due share of scholarly attention in the last few decades. Too often, I think, Milton's own analysis of it in the *De Doctrina* has been neglected:

For what sin can be named, which was not included in this one act? It comprehended at once distrust in the divine veracity, and a proportionate credulity in the assurances of Satan; unbelief; ingratitude; disobedience;

---

[224] *ANCL*, XXIII, 26.
[225] *Bohn*, IV, 39–40; *CE*, XIV, 83.

gluttony, in the man excessive uxoriousness, in the woman a want of proper regard for her husband, in both an insensibility to the welfare of their offspring, and that offspring the whole human race; parricide; theft; invasion of the rights of others, sacrilege, deceit, presumption in aspiring to divine attributes, fraud in the means employed to attain the object, pride, and arrogance.[226]

Every one of these sins is specifically illustrated in *Paradise Lost*.[227] It is a mistake, therefore, to dwell upon one with so great an emphasis that the remainder are forced into the background. Saurat, confusing a result of the Fall with its cause, settles upon sensuality.[228] C. S. Lewis stresses pride and disobedience.[229] Clarence Green finds that "Eve transgresses because her deceived mind misinforms her will . . . Adam, however, transgresses 'against his better knowledge, not deceav'd'. The account of his Fall is voluntaristic: his *will* is primary." [230] Charles Williams, in his introduction to the new World's Classics edition of Milton's *English Poems* (1940), hits upon "a sense of proper dignity, of self admiration, of rights withheld, of injured merit," [231] which is about what Shelley thought. And E. M. W. Tillyard chooses "triviality of mind," or "levity," or, in Adam's case, "uxoriousness." [232] All these views (except perhaps Saurat's) are un-

---

[226] *Bohn*, IV, 254; *CE*, XV, 181–83.

[227] Distrust in the divine veracity, ix, 753–54; credulity in the assurances of Satan, ix, 616, 733–34; unbelief, ix, 773–75; ingratitude, x, 743–46; disobedience, ix, 644–45; gluttony, ix, 739–43; in the man excessive uxoriousness, ix, 908–16; in the woman a want of proper regard for her husband, ix, 545–48, 820–21; in both an insensibility to the welfare of their offspring, x, 979–91; and that offspring the whole human race, ix, 415–16; parricide, ix, 830–33; theft, ix, 780–81; invasion of the rights of others, x, 999–1002; sacrilege, 834–38; deceit, ix, 810–16; presumption in aspiring to divine attributes, ix, 790; fraud in the means employed to attain the object, ix, 977–81; pride, x, 874; and arrogance, x, 876–79. A careful reading of Books ix and x of the epic with this paragraph from the treatise held in mind will demonstrate the truth of my argument far better than this cursory documentation will allow. That Milton had the paragraph in mind as he composed these two books becomes very plain.

[228] *Saurat*, pp. 206–17.

[229] C. S. Lewis, *A Preface to Paradise Lost* (London, New York, and Toronto, 1956), p. 121 ff.

[230] Clarence C. Green, "The Paradox of the Fortunate Fall in *Paradise Lost*," *MLN*, LIII (1938), 557–59.

[231] See *Milton Criticism*, ed. James Thorpe (London, 1951), pp. 252–66.

[232] E. M. W. Tillyard, *Milton* (London, 1956), p. 262. For some interesting views upon the subject in general see John S. Diekhoff, "Eve, the Devil, and *Areopagitica*," *MLQ*, V (1944), 429–34, who argues: "Knowledge useful — indeed necessary — to the salvation of fallen man is worse than useless to innocence and purity"; and the discussion between Professors Millicent Bell and Wayne Shumaker carried on in *PMLA*, LXVIII (1953), 863–83, and LXX (1955), 1185–1203, under the title "The Fallacy of the Fall in *Paradise Lost*."

doubtedly right; but all are at best partial. Surely Milton's own statement in the treatise provides the likeliest key to his characterization of Adam and Eve in *Paradise Lost* as "manifold in sin" (x, 16).

The wages of sin is death. Since the transgression of Adam and Eve, man has been totally mortal. He dies body and soul; he remains dead body and soul until the day of judgment; he is resurrected body and soul; he is judged body and soul; and he enjoys his reward or suffers his punishment body and soul. This is Milton's well-known mortalist heresy. It did not originate with the poet, though the language in which he expresses it is possibly stronger than is usual among theologians; for, as I have shown, an identical doctrine occasioned the fortieth of the Forty-two Articles of 1553: "The souls of them that depart this life do neither die with the bodies nor sleep idly." Though I believe that I have not overstated the Miltonic doctrine, the poet himself, when denying the necessity for purgatory in *The Christian Doctrine*, vitiates his earlier statements concerning the death of the soul until it is clear that he meant only to suggest the sleep of the soul until the resurrection. "And if it be true, as shown in a preceding chapter, that the soul as well as the body sleeps till the day of resurrection, no stronger argument can be urged against the existence of a purgatory." [233] Milton might very well have derived this view, or, indeed, his earlier and more disconcerting satement, from the *De Principiis*: "And if any one imagine that at the end material, *i.e.* bodily, nature will be entirely destroyed, he cannot in any respect meet my view, how beings so numerous and powerful are able to live and to exist without bodies, *since it is an attribute of the divine nature alone — i.e. of the Father, Son and Holy Spirit — to exist without any material substance, and without partaking in any degree of a bodily adjunct*." [234] Of death and resurrection, moreover, Origen says:

But how do they [believers in Christianity who do not see eye to eye with Origen upon the resurrection] understand the declaration of the apostle, "We shall all be changed"? This transformation certainly is to be looked for, according to the order which we have taught above; and in it, undoubtedly, it becomes us to hope for something worthy of divine grace; and this we believe will take place in the order in which the apostle describes the sowing in the ground of a "Bare grain of corn, or of any other fruit," to which "God gives a body as it pleases Him," as soon as the grain of corn is dead. For in the same way also our bodies are to be supposed to fall into the earth like a grain; and (that germ being implanted in them which con-

---

[233] *Bohn*, IV, 318; *CE*, XV, 341.
[234] *ANCL*, X, 58–59. Italics mine.

tains the bodily substance) although the bodies die, and become corrupted, and are scattered abroad, yet by the word of God, that very germ which is always safe in the substance of the body, raises them from the earth, and restores and repairs them, as the power which is in the grain of wheat, after its corruption and death, repairs and restores the grain into a body having a stalk and ear.[235]

If soul cannot exist without body, and if body "die" and be subject to corruption and dissolution, then soul "dies" too. But in Origen's thought body does not entirely die — it contains an immortal germ or seed within it which will enable it to rise a spiritual body at the resurrection. If then once more the body live, so too may the soul. Origen and Milton hold identical mortalist theories. Each speaks of the death of the soul and body; and each means, in reality, the dormant state, or sleep, of soul and body. Each insists that body and soul sleep until the day of the last judgment.

In *Paradise Lost*, Adam's speech on death may well illustrate the logical process by means of which Milton himself arrived at his mortalist belief.

> . . . Yet one doubt
> Persues me still, least all I cannot die,
> Least that pure breath of Life, the Spirit of Man
> Which God inspir'd, cannot together perish
> With this corporeal Clod; then in the Grave,
> Or in some other dismal place, who knows
> But I shall die a living Death? O thought
> Horrid, if true! yet why? it was but breath
> Of Life that sinnd; what dies but what had life
> And sin? the Bodie properly hath neither.
> All of me then shall die: let this appease
> The doubt, since human reach no further knows.
>
> x, 782–93

Death, the punishment for sin, is divided by Milton into four categories. The first consists of "all those evils which lead to death, and which it is agreed came into the world immediately upon the fall of man. . . ."[236] The second is spiritual death, "the loss of divine grace, and that innate righteousness, wherein man in the beginning lived unto God."[237] The third is the simultaneous and complete death of the body and the soul, a state which lasts until the last judgment.[238] All mankind must suffer these three phases of death; but the fourth is reserved for the lost. It is the eternal

---

[235] *Ibid.*, p. 139.
[236] *Bohn*, IV, 264; *CE*, XV, 203.
[237] *Bohn*, IV, 264–65; *CE*, XV, 205.
[238] *Bohn*, IV, 271; *CE*, XV, 219.

damnation and punishment of souls condemned to Hell at the judgment.[239]

CHRIST

The word "Christ" does not appear in *Paradise Lost*. In the present discussion, the name will identify the incarnate Son of God as he
came to men on earth. In the epic the Son is called Word, Son,
Lord, Messiah, and Saviour; to these titles Logos and Christ are
added in the treatise — the primary meaning of Christ being "the
anointed," while the secondary meaning is "Christ incarnate."
Though all these names are correctly applied to him who was the
first of the whole creation, it is helpful to narrow them down to the
three which represent chronologically differentiated phases of his existence: the Word or Logos is he who was literally begotten; the Son
is he who was metaphorically begotten and manifested to the angels;
Christ is he who was begotten in the flesh and manifested to men.

According to the orthodox view, as Milton explains it in *The
Christian Doctrine*, "two natures are so combined in the one person of Christ, that he has a real and perfect subsistence in the one
nature independently of that which properly belongs to the other;
insomuch that two natures are comprehended in one person." [240]
This is what is known as the "hypostatic union." Milton quotes Zan-
chius to make plain the orthodox doctrine:

"He took upon him not man, properly speaking, but the human nature.
For the Logos being in the womb of the Virgin assumed the human nature
by forming a body of the substance of Mary, and creating at the same time
a soul to animate it. Moreover, such was his intimate and exclusive assumption of this nature, that it never had any separate subsistence, independent
of the Logos; but did then first subsist, and has ever since subsisted, in the
Logos alone."[241]

Milton scoffs at these "arcana." For him the orthodox system fails
in that the union of God and man is incomplete. In other words, God
is linked only with man's nature, not with man; and man is not
linked with God at all. Milton substitutes the following:

There is then in Christ *a mutual hypostatic union* of two natures, that is
to say, of two essences, of two substances, and consequently of two persons;
nor does this union prevent the respective properties of each from remaining individually distinct.[242]

---

[239] *Bohn*, IV, 488; *CE*, XVI, 369.
[240] *Bohn*, IV, 290; *CE*, XV, 267.
[241] *Bohn*, IV, 290–91; *CE*, XV, 267.
[242] *Bohn*, IV, 292; *CE*, XV, 271.

And a little farther on:

. . . the Son of God, our Mediator, was made flesh, that he is called both God and Man, and is such in reality; which is expressed in Greek by the single and appropriate term Θεάνθρωπος.[243]

Origen's conception of the nature of Christ is identical with Milton's. Quasten, in *Patrology*, remarks: "It remains Origen's merit to have given to Greek Christology the scientific terms, *physis, hypostasis, ousia, homousios,* and *theanthropos.*"[244] In *The Christian Doctrine* Milton uses all these terms except the first. Of these the last is the most important, since it pins down exactly Milton's idea of Christ. Origen writes in the *De Principiis*:

This substance of a soul, then, being intermediate between God and the flesh — it being impossible for the nature of God to intermingle with a body without an intermediate instrument — the God-man Θεάνθρωπος is born, as we have said, that substance being the intermediate to whose nature it was not contrary to assume a body. But neither, on the other hand, was it opposed to the nature of that soul, as a rational existence to receive God, into whom, as stated above, as into the Word, and the Wisdom, and the Truth, it had already wholly entered. And therefore deservedly it is also called, along with the flesh which it had assumed, the Son of God, and the Power of God, the Christ, and the Wisdom of God, either because it was wholly in the Son of God, or because it received the Son of God wholly into itself.[245]

If, at the appointed time, the Son is made "very man" as Christ, if Christ should not be regarded merely as the Son clothed in flesh, then, both Origen and Milton hold, when Christ dies on the cross, his soul perishes with his body — the whole being dies. Origen says:

. . . the Son of God, through whom all things were created, is named Jesus Christ and the Son of man. For the Son of God also is said to have died — in reference, viz., to that nature which could admit of death; and He is called the Son of man, who is announced as about to come in the glory of God the Father, with the holy angels. And, for this reason, throughout the whole of Scripture, not only is the divine nature spoken of in human words, but the human nature is adorned by appellations of divine dignity. More truly indeed of this than of any other can the statement be affirmed, "They shall both be in one flesh, and are no longer two, but one flesh."[246]

Origen bases his contention that Christ died completely upon the premise that the resurrection is fact — the logic is uncomplicated and irrefutable once the premise is granted. "For he who really died,

---

[243] *Bohn*, IV, 293; *CE*, XV, 273.
[244] Johannes Quasten, *Patrology* (Westminster, Md., 1950–60), II, 81.
[245] *ANCL*, X, 109.
[246] *Ibid.*

actually arose, if he did arise; whereas he who appeared only to have died, did not in reality arise." [247]

Origen's phrase "to that nature which could admit of death" is strongly reminiscent of Milton's "All that of me can die" (*P.L.*, iii, 246); and the meaning of both phrases is exactly the same. Milton's phrase appears in the following passage, in which the Son, offering himself as man's redeemer before the Fall, speaks these words:

> Account mee Man; I for his sake will leave
> Thy bosom, and this glorie next to thee
> Freely put off, and for him lastly die
> Well pleas'd; on mee let Death wreck all his rage;
> Under his gloomie power I shall not long
> Lie vanquisht; thou hast givn me to possess
> Life in my self for ever, by thee I live,
> Though now to Death I yield, and am his due
> *All that of me can die*; yet that debt paid,
> Thou wilt not leave me in the loathsom grave
> His prey, nor suffer my unspotted Soule
> For ever with corruption there to dwell;
>
> iii, 238–49 (italics mine)

Professor Kelley interprets the phrase thus: ". . . on account of our sins, even the soul of Christ was for a short time subject unto death." [248] Saurat holds that because the Son's "soul — his life — is unspotted, therefore he shall not die." [249] Professor Merritt Hughes offers this note on the passage: ". . . the words are traditional in this connection and occur without theological surcharge about the Son's immunity to death in Serafine Salandra's Adamo caduto (Cozanza, 1647), V, vii, p. 123. Milton is not splitting theological hairs; he is dealing with the justice of Christ's incarnation and crucifixion, which — as Beatrice explains to Dante in Paradiso VII, 40–42 — can be explained only on the ground that in assuming human nature Christ became guilty of all human sin." [250] From this — especially from the expression "immunity to death" — I take it that Professor Hughes thinks Christ does not totally die. Surely the doctrine Hughes articulates is orthodox. In the treatise, however, Milton states his heretical position on the question without ambiguity: "The fact, that Christ became a sacrifice both in his divine and human nature, is denied by none; and as it was requisite that the whole of the sacrifice

[247] *Ibid.*, XXIII, 22.
[248] *Kelley*, p. 32.
[249] Denis Saurat, "Two Notes on Milton," *RES*, XII (1936), 324.
[250] *John Milton: Complete Poems and Major Prose*, ed. Merritt Y. Hughes (New York, 1957), p. 264n.

should be slain, Christ, who was the sacrificial lamb, must be considered as *slain in the whole of his nature*." [251] Since Christ is a being,
in whom are inextricably united God and man, he may act as God
or he may act as man; but he cannot separate his one nature of God-
man into two. Therefore, when Christ dies, he dies body and soul. He
dies totally, as all men die, because he is a man.[252] He dies as God,
too; because in him God and man are united in a single being. This
is, I think, a fair précis of what Milton says in the *De Doctrina*. Nor
is there anything in the Son's speech which contradicts the clear import of the statement in the treatise. "On mee let Death wreck all
his rage" — *all* Death's rage would surely imply total death. "Under
his gloomie power I shall not long / Lie vanquisht" — for a time, at
least, Christ is vanquished by Death. "Though now to Death I yield,
and am his due" also implies total death. A debt cannot be spoken
of as paid (line 246) until it is completely discharged. Christ will be
unable to rise from the grave unless God intervenes (lines 247–49).
Finally, should God fail to intervene, Christ's *soul* would dwell forever with corruption. Against this evidence, apparently, we have
"thou hast givn me to possess / Life in my self for ever" and "All that
of me can die." For if Christ has been granted eternal life, he cannot even for a moment die; and the latter phrase certainly seems
to have a partitive sense.

But the speaker of the lines is not the incarnate Christ; he is the
Son, the anointed Christ, who here offers *later* to become the God-
man, *later* as Christ to be the sacrificial lamb, *later* to be raised from
the grave. Christ incarnate may die in his total nature; the Son will
not. To the Son has been given life forever, not to Christ. The idea
of the Son's ubiquity, which, as I have already demonstrated, was
held by both Origen and Milton, makes plausible what might otherwise seem a sophistical argument.

After the ascension, Milton says, the "human nature of Christ,
although exalted to a state of the highest glory, exists nevertheless
in one definite place, and has not, as some contend, the attribute of
ubiquity." [253] It is clearly indicated here that the divine nature of
Christ enjoys ubiquity to the extent that he had this attribtue before the incarnation. Milton probably has in mind such Scriptural

[251] *Bohn*, 306; *CE*, XV, 309. Italics mine.
[252] William B. Hunter, "Milton on the Incarnation: Some More Heresies,"
JHI, XXI (1960), 349–69, shows Milton to be following the Nestorian heresy in
arguing for the mutual hypostatic union, and the Theopaschite heresy when he
maintains that the divine nature suffered and died.
[253] *Bohn*, IV, 308; *CE*, XV, 315.

passages as Matt. xviii, 20: "For where two or three are gathered to-gether in my name, there am I in the midst of them."

Identification of the redeeming Christ as a second Adam is made in Origen's commentary upon John: "He is not only the firstborn of all creation, but is also designated the man, Adam. For Paul says He is Adam: 'The last Adam was made a life-giving spirit.'"[254] In *Paradise Lost* Christ is designated a second Adam:

> Not higher that Hill nor wider looking round,
> Whereon for different cause the Tempter set
> Our second *Adam* in the Wilderness,
> To shew him all Earths Kingdoms and thir Glory.
>
> xi, 381–84

Milton explores the paradox of the two Adams. The first "Brought Death into the World" (i, 3); and the second is enjoined by God:

> . . . Be thou in Adam's room
> The Head of all mankind, though Adam's Son.
>
> iii, 285–86

ESCHATOLOGY

For Origen, as I have indicated, the world is eternal. It is made anew over and over as a training school for souls fallen into sin. There were, he contends, worlds before this; and others will follow. Because sentient beings are invested from eternity with free will, some will always fail and be forced down the chain of being away from holiness and from God. Within each world, the good aid their weaker fel-lows; eventually all come to redeem their sins and to ascend ardu-ously toward God. Since goodness preponderates in each universe, even the worst souls recognize their error and attain holiness. When-ever a world comes to its end, God is "all in all." But individuals yet retain their free will; in time one is sure to fall and others to ac-company him; a new world becomes necessary; and a new cycle be-gins. Thus cosmic history, like Fortune's wheel, swings through its prodigious revolutions. In support of these Origenic concepts I offer the following excerpt from the *De Principiis*:

But in the meantime, both in those temporal worlds which are seen, as well as in those eternal worlds which are invisible, all those beings are ar-ranged, according to a regular plan, in the order and degree of their merits; so that some of them in the first, others in the second, some in the last times, after having undergone heavier and severer punishments, endured for a lengthened period, and for many ages, so to speak, improved by this stern method of training, and restored at first by the instruction of the

---

[254] *Comm. John*, p. 322.

angels, and subsequently by the powers of a higher grade, and thus advancing through each stage to a better condition, reach even to that which is invisible and eternal, having travelled through, by a kind of training, every single office of the heavenly powers. From which, I think, this will appear to follow as an inference, that every rational nature may, in passing from one order to another, go through each to all, and advance from all to each, while made the subject of various degrees of proficiency and failure according to its own actions and endeavors, put forth in the enjoyment of its power of freedom of will.[255]

Milton, of course, does not include in his serious theology the theory of the cyclic universe; for him the world had its beginning and will have its end. Nevertheless, in at least two passages in *Paradise Lost*, Milton suggests that subsequent universes may be created:

> Space may produce new Worlds;
>
> i, 650

> . . . Into this wilde Abyss,
> The womb of Nature and perhaps her Grave,
> Of neither Sea, nor Shore, nor Air, nor Fire,
> But all these in thir pregnant causes mixt
> Confus'dly, and which thus must ever fight,
> Unless th' Almighty Maker them ordain
> His dark materials to create more Worlds,
>
> ii, 910–16

In *Paradise Lost*, Adam sees the world as a training school for virtue:

> Henceforth I learne, that to obey is best,
> And love with feare the onely God, to walk
> As in his presence, ever to observe
> His providence, and on him sole depend,
> Merciful over all his works, with good
> Still overcoming evil, and by small
> Accomplishing great things, by things deemd weak
> Subverting worldly strong, and worldly wise
> By simply meek; that suffering for Truths sake
> Is fortitude to highest victorie,
> And to the faithful Death the Gate of Life;
>
> xii, 561–71

The idea that good spirits aid lesser creatures appears more than once in *Paradise Lost*. Adam tells Eve of the millions of spirits who night and day walk the earth.[256] Raphael and Michael are sent for the express purpose of aiding Adam and Eve.[257] Our first parents are guarded from harm, ineffectually, it is true, by an angelic watch.[258]

---

[255] *ANCL*, X, 57–58.
[256] *P.L.*, iv, 677–78.
[257] *Ibid.*, Books v–viii, xi–xii.
[258] *Ibid.*, Book iv.

Despite his theory that this world is but one in a continuing cycle, Origen believes that Christ will appear as judge when our particular universe draws to its close: "The end of the world, then, and the final consummation, will take place when every one shall be subjected to punishment for his sins; a time which God alone knows, when He will bestow on each one what he deserves. We think, indeed, that the goodness of God, through His Christ, may recall all His creatures to one end, even His enemies being conquered and subdued." [259] Chapter XXXIII of the first book of the *De Doctrina* deals very largely with Christ's function as judge. Christ's role in the last judgment is detailed in the epic, Book xii, 451–65.

To every man, Milton held, God gives knowledge of the right; and, therefore, every man is responsible to himself. Written in his heart is the law of God; and by that law is he finally to be judged. "The rule of judgement will be the conscience of each individual, according to the measure of light which he has enjoyed." [260] In *Paradise Lost*, God says:

> And I will place within them as a guide
> My Umpire *Conscience*, whom if they will hear,
> Light after light well us'd they shall attain,
> And to the end persisting, safe arrive.
>
> iii, 194–97

Origen does not name the principle, but it is nonetheless a tenet in his theology: "It is not therefore matter of surprise that the same God should have sown in the hearts of all men those truths which he taught by the prophets and the Saviour, in order that at the divine judgment every man may be without excuse, having the 'requirements of the law written upon his heart. . . .' " [261]

In Origen's system, when a cycle is fulfilled and when all beings have worked their way upward into goodness, there comes a static period in which God is, as he was before the beginning, "all in all": ". . . this transmutation of the form of the present world . . . will undoubtedly be prepared for those who are walking along that way which we have pointed out . . . and are tending to that goal of happiness to which, it is said, even enemies themselves are to be subjected, and in which God is said to be 'all and in all.' " [262] Milton, too, of course, believes that God will ultimately reassume the complete integrity which, to carry out his plan — the manifestation of his

---

[259] *ANCL*, X, 54.
[260] *Bohn*, IV, 483; *CE*, XVI, 357.
[261] *ANCL*, X, 401.
[262] *Ibid.*, p. 58.

glory and goodness — he voluntarily disturbed.[263] Twice in *Paradise Lost* (iii, 341; vi, 732) the phrase "all in all" is employed. Origen, as I have indicated, holds that God can not long remain in this state, since the retention of free will by rational beings makes inevitable another Fall. Origen's singular view may be faintly reflected in Satan's soliloquy outside the walls of Eden:

> O had his powerful Destiny ordaind
> Mee some inferiour Angel, I had stood
> Then happie; no unbounded hope had rais'd
> Ambition. Yet why not? som other Power
> As great might have aspir'd, and mee though mean
> Drawn to his part;
>
> iv, 58–63

The implication of these lines is surely that rebellion against God is bound to happen; for Satan recognizes that even without ambition's spur he would have fallen, following the lead of another. Thus Satan himself seems to affirm that evil would have entered the cosmos without his instigation.

Origen's belief in a recurrent or cyclical universe made it impossible for him to be a millenarian. As I have shown, millenarianism represented the orthodox position in ante-Nicene times; the majority of the early Fathers (including Papias, "Barnabas," "The Shepherd," Justin, Irenaeus, Hippolytus, Tertullian, Commodianus, Victorinus of Pettau, Lactantius, and Septimus Severus) subscribed to it. About A.D. 260, Nepos, an Egyptian bishop, attempted to overthrow the Origenistic eschatology and to vindicate, by reference to the Bible and especially to Revelation, the chiliastic interpretation. But Dionysius, Bishop of Alexandria, successfully refuted the followers of Nepos, asserting that the prophets must be understood as having written allegorically. From this time (the middle of the fourth century) until late in the Middle Ages, the Greek Church denied the canonicity of the Book of Revelation, fearing that its authority might encourage the spread of millenarianism. The more conservative Western Church, on the other hand, gave official sanction to the doctrine until it was superseded by the Augustinian view that, as the Catholic Church was an empirical form of the kingdom of Christ, so his thousand-year reign should be held to have begun with his first advent. Yet the old millenarianism continued to crop up, particularly in the lower strata of Christian society, usually as the chief tenet in a sect hostile to the secularized Church. The Anabaptists,

---

[263] *Bohn,* IV, 491–94; *CE,* XVI, 375–81.

the early Lutherans, and other Reformed sects adopted the chiliastic eschatology, though their interpretations of it were often at variance with the convictions of the early Fathers.[264]

Milton declares in *The Christian Doctrine*: "It appears that the *judgement* . . . will not be confined to a single day, but will extend through a great space of time; and that the word is used to denote, not so much a judicial inquiry properly so called, as an exercise of dominion; in which sense Gideon, Jephthah, and the other judges are said to have judged Israel during many years." [265] Among the proof texts which Milton quotes is Rev. xx, 7: ". . . but they shall be priests of God and of Christ, and shall reign with him a thousand years." Milton continues: "After the expiration of the thousand years Satan will rage again, and assail the church at the head of an immense confederacy of its enemies but will be overthrown by fire from heaven, and condemned to everlasting punishment." [266] Though Milton's millenarian position is here unequivocal, *Paradise Lost* contains no similarly explicit affirmation of the view. Yet the opportunity to include it is surely present at the end of Book xi; in Gabriel's account of the end of the world, Book xii, 458 ff. and 537 ff.; and in Book iii, 254 ff.

The passage in Book iii, however, offers a cryptic allusion to the chiliastic persuasion. Looking forward to the judgment, the Son reminds his Father that

> I through the ample Air in Triumph high
> Shall lead Hell Captive maugre Hell, and show
> The Powers of darkness bound. Thou at the sight
> Pleas'd, out of Heaven shalt look down and smile.
> While by thee rais'd I ruin all my Foes,
> Death last, and with his Carcass glut the Grave:
> Then with the multitude of my redeemd

---

[264] Milton's heretical mortalist views are by this time well known. A series of articles has recently appeared upon the subject. See, for example, William B. Hunter, "Milton's Materialistic Life Principle," *JEGP*, XLV (1946), 68–76; Nathaniel H. Henry, "Milton and Hobbes: Mortalism and the Intermediate State," *SP*, XLVIII (1951), 234–49; C. A. Patrides, "*Paradise Lost* and the Mortalist Heresy," *N&Q*, n.s., IV (1957), 250; George L. Mosse, "Puritan Radicalism and the Enlightenment," *Church History*, XXIX (1960), 424–39; and George Williamson, *Seventeenth Century Contexts* (London, 1960). Henry, Mosse, and Williamson link Milton's mortalism with contemporary writers and sects — with Overton, the Ranters, the Baptists, the Mennonites, and the Socinians. Henry notes (p. 224) that Bishop Hall had traced the mortalist belief back to Origen. Patrides admits the mortalism in *The Christian Doctrine* but questions whether it appears in *Paradise Lost*.

[265] *Bohn*, IV, 486; *CE*, XVI, 363.

[266] *Ibid*.

> Shall enter Heav'n *long absent,* and returne,
> Father, to see thy face,
>
> iii, 254–62 (italics mine)

Milton cannot mean by the phrase "long absent" the period of Christ's ministry on earth, since, obviously, Christ does not after it enter Heaven with his redeemed. The phrase must, then, refer to the time subsequent to the second advent. The fact that Milton does not here or elsewhere in the epic specify a thousand-year reign leads one to suspect that his chiliasm was figurative rather than literal.

Milton seems unaware of one problem inherent in his eschatology. God's being once again the Absolute precludes the possibility of the separate existence of any matter or being. Though Milton does not explicitly foretell the reabsorption of matter into God as he does the reabsorption of worthy beings, the intrinsic purity of Heaven and Chaos (including the matter which now forms the world) makes quite possible such a total reunion. But if fallen angels and evil men are to be eternally punished, Hell must forever exist; and it cannot then logically become a part of an infinitely good God.[267]

---

[267] As Allan H. Gilbert says in "The Problem of Evil in *Paradise Lost*," *JEGP,* XXII (1923), p. 177, "Milton was not a romantic sentimentalist, and hence did not feel that he must make Satan good at last, like the villain in the last scene of a comedy." Satan, Gilbert suggests, is used by Milton not to show the origin or the end of evil so much as to personify its present existence.

CHAPTER FIVE

MILTON'S MUSE

The meaning, not the Name I call:
P.L., vii, 5

The problem of identifying Milton's epic Muse may seem to be included arbitrarily in this study of Milton's theology and its relationship to the doctrines of Origen as a representative ante-Nicene Father. I am convinced, however, that the problem is a theological one and that accordingly it should be approached from within the framework of Milton's systematic theology; the solution of the Muse's identity at once depends upon and augments our understanding of the poet's beliefs. The identification which I propose did not occur to me until with the aid of primitive Christianity in general and Origen in particular I gained new insight into Milton's religious thought. In exploring the subject of the Muse I have relied exclusively upon theological tools — the Bible, the *De Doctrina*, and the writings of Origen.

The facts about the Muse are contained, of course, in approximately a hundred lines from the two epics; illumination must stem first from Scriptural texts which inspired the lines. But such light as may be gained from an intensive reading of the lines themselves and from their Biblical sources will be only partial. The speculative, daring, and individual interpretation which Milton gives in *The Christian Doctrine* to theological questions ultimately affords the only criteria from which conclusions about the meaning of the poetic passages may be formed. These passages occur near the beginnings of Books i, iii, vii, and ix of *Paradise Lost* and Book i of *Paradise Regained*. In addition to the matter of the Muse's identity, there are two subsidiary areas of disagreement among those who have studied the lines: some contend that more than one Muse is referred to; and some doubt that certain lines refer to the Muse at all. It will be my position that only one Muse is invoked by the poet — this is rather easily proved — and that the major part of the invocation in Book iii of *Paradise Lost* very probably is not addressed to that Muse.

The Muse is named in Book vii — Urania. Milton's Urania is, to be sure, not the Greek Muse of astronomy; but neither may it be associated with the traditional Christian Muse introduced by Du Bartas in *La Muse Chrétienne* nor with Spenser's Urania in *The Teares of the Muses* (called Sapience in *An Hymne of Heavenly Beautie*). The choice of name was certainly not accidental, but Milton cautions the reader, "The meaning, not the Name I call."

By far the most common assumption is that Milton meant to suggest the third person of the Trinity, the Holy Spirit. The assumption is natural because, according to Newton, Milton's wife thus identified the Muse, because in *The Reason of Church Government* Milton remarks that great poetry may be written only with the aid of "that Eternal Spirit, who can enrich with all utterance and knowledge," [1] and because in his invocation to the Muse in Book i, Milton describes the "Spirit" as "Dove-like," an epithet which reminded commentators of the descent of the Holy Spirit upon Christ at his baptism. But however natural, this interpretation cannot be credited. Milton uses the word "Spirit" eclectically; he applies it to God, to the Son, to the Spirit, to angels, and to Satan and his followers. Assuredly, in *The Reason of Church Government*, the Holy Ghost is not "that eternal Spirit" who "sends out his seraphim with the hallowed fire of his altar to touch and purify the lips of whom he pleases"; for the Holy Spirit, Milton declares, is itself sent or given by God or the Son — no other being is sent by it. The most cogent reason for disallowing the identification of the Muse with the Holy Spirit is Milton's statement in the *De Doctrina*: "Why do we not call upon the Spirit himself, if he be God, to give himself to us? He who is sought from the Father, and given by him, not by himself, can neither be God, nor an object of invocation." [2] If the Holy Spirit cannot be invoked, obviously it is not the Muse of the epics.

Professor Kelley, recognizing these facts, proposes that Milton "invoked a personification of the various attributes of God the Father,

---

[1] *The Prose Works of John Milton*, ed. J. A. St. John (London, Henry G. Bohn, 1848–53), II, 481. Future reference will be to *Bohn* by volume and page number. I also cite the Columbia Edition by volume and page number: *CE*, III, 241.

[2] *Bohn*, IV, 165; *CE*, XIV, 395.

and thus turned for inspiration and knowledge not to what he considered a subordinate figure but rather to the Father himself — the very fountainhead of all wisdom and enlightenment." [3]

This interpretation seems to me as alien to Milton's theology as the identification of Urania as the Holy Spirit. To equate the Muse with the Absolute, the eternal God who cannot be comprehended by men or angels except through the Logos, is unthinkable. Further, if Milton "turned for inspiration . . . to the Father himself," as Kelley asserts, then God becomes the sister of his own Wisdom, he is born in Heaven, and, playing before himself, he pleases himself with his own song. For thus these well-known lines would force us to conclude:

> . . . Heav'nly born,
> Before the Hills appear'd, or Fountain flow'd,
> Thou with Eternal Wisdom didst converse,
> Wisdom thy Sister, and with her didst play
> In presence of th' Almighty Father, pleas'd
> With thy Celestial Song.
>
> P.L., vii, 7–12

Kelley is admittedly somewhat diffident about his solution to the problem of the Muse's identity; in fact, he is by no means positive that Milton thought of the Muse in theological terms. And while other commentators, with varying degrees of confidence, have put forward different solutions from those so far mentioned here, many apparently agree with Dr. Tillyard that the mystery may be finally inscrutable.[4] Yet in his invocations Milton has given us a number of hints which become quite clear in the light of statements from *The Christian Doctrine*. By adducing lines from the epics, by tracing their sources to the Bible, by explicating their meanings with the aid of the treatise and of passages in the poems, and by calling upon Origen for support in my interpretation, I propose to demonstrate that Milton's Muse is without question the Logos.

Throughout the following discussion the reader should bear continually in mind this important tenet from *The Christian Doctrine*: ". . . the Word is both Son and Christ, that is, as I say, *anointed*;

---

[3] Maurice Kelley, *This Great Argument* (Princeton, N.J., 1941), p. 118. Future reference will be to *Kelley*.

[4] Jackson I. Cope, in "Milton's Muse in *Paradise Lost*," *MP*, LV (1957), 6–10, suggests that the Muse is "the Celestial Light shining inward that men 'may see and tell / Of things invisible to mortal sight,' that with which 'they which see not might see.'" Martin A. Larson, "Milton and Servetus: A Study in the Sources of Milton's Theology," *PMLA*, XLI (1926), 891–934, argues that "Milton's Muse is nothing less than God himself, a God that is a *modal* Trinity."

and as he is the image, as it were, by which we see God, so he is the word by which we hear him." [5]

Lines 6–10 of *Paradise Lost*, Book i, offer us the first opportunity to identify Milton's Muse.

> Sing Heav'nly Muse, that on the secret top
> Of Oreb, or of Sinae, didst inspire
> That Shepherd, who first taught the chosen Seed,
> In the Beginning how the Heav'ns and Earth
> Rose out of Chaos:

"That Shepherd" is, of course, Moses, who first taught the ancient Israelites ("the chosen Seed") about the beginnings of Heaven and earth as recorded in Genesis. He alone ("secret top") on Oreb heard the voice of God from the burning bush (Exod. iii, 1–2); and on Sinai, when it was death to anyone else who touched the mount, he received the tablets of the law (Exod. xix, 3). In his argument for identifying the Muse as "a personification of the various attributes of God the Father," Kelley asserts that it was God who inspired Moses on Sinai. His authority is *P.L.*, xii, 227–30.

> God from the Mount of *Sinai*, whose gray top
> Shall tremble, he descending, will himself
> In Thunder, Lightning and loud Trumpet's sound
> Ordain them Laws;

These lines would appear conclusive. Within five lines, however, indeed in the very next sentence, Milton explains what he means more fully:

> . . . But the voice of God
> To mortal ear is dreadful; they beseech
> That *Moses* might report to them his will,
> And terror cease; he grants what they besought,
> *Instructed that to God is no access*
> *Without Mediator,*
>
>   xii, 235–40 (italics mine)

From the treatise it may be discovered that

THE CHRISTIAN DOCTRINE is that DIVINE RELEVATION disclosed in various ages by CHRIST (though he was not known under that name in the beginning). . . .

Under the name of CHRIST are also comprehended MOSES and the prophets, who were his forerunners, and the Apostles whom he sent.[6]

---

[5] *Bohn*, IV, 168; *CE*, XIV, 401.

[6] *Bohn*, IV, 10–11; *CE*, XIV, 17. This is a most difficult passage. When Milton writes that under the name of Christ are also comprehended Moses, the prophets, and the Apostles, he does not mean that these men were in actuality Christ but simply that through them the teachings of Christ were transmitted to men. A being cannot logically be considered his own forerunner, nor can he properly

And, most significantly, the *De Doctrina* has this to say about Moses'
reception of God upon the twin mountain: "Deut. iv. 33. 'did ever
people hear the voice of God speaking out of the midst of the fire,
as thou hast heard, and live?' Yet it is said, Exod. xxxiii. 20. 'there
shall no man see me, and live.' . . . It follows therefore that whoever was heard or seen, it was not God. . . ."[7]

The invocation from *Paradise Lost* continues:

> . . . Or if *Sion* Hill
> Delight thee more, and *Siloa's* Brook that flow'd
> Fast by the Oracle of God; I thence
> Invoke thy aid to my advent'rous Song,
>
> i, 10–13

"*Sion* Hill" and "*Siloa's* Brook" are signposts directing toward the
Logos as the Muse. The second Psalm reads: "Yet have I set my
king upon my holy hill of Zion. I will declare the decree: the LORD
hath said unto me, Thou art my Son; this day have I begotten thee."
Upon these verses Milton bases his entire discussion of the metaphorical generation of the Son in the *De Doctrina*. The "Oracle of
God" is the temple in Jerusalem "fast by" the brook and the pool
of "*Siloa*" associated with Christ's healing of the blind man in John ix.
As Jesus left the temple (John viii, 59), he met a man blind from
birth who was enabled to see when he washed in the nearby pool
of Siloam. The spirit invoked by Milton from "thence" must be the
spirit of the Logos.

Milton next addresses and identifies his Muse in lines 17–19:

> And chiefly Thou O Spirit, that dost prefer
> Before all Temples th' upright heart and pure,
> Instruct me for Thou know'st;

Kelley is surely correct in saying that the word " 'chiefly' (l. 17) is
to be interpreted as 'above all' (NED., i), and the passage paraphrased 'And do thou, O Spirit, above all instruct me. . . .' "[8] Biblical texts underlying Milton's lines include:

1. I Cor. iii, 16: Know ye not that ye are the temple of God, and that
the Spirit of God dwelleth in you?

2. I Cor. vi, 19: What? know ye not that your body is the temple of the
Holy Ghost which is in you, which ye have of God, and ye are not your own?

3. II Cor. vi, 16: And what agreement hath the temple of God with
idols? for ye are the temple of the living God; as God hath said, I will

---

be said to send himself. The Spirit of Christ led the prophets and the Apostles,
who are thus comprehended under his name as doing his work — they are not
to be considered as embodiments of the Son of God.

[7] *Bohn*, IV, 108; *CE*, XIV, 249–51.

[8] *Kelley*, p. 116.

dwell in them, and walk in them; and I will be their God, and they shall be my people.

4. John xiv, 23: Jesus answered and said unto him, If a man love me, he will keep my words: and my Father will love him, and we will come unto him, and make our abode with him.[9]

Milton treats these passages together in *The Christian Doctrine*; he interprets the first three in the light of the last: "The third place is 1 Cor. iii. 16 compared with vi. 19. and 2 Cor. vi. 16. 'the temple of God . . . the temple of the Holy Ghost.' But neither is it here said, nor does it in any way follow from hence, that the Holy Spirit is God; for it is not because the Spirit alone, but because the Father also and the Son *make their abode with us*, that we are called the *temple of God*."[10] Thus Milton argues that Father, Son, and Holy Ghost dwell in the upright heart and pure. But since the Father cannot be seen nor heard, since the Holy Spirit must not be invoked, the Muse who prefers "Before all Temples th' upright heart and pure" is the Logos. Elsewhere in the *De Doctrina*, Milton reasserts his belief that it is the Logos who inspires men with God's Spirit: ". . . the Spirit signifies a divine impulse or light, or voice, or word transmitted from above either through Christ, who is the Word of God, or by some other channel."[11] Commenting upon a number of Biblical texts containing reference to the Holy Ghost, Milton writes: "It appears to me, that these and similar passages cannot be considered as referring to the express person of the Spirit, both because the Spirit was not yet given, and because Christ alone, as has been said before, is, properly speaking, and in a primary sense, the Word of God, and the prophet of the Church. . . ."[12]

In at least two passages from *Paradise Lost* Milton declares that the Son dwells within men to inspire them.

> Thus far to try thee, *Adam*, I was pleas'd,
> And find thee knowing not of Beasts alone,
> Which thou hast rightly nam'd, but of thyself,
> Expressing well the spirit within thee free,
> My image, not imparted to the Brute,
>
> viii, 437–41

The speaker of these lines is, of course, the Son. Again, when Michael shows Adam what the future of mankind will be, the angel remarks:

---

[9] Ps. xviii, 25–26, also deserves mention here: ". . . with an *upright* man thou wilt show thyself *upright*; With the *pure* thou wilt show thyself *pure* . . ." (italics mine).

[10] *Bohn*, IV, 161; *CE*, XIV, 383.

[11] *Bohn*, IV, 155; *CE*, XIV, 367.

[12] *Bohn*, IV, 155; *CE*, XIV, 369.

Those Tents thou saw'st so pleasant, were the Tents
Of wickedness, wherein shall dwell his Race
Who slew his Brother; studious they appear
Of Arts that polish Life, Inventors rare,
Unmindful of thir Maker, though his Spirit
Taught them, but they his gifts acknowledg'd none.

xi, 607–12

It is the Spirit of the Son, the maker of man, which instructs even the inhabitants of the tents of wickedness, though they will not acknowledge his gifts.

The next lines from *Paradise Lost* which help to identify the Muse paraphrase the beginning of the Biblical creation story in Gen. i, 2: "And the earth was without form and void; and darkness was upon the face of the deep. And the Spirit of God moved upon [margin: "was brooding upon"] the face of the waters."

. . . Thou from the first
Wast present, and with mighty wings outspread
Dove-like satst brooding on the vast Abyss
And mad'st it pregnant:

i, 19–22

Two passages from *The Christian Doctrine* illuminate these lines. The first is from Milton's chapter on the Holy Spirit.

When the phrase, the Spirit of God, or the Holy Spirit, occurs in the Old Testament, it is to be variously interpreted; sometimes it signifies God the Father himself . . . sometimes the power and virtue of the Father, and particularly that divine breath or influence by which everything is created and nourished. In this sense many both of the ancient and modern interpreters understand the passage in Gen. i. 2. "the Spirit of God moved upon the face of the waters." Here, however, it appears to be used with reference to the Son, through whom the Father is so often said to have created all things.[13]

Oddly enough, Kelley denies the significance of this commentary as a gloss upon *P.L.*, i, 19–22, because he maintains that in Milton's second and fuller treatment of the same Scriptural text Milton contradicts his own earlier interpretation. It seems to me that the second treatment merely expands the first and that Kelley has not considered it in its entirety. I quote it in full:

AND SPIRIT. Gen. 1. 2. "the spirit of God moved upon the face of the waters;" that is, his divine power, rather than any person, as has been already shewn in the sixth chapter, or the Holy Spirit. For if it were a person, why is the Spirit named, to the exclusion of the Son, by whom we so often read that the world was created? unless, indeed, that Spirit were Christ, to whom, as has been before proved, the name of Spirit is sometimes given in the

---

[13] *Bohn*, IV, 151–52; *CE*, XIV, 359–61.

Old Testament. However this may be, and even if it should be admitted to have been a person, it seems at all events to have been only a subordinate minister: God is first described as creating the heaven and the earth; the Spirit is only represented as moving upon the face of the waters already created. So Job xxvi. 13. "by his Spirit he hath garnished the heavens." Psal. xxxiii. 6. "by the word of Jehovah were the heavens made, and all the host of them by the breath (*spiritu*) of his mouth." Now the person of the Spirit does not seem to have proceeded more from the mouth of God than from that of Christ, who "shall consume that wicked one with the spirit of his mouth," 2 Thess. ii. 8. compared with Isai. xi. 4. "the rod of his mouth." [14]

As I understand these two passages from the treatise, they preach an identical doctrine concerning the brooding Spirit. In each Milton first identifies the Spirit as the Spirit of God rather than as the third person. In each he goes on to remark that in this particular event the Spirit is received by the Son as the gift of the Father. The Son then makes use of the Father's Spirit in the creation. Both commentaries completely accord with Milton's carefully worked out theory of the relationship among the Father, the Son, and the Spirit. Thus the brooding, dove-like Spirit of *Paradise Lost,* Book i, is more intimately and directly linked with the Son than with either the Father or the Holy Ghost.

Kelley cites *P.L.*, vii, 165–66, as corroboration of his contention that the Muse is the Father; again I feel that he is misreading Milton's intention. I quote the lines in context:

> And thou my Word, begotten Son, by thee
> This I perform, speak thou, and be it done:
> My overshadowing Spirit and might with thee
> I send along, ride forth, and bid the Deep
> Within appointed bounds be Heav'n and Earth,
>
> vii, 163–67

Do not these lines say, simply: (1) the Father wills the creation — the Son performs it; (2) the Father gives his Spirit and might to the Son; (3) the Son is to utilize that power and Spirit in the creation? It should be noticed, too, that these lines are concerned with the preparation for the creation rather than with the actual event. Between these lines and those which describe the dove-like brooding of the Spirit over the embryonic universe there is only the connection of cause and effect. In these lines God gives his Spirit to the Son; in those, the Son puts forth God's gift and creates.

The invocation to the Muse in Book i yields one further hint of her identity.

---

[14] *Bohn*, IV, 175; *CE*, XV, 13–15.

> Say first, for Heav'n hides nothing from thy view
> Nor the deep tract of Hell,
>
> i, 27–28

These lines rule out the possibility that the Muse is the Holy Spirit, described in the *De Doctrina* as a limited being: "But even if it filled with its presence the whole circle of the earth, with all its heavens, that is, the entire fabric of this world, it would not follow that the Spirit is omnipresent. For why should not the Spirit easily fill with the influence of its power, what the Sun fills with its light; though it does not necessarily follow that we are to believe it infinite?" [15] The Father is, of course, by definition he who fills everything; and to his Son he grants the attribute of omnipresence, though in respect to its being a gift which can be withdrawn, the Son's omnipresence is inferior to the Father's.[16] Lines from Book iii of *Paradise Lost* affirm the Miltonic conception of the Son's ability to see all things at one view.

> Now had th' Almighty Father . . .
>
> . . . . .
>
> . . . bent down his eye,
> His own works and their works at once to view:
>
> . . . . .
>
> . . . On Earth he first beheld
> Our two first parents . . .
>
> . . . . .
>
> . . . he then surveyed
> Hell and the Gulf between, and *Satan* there
> Coasting the wall of Heav'n . . .
>
> . . . . .
>
> Him God beholding . . .
>
> . . . . .
>
> Thus to his only Son foreseeing spake.
> Only begotten Son, seest thou. . . .
>
> iii, 56–80

The superb opening lines of Book iii have perplexed rather than assisted those commentators who have attempted to deduce from them the identity of the Muse. Actually, only three lines (19–21) of the fifty-five which make up the exordium refer to the Muse. Two kinds of light, mundane and ethereal, are pictured in the lines; but at no time is the light equated directly with any being. Book iii begins:

> Hail holy Light, offspring of Heav'n first-born
> Or of th' Eternal Coeternal beam

[15] *Bohn*, IV, 162; *CE*, XIV, 387.
[16] *Bohn*, IV, 134; *CE*, XIV, 315.

> May I express thee unblam'd? since God is Light,
> And never but in unapproached Light
> Dwelt from Eternity, dwelt then in thee,   5
> Bright effluence of bright essence increate.[17]

These first six lines are concerned with celestial light, that in which God dwells and unto which no man can approach. They cannot point either to the Son or to the Spirit because the object of description is eternal; and, in Milton's system, even the Son had his beginning in time. They cannot directly refer to the Father, because God dwells *in* the light which is *coeternal* with him. The light is that which emanates from the uncreated essence of God.

The second six lines are concerned with the physical light which is visible to mankind.

> Or hear'st thou rather pure Ethereal stream,
> Whose Fountain who shall tell? before the Sun,
> Before the Heavens thou wert, and at the voice
> Of God, as with a mantle did'st invest   10
> The rising world of waters dark and deep,
> Won from the void and formless infinite.

According to Genesis and according to Milton, light existed independent of a luminary before the sun. At the *fiat lux*, it invested the darkness of the newly created world. [18]

The next six lines serve as a transition between the account of the dark regions of Hell and Chaos and the bright scenes of the world and of Heaven. These lines depict the gradual increase of light which the poet experiences as, in his fancy, he traverses the reaches of extrastellar space between Hell and Heaven.

> Thee I revisit now with bolder wing,
> Escap't the *Stygian* Pool, though long detain'd
> In that obscure sojourn, while in my flight   15
> Through utter and through middle darkness borne
> With other notes than to th' *Orphean* Lyre
> I sung of *Chaos* and *Eternal* Night,

The word "revisit" alone is ample proof that Milton is not speaking of any person of the Trinity; and it also eliminates the possibility

---

[17] William B. Hunter, in "The Meaning of 'Holy Light' in *Paradise Lost* III," *MLN*, LXXIV (1959), 589–92, argues that the Father in *P.L.*, iii, 1 ff., is the source of light and that the Son who is Light emanates from him: "I wish to urge that the collocation of the two images light-sun and stream-fountain reveals that Milton had in mind the identification of this Holy Light with the Son of God." Now this is surely mistaken; for lines 3–6 tell us that God dwelt in light which flows out from his own bright essence from eternity; and, in Milton's system, as we have seen, the Son is not eternal, nor can God ever have dwelt within (line 5) his own Son.

[18] *P.L.*, vii, 243–52.

that he has the Muse in mind. Patently, he cannot revisit one who has never left him.

Lines 19–21 do, however, refer to the Muse; and they clearly point to her identity as the Logos.

> Taught by the heav'nly Muse to venture down
> The dark descent, and up to reascend,   20
> Though hard and rare:

These lines are firmly grounded upon Biblical sources:

Rom. x, 6–7: But the righteousness which is of faith speaketh on this wise, Say not in thine heart, Who shall ascend into heaven? (that is, to bring Christ down from above:) Or who shall descend into the deep? (that is, to bring up Christ from the dead.)

Eph. iv. 9–10: (Now that he ascended, what is it but that he also descended first into the lower parts of the earth? He that descended is the same also that ascended up far above all heavens, that he might fill all things.)

The next six lines again refer to physical light, which the poet laments his inability to see.

> . . . thee I revisit safe,
> And feel thy sovran vital Lamp; but thou
> Revisit'st not these eyes, that roll in vain
> To find thy piercing ray, and find no dawn;
> So thick a drop serene hath quencht thir Orbs,   25
> Or dim suffusion veil'd.

Again, precisely as in line 13, the word "revisit" in line 21 obviates the assumption that "thee" means any person of the Trinity or the Muse; and no being or spirit can be logically thought of as physically illuminating with "piercing ray" the vainly rolling eyes of the poet.

The one passage in the exordium to Book iii which seems to me ambiguous is the concluding five lines, wherein the blind poet, "Presented with a Universal blanc" and admitting that for him was "wisdom at one entrance quite shut out," asks for interior illumination.

> So much the rather thou Celestial Light
> Shine inward, and the mind through all her powers
> Irradiate, there plant eyes, all mist from thence
> Purge and dispense, that I may see and tell
> Of things invisible to mortal sight.   55

The "things invisible to mortal sight" of which the poet, with the aid of celestial light, hopes to be able to "see and tell" are, we know, the events recounted in the remainder of Book iii. These lines, I suggest, link two kinds of light, earthly and heavenly, with the interior and figurative illumination of the poet's understanding which he seeks from the Muse. Between light of whatever kind and the Logos, I am sure that there was for the poet a vital nexus. As physical light in Genesis is "offspring of Heav'n first-born," so is the Logos "the first of the whole creation." The opening chapter of John familiarizes us with the concept of the Word as light: "In him was life; and the life was the light of men." The eighth chapter reinforces the idea: "I am the light of the world: he that followeth me shall not walk in darkness, but shall have the light of life." Psalm cxix says, "Thy word is a lamp unto my feet, and a light unto my path." In *The Christian Doctrine* Milton equates Christ with light.[19] It is the Son in *Paradise Lost* who invests with light "the rising world of waters dark and deep." It is the Son who circumscribed the world with the golden compasses and thus "Won from the void and formless infinite" the pendant world. The word "celestial" (line 51) is used only once in the Bible, where it leads to the Son: I Cor. xv, 40, 45, 47.

The invocation which opens Book vii is perhaps the most familiar and certainly the most circumstantial of Milton's references to the Muse. From the initial lines we discover that the Muse is named Urania, that she is not the Muse of astronomy, that she is from Heaven, and that she was born in Heaven.

> Descend from Heav'n *Urania* . . .
> The meaning, not the Name I call . . .
>   . . . . .
> . . . Heav'nly born,
>
> vii, 1–7

The name Urania means "heavenly"; Milton may be translating it as "Heav'nly born."[20] The next five lines in the poem, of all descriptions of the Muse, offer the most informative characterization.

> Before the Hills appear'd, or Fountain flow'd,
> Thou with Eternal Wisdom didst converse,
> Wisdom thy Sister, and with her didst play
> In presence of th' Almighty Father, pleas'd
> With thy Celestial Song.

---

[19] *Bohn*, IV, 102, 138–39, 144, 148; *CE*, XIV, 235, 327, 341, 351.

[20] In the Greek the name "Urania" is often used as an epithet of Aphrodite. The Muse of Book vii is identical with that which was invoked in Book i because Milton writes in lines 30–31, ". . . still govern thou my Song, / *Urania*." The three lines in the exordium to Book iii, which certainly treat of the Muse, link her with the Urania of Book vii by the use of the adjective "heav'nly." The "Celestial Patroness" of Book ix, 21, is surely a reference to the same figure. In *P.R.*, 1, 11–12, Milton writes, ". . . inspire, / As thou art wont, my prompted Song," and thus links the Muse of the shorter epic with that of the longer.

As every student of Milton knows, the Biblical sanction for these lines is the eighth chapter of Proverbs. Yet the full nature of the connection between this source and the lines has not previously been explored. To elucidate this connection I present in parallel columns the verses from Proverbs which are germane and the verses to which the marginal notations of the King James Version direct us. Every verse to which we are directed is central to the Miltonic conception of the Logos. I have italicized those portions of verses from Proverbs echoed in the quoted lines from *Paradise Lost.*

1 Doth not Wisdom cry?	
22 The LORD possessed me in the beginning of his way, before his works of old.	
23 I was [k]set up from everlasting, from the beginning, or ever the earth was.	[k]Ps. 2.6: Yet have I set my king upon my holy hill of Zion.
24 When there were no [l]depths, I was brought forth; *when there were no fountains abounding with water.*	[l]Ge. 1.2: And the earth was without form, and void; and darkness was upon the face of the deep. And the Spirit of God moved upon the waters.
25 Before the mountains were settled; [m]*before the hills* was I brought forth:	[m]Ps. 90.2: Before the mountains were brought forth, or ever thou hadst formed the earth and the world, even from everlasting thou art God.
27 When he prepared the heaven, I was there: when he set a compass upon the face of the depth.	
30 [q]*Then I was by him, as one brought up with him: and I was daily his delight, rejoicing always before him.*	[q]Jn. 1.1, 3: In the beginning was the Word, and the Word was God. All things were made by him; and without him was not any thing made that was made.

Bishop Sumner says of Prov. viii: "All the Christian writers, from the earliest times, apply this text to Christ; and expressions in it are even quoted by those who deny his divinity." [21] For the orthodox reader, in other words, Wisdom is Christ and Christ is the speaker of the verses. It is Christ who cries that God, in the beginning of his way, possessed him; Christ who was set up from everlasting, who was brought forth before the depths, before the fountains, before the hills. When God made Heaven and earth, Christ was with the Father and was daily his delight, rejoicing always before him. Two per-

[21] But, as we have seen, Origen identifies the speaker in Prov. viii as Wisdom herself.

sons, and only two, are introduced in the passage as it is understood by the orthodox Christian: God the creator and his Son who is called Wisdom.

But Milton is not an orthodox Christian; nor is his reading of Proverbs the usual reading. In *The Christian Doctrine,* he writes: "As to the eighth chapter of Proverbs, it appears to me that it is not the Son of God who is there introduced as the speaker, but a poetical personification of wisdom." [22] This is precisely what Origen says:

And therefore we must believe that Wisdom was generated before any beginning that can be either comprehended or expressed. And since all the creative power of the coming creation was included in this very existence of Wisdom . . . having been formed beforehand and arranged by the power of foreknowledge; on account of these very creatures which had been described, as it were, and prefigured in Wisdom herself, does Wisdom say, in the words of Solomon, that she was created the beginning of the ways of God, inasmuch as she contained within herself either the beginnings, or forms, or species of all creation.[23]

In Milton's theology, as we have seen, Wisdom is equated with the internal efficiency of God, with God's decrees. Internal efficiency, or the decree, precedes external efficiency, the Son, who is brought into being as the result of the decree. Thus, as Milton understood the passage from Proverbs, three persons are mentioned: Wisdom, the speaker; Word, who created all things; and God, with whom was the Word in the beginning. With Milton's three entities in mind rather than the two of the orthodox, the interpretation of Proverbs is substantially changed.

[1] Doth not Wisdom cry. . . . [22] The Logos possessed me in the beginning of his way, before his works of old. [23] I, Wisdom, was set up from everlasting, from the beginning, or ever the earth was. [24] I, Wisdom, existed before the depths, before the fountains, [25] before the mountains and the hills. [27] When the Logos prepared the heaven, I, Wisdom, was there; when the Logos set a compass upon the face of the depth. [30] Then I, Wisdom, was by the Logos, as one brought up with him. . . .

Before completing the paraphrase, let me pause a moment to discuss some ramifications of this reading. If Wisdom is the speaker of the lines as Milton suggests, the person of whom she speaks must be the Logos. The Father, in the Miltonic system, cannot be said to have had a "beginning of his way" (verse 22); the Logos, as creator, brought forth the fountains (verse 24), the mountains and hills

---

[22] *Bohn,* IV, 174; *CE,* XV, 13.

[23] *Ante-Nicene Christian Library,* ed. Alexander Roberts and James Donaldson (Edinburgh, various dates), X, 19. Future reference will be to *ANCL* by volume and page number.

(verse 25), the heavens and the world ("set a compass upon the face of the depth," verse 27); and only the Logos can have been "as one brought up with" Wisdom, for the eternal Father was never brought up in any sense. The verses to which the reader of the Authorized Version is directed reinforce this identification. The phrase in Ps. xc, 2 (marginal note m), "from everlasting to everlasting, thou art God," would not be understood by Milton as referring to the eternal God for two reasons. (1) The *De Doctrina* asserts: "But all the words used in Scripture to denote eternity, often signify only of old time, or antiquity." Milton quotes examples and concludes: "From these and many similar texts it appears that the idea of eternity, properly so called, is conveyed in the Hebrew language rather by comparison and deduction than in express words." [24] (2) Within this verse from Psalm xc is contained the identifying information that the God of the verse is he who created the mountains and formed the earth — and that God for Milton is the Logos, not the Father. But in the verses indicated by the marginal notes a third entity, the Father, is added to the two already mentioned in Proverbs: "Yet have *I* set *my* king upon *my* holy hill of Zion." The king is certainly the Logos, but the pronouns refer to God. This verse, it will be remembered, is central to Milton's discussion of the metaphorical generation of the Son in *The Christian Doctrine*. In my explication of Milton's reading of Gen. i, 2, I have already demonstrated that the "Spirit" of this verse is the Son. Let us now return to the paraphrase of Prov. viii, 30. The marginal note points to John i, 1, 3, wherein the Logos is intimately linked with God. Milton, however, denies the orthodox Trinitarian reading of "the Word was God," which argues that God and the Word are one person. Milton's comment upon the verses is, in part, as follows:

The Word was with God, and was God, — namely, because he was with God, that is, in the bosom of the Father, as it is here expressed v. 18. Does it follows therefore that he is one in essence with him with whom he was? It no more follows, than that the disciple *who was lying on Jesus' breast,* John xiii. 23 was one in essence with Christ. Reason rejects the doctrine; Scripture nowhere asserts it; let us therefore abandon human devices, and follow the evangelist himself, who is his own interpreter. Rev. xix. 13. "his name is called the Word of God" — that is, of the one God: he himself is a distinct person.[25]

Verse 30 of the eighth chapter of Proverbs, to continue my earlier paraphrase, might be expected to read: "Then I, Wisdom, was by the

[24] *Bohn*, IV, 23; *CE*, XIV, 45–47.
[25] *Bohn*, IV, 110; *CE*, XIV, 253–55.

Logos, as one brought up with the Logos; and I, Wisdom, was daily the delight of the Logos, rejoicing always before him." But here, as the lines from *Paradise Lost* which brought about the entire discussion clearly demonstrate, Milton has been influenced by the verse from John i to which he was directed by the marginal note; and he introduces a third entity, the Father, into his reading of Proverbs. The relationship between Father and Son in the beginning also brought to his mind one of the most familiar of all Biblical verses, Matt. iii, 17: "And lo a voice from heaven, saying, This is my beloved Son, in whom I am well pleased." [26] Thus Milton can be seen in actuality to have paraphrased Prov. viii, 30, following an intricate logic all his own: "Then I, Wisdom, was by the Logos, as one brought up with him; and I was daily God's delight, rejoicing always before him." [27]

In the eighth chapter of Proverbs, as it was understood by Milton, then, Wisdom is the speaker; but the subject of her speech is "The Lord" of verse 22. That Lord — the citations show it, the verses to which the reader is directed by the marginal notes corroborate it — is he who was in the beginning (but not eternally) with the Father, who was made a king at the time of his metaphorical generation upon the holy hill of Zion, who created all things, who centered the compass in the deep to describe the vast sphere of the world, who brooded upon the rising world of waters dark and deep, who was the beloved Son in whom the Father is well pleased, who is, without question, the Logos. The Logos was *by* Wisdom in the beginning ("in the beginning of his way, before his works of old," verse 22); Wisdom was his "Sister" ("as one brought up with him," verse 30); and the Logos and Wisdom played before God ("daily his delight," verse 30, and "the Word was with God," John i, 1) who was pleased ("my beloved Son, in whom I am well pleased," Matt. iii, 17) with his "Celestial Song." Even the word "Song" is reminiscent of the Word, who makes God's Wisdom known. All this is in complete accord with Milton's system as I have earlier outlined it.

Book ix of *Paradise Lost* adds nothing new to our understanding of the Muse except that she visits the poet nightly.[28]

---

[26] Cf. Matt. xii, 18; xvii, 5; Mark i, 11; Luke iii, 22; II Pet. i, 17.

[27] In this paraphrase I intend no overtone of the "sexual" theory of God's creativity first propounded by Saurat in *Milton: Man and Thinker* (London, 1946), p. 240.

[28] In the Bible, night is the usual time for spiritual visitations and for heavenly visions. See Num. xxii, 20; II Chron. i, 7; Gen. xx, 3; xxxi, 24; Job xxxv, 10; Pss. xlii, 8; lxxvii, 6; Isa. xxx, 20; etc.

I anticipate two objections to the identification of Urania as the Logos. The first derives from the fact that in *Paradise Regained* Christ is led into the wilderness by the spirit who is Milton's Muse:

> Thou Spirit who led'st this glorious Eremite
> Into the Desert, his Victorious Field
> Against the Spiritual Foe, and brought'st him thence
> By proof th' undoubted Son of God, inspire,
> As thou art wont, my prompted Song, else mute,
>
>   *P.R.*, i, 8–12

That this spirit is Urania is, of course, established by the last quoted line. In his *Milton's Semitic Studies*, Professor H. F. Fletcher equated the "Spirit" of these lines with "that aspect of the Holy Spirit" who, in Milton's words from the *De Doctrina*, "was sent by the Father to lead the Israelites into the land of Canaan." Commenting upon this identification, Kelley quite rightly points out that the "aspect of the Holy Spirit" chosen by Fletcher is not really the third person but rather the Spirit of Christ. Kelley continues: "If, therefore, we accept Mr. Fletcher's connecting of the Muse in *Paradise Regained* with this passage, we are faced with the absurdity of Christ's being led into and brought out of the wilderness by a Spirit who was Christ himself." [29] What Professor Fletcher said, I assert with confidence: the spirit who led Christ into his trial in the wilderness in *Paradise Regained* is Christ's own Spirit. It was given to Christ at the time of his baptism in the River Jordan when the power and virtue of the Father are bestowed upon the Son, symbolized by the descending dove and the voice from Heaven declaring, "This is my beloved Son, in whom I am well pleased." [30] From this moment forth, when Christ begins his ministry upon earth, the Spirit is his, the gift of the Father; and it is by this Spirit within himself that the Son is led into the wilderness. This, it seems to me, is what Milton intends in the following lines:

> Meanwhile the Son of God . . .
>
>   . . . .
>
> Musing and much revolving in his breast,
> How best the mighty work he might begin
> Of Saviour to mankind, and which way first
> Publish his Godlike office now mature,
> One day forth walk'd alone, the Spirit leading;
>
>   *P.R.*, i, 183–89

Had Milton intended to present two beings as present in this scene, he surely would not have used the word "alone." *Paradise Lost* and

---

[29] *Kelley*, p. 114.
[30] See the discussion in *Bohn*, IV, 154–55; *CE*, XIV, 367.

the *De Doctrina*, as I have shown, concur in stating that even before the Fall, the Son was promised as man's deliverer, who would alone and unaided bruise the serpent's head. This is the tenor of the dialogue between Father and Son in Book iii of *Paradise Lost*; and this is the serious doctrine of Christ's sacerdotal function as it is propounded in Chapter XV of the first book of *The Christian Doctrine*.

The second objection which I foresee to my identification of the Muse as the Logos is that Urania should not be equated with the Son, a masculine being. This objection, obviously, might be made with equal force against the supposition that the Muse is God or the Holy Ghost. But spirits, we are told in *Paradise Lost* and in *The Christian Doctrine*, may assume any form they desire – and either gender. Moreover, Origen (I have shown this earlier, in my discussion of the Word) offers a precedent for treating the Word as a feminine being:

> Now, in the same way in which we have understood that Wisdom was the beginning of the ways of God, and is said to be created, forming beforehand and containing within herself the species and beginnings of all creatures, must we understand her to be the Word of God, because of her disclosing to all other beings, *i.e.* to universal creation, the nature of the mysteries and secrets which are contained within the divine disdom; and on this account she is called the Word, because she is, as it were, the interpreter of the secrets of the mind. And therefore that language which is found in the *Acts of Paul*, where it is said that "here is the Word a living being," appears to me to be rightly used.[31]

The arguments which I have based upon hints concerning his Muse scattered by Milton in four books of *Paradise Lost* and one of *Paradise Regained* are certainly not individually conclusive. Their impact is cumulative. To identify the Muse as God the Father runs counter to Milton's concept of the absolute nature of the Deity; to suppose that the Muse is the person of the Holy Spirit is to ignore Milton's succinct denial that the Spirit may be invoked; to equate the Muse with any lesser spirit seems arbitrary when one remembers that Urania existed in the beginning and with her sister Wisdom played before God; and to assume that Milton did not think of his Muse in theological terms appears to me entirely untenable in view of the Biblical allusions upon which the invocations are constructed. The identification of the Muse as the Logos is consonant with Milton's systematic theology, as well as with his poetic theology. It demonstrates a fact which I feel has not been sufficiently recognized by students of Milton: that the Son, because of his functions as agent, mediator, judge, prophet, and priest, because of his closeness to

---

[31] *ANCL*, X, 20.

mankind as *theanthropos,* is the most important figure in Milton's religious thought. August and remote behind the Son exists the unknowable Father, from who is all power; but the comprehensible Son is illumination, intelligence, action, strength, compassion, and love. Speaking of Christ's prophetical function, Milton asserts that it consists of two parts, "one external, namely the promulgation of divine truth; and the other internal, to wit, the illumination of the understanding." [32] What more fitting spirit than Christ's might be found to serve as the Muse of the two great epics?

---

[32] *Bohn,* IV, 299; *CE,* XV, 289.

CHAPTER SIX

CONCLUSIONS

In this study I have touched upon a number of problems familiar to Miltonists and perhaps introduced a few new ones. The points which I have made will not be further belabored here, for I have had my say.

It is hoped that this work will not be considered as a study of the influence of one man upon another, for the dangers which on every hand beset the author of such a project are magnified when the beneficiary of the supposed influence is so learned a poet as Milton. In any case, matching Origen's lost Greek, translated loosely into Latin by Rufinus and then into English by the Reverend Frederick Crombie, with Bishop Sumner's Englishing of Milton's Latin would travesty the often legitimate search for verbal parallels. Yet the ideas of the Alexandrian, blurred as they may be by multiple translation, survive intact enough so that comparisons between them and Milton's seem to me worthwhile. It has been my intent, however, to present Origen only as representative of a particular way of thought, of an intellectual climate. I have tried to show this climate congenial to the mind of Milton. Through the ages Origen's theological conjectures have appealed to strong intellects. Jerome, Augustine, Aquinas, Scotus, Erasmus, Newman, Harnack — these are men who have responded to his genius. Milton's mind, exceptional in its power, likewise, I believe, felt the attraction.

In a very real sense Milton, though he occasionally denigrated the antiquarian, was one himself. His astronomy was Aristotle's and Ptolemy's, not Kepler's and Newton's. His medicine was Galen's, not Harvey's. Very little of his science cannot be found in *De Proprietatibus Rerum*. I am convinced that in theology, too, he looked backward.

It is a major contention of this study that Milton's religious views were those of the Christian writers before the Council of Nicea. These writers dealt with many subjects not accounted theological. They were grounded, as was Milton, in the ancient Greek learning, especially that of Plato and Aristotle. Like the poet they were acquainted with early neo-Platonism. They incorporated elements of Greco-Judaic lore into their theologies, drawing from Philo and Josephus.

Milton cites Origen to argue that women may divorce their husbands and marry again. He uses Origen's biography in his contention that the laity have rights and duties which have been usurped by the bishops. Milton's poetry is instinct with the same lore which animates the thought of Origen: the phoenix symbol, Satan's rule over the north, Greek and Roman gods made demons, Belial and Mammon changed from abstractions into devils, the feasting of angels, the repentance of devils, the intelligence of ants and bees, the laughter of God, God's darkness, the theft from Moses of Greek philosophy, the flight of oracles at Christ's advent, the power of precious stones, demons regarded as a source of augury, the mystery of Jacob's ladder, the devil in the serpent, Moses as a type of Christ, the influence of the stars and planets on men. My list of minor correspondences such as these might be greatly lengthened and yet prove nothing; certainly sources other than Origen, pagan as well as Christian, might be readily substituted. But Milton and Origen agree also to a very marked extent in serious doctrine. Milton's two major heresies, according to Professor Conklin, mortalism and pantheistic materialism, are certainly present in Origen and central to his system. Like Milton, Origen is a subordinationist. And each of the following is a tenet in the faith of both.

The Bible is simple enough to be understood by all, difficult enough to tax the abilities of gifted men, who labor with the aid of the Spirit to unfold its mysteries.

The exegete is bound to be guided in delineating God by the complete list of his attributes.

God has accommodated his Word to finite understandings.

God is invisible and inaudible even to the Son.

God's omnipotence is limited only in that he cannot contradict himself.

God, the Absolute, qua God, cannot create.

Wisdom exists eternally as an attribute of God.

Wisdom becomes an entity — feminine in gender, like God unmanifest.

Wisdom, not the Son of God, is the speaker in the eighth chapter of Proverbs.

God's foreknowledge is his Wisdom.

The cosmos results from the Wisdom of God; in a sense it emanates from that Wisdom.

Matter, the total material of the cosmos, is *ex deo*, the substance of God freed from his beneficent control.

The cosmos lies within the infinite God.

Matter per se is not evil; but evil beings may make it so.

Matter, though indestructible, is fortunately alterable in its grosser manifestations.

Matter has the remarkable capability of receiving forms.

The Word or Logos is Wisdom manifested.

The Word is self-generated and invisible.

The Holy Spirit, a relatively unimportant being, is created by the Logos, who is vastly superior to it.

Heaven may be conceived in four ways: as a real place above and outside the universe; as the Platonic world of idea or essence; as a climate in the mind; and as a state of being "all in all" with God.

Heaven was created before the world.

Though angels are not arranged hierarchically in their traditional orders, they achieve rank in Heaven through merit.

Hell is a real place, but, more importantly, it is, like Heaven, a state of mind.

The chief punishment of the damned is their alienation from God, which is metaphorically illustrated by the physical torments of Hell.

The Son was begotten literally and metaphorically.

The Son achieved his place in Heaven through his own merit.

Not in essence, but in thought, harmony, and identity of will, the Son is one with God. Like everything else in creation, the Son is of the substance of God.

Prior to his incarnation, the Son is ubiquitous.

Before the Fall the Son promises man's redemption.

All great men, pagan as well as Christian, are inspired by the Son.

Evil is not a positive force — it is merely the negation of good.

Evil may be known to God or man and, if not approved, be without effect.

There is no value in a cloistered virtue — upon this precept, ultimately, depends the paradox of the fortunate Fall.

Evil results from the free choice of free wills. The primal sin of both angels and men is disobedience of God's law. Reason is goodness; unreason is evil.

Satan, before his fall, was pre-eminent among the angels, existing as light (Lucifer). God's gifts he considered as his by right. He fell through pride and an aspiration to become God.

Like angels, demons achieve positions through merit.

The gods of the nations are demons; to men they owe their status as gods.

Upon the birth of Christ, the demons lost much of their power over men; and the oracles, who are inspired by demons, ceased their activities.

Evil beings are not all punished in the same degree.

Good men cannot be harmed by demons, though they can corrupt matter and put it to evil uses.

As an animal trainer rules his charges, so the Son rules demons through fear.

The Son is the creator of the world, which with its inhabitant, man, a creature midway between angel and devil, was made in order to manifest God's goodness.

Adam is the type of mankind; mankind's future is contained in him.

Man dies body and soul. He remains dead until the judgment, when he rises body and soul; and his body is changed into an immortal body capable of becoming one with God.

God's foreknowledge in no way influences the fall of man.

Christ is the *theanthropos,* a mutual hypostatic union of God and man.

Christ is the second Adam.

Like all men, Christ incarnate dies body and soul; and he is resurrected body and soul. Yet, since the Son as Logos exists in Heaven even while the incarnate Christ performs his mission and undergoes his sacrifice upon earth, the Son is immortal.

The world is a training school for virtue.

At the time of the resurrection, men will be judged by what they know of themselves — they will damn or save themselves in the light of their divinely given consciences — Milton calls this "the rule of judgment."

After the last days, God will again be as he was in the beginning, "all in all."

To assert that any of these ideas can be found only in Origen would indeed be rash; and it would be likewise presumptuous to maintain that most of them originated with him. Like historians, mathematicians, or poets, theologians stand upon the shoulders of those who have gone before them. Yet while the beginnings of the study of history, mathematics, and poetry are lost in ancient mists, Christian theology had its beginnings well within historic times. As the first to attempt a systematic organization of the Christian faith, Origen worked as a pioneer in a pristine field, clearing a vast area which later thinkers intensively cultivated. Augustine, Jerome, Aquinas, and Duns Scotus frequently admit their indebtedness to him. Not only did much of his thought find a direct though uncredited way into orthodox theology; but also many of his conjectures which were deemed heretical helped to shape, in the flames of controversy, the rigid framework of Christian doctrine. In the *Contra Celsum* (*ANCL*, XXXIII, xii), Origen himself taught that "heresies of different kinds have never originated from any matter in which the principle involved was not important and beneficial to human life."

Milton does not treat many theological particulars upon which Origen delivered himself at some length. The poet was no man's disciple. But it seems to me that the resemblances between his theology and that of the earliest Christian Fathers as summed up in Origen are too numerous to be coincidental. I suggest that the writings of the Alexandrian were for Milton a fruitful aid to the formulation of his own doctrine. We may be certain that the poet accepted no precept which could not to his own satisfaction be proved from Scripture and elucidated by the light of the Holy Spirit within himself. Nevertheless, it seems to me most probable that Origen was foremost among the writers whom Milton had in mind when he wrote in the Dedication to *The Christian Doctrine*:

I had not even read any of the works of heretics, so called, when the mistakes of those who are reckoned for orthodox, and their incautious handling of Scripture first taught me to agree with their opponents whenever those opponents agreed with Scripture. If this be heresy, I confess with St. Paul, Acts xxiv. 14. "that after the way which they call heresy, so worship I the God of my fathers, believing all things which are written in the law and the prophets" — to which I add, whatever is written in the New Testament. Any other judges or paramount interpreters of the Christian belief, together with all implicit faith, as it is called, I, in common with the whole Protestant Church, refuse to recognise.

BIBLIOGRAPHY

BOOKS

Adams, Robert, *Ikon: John Milton and the Modern Critics* (Ithaca, N.Y., 1955).

Allen, Don Cameron, *The Harmonious Vision* (Baltimore, 1954).

Ante-Nicene Christian Library: Translations of the Writings of the Fathers down to A.D. 325, ed. Alexander Roberts and James Donaldson (Edinburgh, various dates).

Aquinas, St. Thomas, *Basic Writings of Saint Thomas Aquinas*, ed. Anton C. Pegis (New York, 1945).

Aristotle, *The Student's Oxford Aristotle*, tr. W. D. Ross (London, New York, and Toronto, 1942).

Augustine, St., *The Confessions of St. Augustine*, tr. Edward B. Pusey (New York, 1953).

Barker, Arthur E., *Milton and the Puritan Dilemma, 1641–1660* (Toronto, 1942).

Barton, William E., *Congregational Creeds and Covenants* (Chicago, 1917).

Bigg, Charles, *The Christian Platonists of Alexandria* (Oxford, 1886).

Bréhier, Émile, *The Philosophy of Plotinus*, tr. Joseph Thomas (Chicago, 1958).

Broadbent, J. B., *Some Graver Subject: An Essay on Paradise Lost* (London, 1960).

Burgess, Thomas, *Protestant Union* (London, 1826).

Bush, Douglas, *Paradise Lost in Our Time* (Ithaca, N.Y., 1945).

Cadiou, René, *Origen: His Life at Alexandria*, tr. John A. Southwell (St. Louis and London, 1944).

Conklin, George N., *Biblical Criticism and Heresy in Milton* (New York, 1949).

Corcoran, Sister Mary Irma, *Milton's Paradise with Reference to the Hexameral Background* (Washington, D.C., 1954).

Curry, Walter Clyde, *Milton's Ontology, Cosmogony, and Physics* (Lexington, Va., 1957).

Danielou, Jean, *Origen*, tr. Walter Mitchell (London and New York, 1955).

Diekhoff, John S., *Milton on Himself* (New York, 1939).

Dreyer, J. L. E., *A History of Astronomy from Thales to Kepler* (New York, 1953).

The Early Christian Fathers, ed. and tr. Henry Bettenson (London, New York, and Toronto, 1956).

The Book of the Secrets of Enoch, tr. W. R. Morfill, ed. R. H. Charles (Oxford, 1896).

Fairweather, William, *Origen and Greek Patristic Theology* (New York, 1901).

The Fathers of the Church, ed. Ludwig Schoop *et al.* (New York, 1948).

Fletcher, Harris Francis, *Milton's Rabbinical Readings* (Urbana, Ill., 1930).

————, *Milton's Semitic Studies and Some Manifestations of Them in His Poetry* (Chicago, 1926).

————, *The Use of the Bible in Milton's Prose* (Urbana, Ill., 1929).

Frye, Roland Mushat, *God, Man, and Satan* (Princeton, N.J., 1960).

Gilbert, Allan H., *On the Composition of Paradise Lost* (Chapel Hill, N.C., 1947).

Good, John Walter, *Studies in the Milton Tradition,* in *University of Illinois Studies in Language and Literature* (Urbana, Ill., 1915), I, 93–402.

Green, E. Tyrrell, *The Thirty-nine Articles and the Age of the Reformation* (London, 1896).

Grierson, Sir Herbert J. C., *Milton & Wordsworth, Poets and Prophets* (London, 1956).

Hanford, James Holly, *John Milton, Englishman* (New York, 1949).

Harnack, Adolph, *History of Dogma,* tr. Neil Buchanan (Boston, 1895).

Harris, C. R. S., *Duns Scotus* (Oxford, 1927).

Hartwell, Kathleen Ellen, *Lactantius and Milton* (Cambridge, Mass., 1929).

Jerome, St., *Letters and Select Works of St. Jerome,* tr. W. H. Fremantle, in *A Select Library of Nicene and Post-Nicene Fathers of the Christian Church,* 2nd ser., ed. Philip Schaff and Henry Wace (New York, Oxford, and London, 1893), VI.

Kelley, Maurice, *This Great Argument* (Princeton, N.J., 1941).

Lamson, Alvan, *The Church of the First Three Centuries* (Boston, 1860).

Lewis, C. S., *A Preface to Paradise Lost* (London, New York, and Toronto, 1956).

Mathers, S. L. MacGregor, *Kabbala Denudata: The Kabbalah Unveiled* (New York, 1912).

Maimonides, Moses, *The Guide for the Perplexed,* tr. M. Friedlander (New York, 1956).

Martyn, W. Carlos, *Life and Times of John Milton* (New York, 1866).

Milton, John, *John Milton: Complete Poems and Major Prose,* ed. Merritt Y. Hughes (New York, 1957).

————, *The Poetical Works of John Milton,* ed. Helen Darbishire (London, 1958).

————, *The Prose Works of John Milton,* ed. J. A. St. John (London, Henry G. Bohn, 1848–53).

————, *The Works of John Milton,* ed. F. A. Patterson *et al.* (New York, Columbia University Press, 1931–42).

Milton Criticism: Selections from Four Centuries, ed. James Thorpe (London, 1951).

Milton Memorial Lectures, 1908, ed. Percy W. Ames (London, 1909).

A New Commentary on Holy Scripture, ed. Charles Gore, Henry Leighton Goudge, and Alfred Guillaume (New York, 1946).

Origen, *Origen's Commentaries on John, Books I–IX, and Matthew, Books*

I, II, and X–XIV, in The Ante-Nicene Fathers. Translations of the Writings of the Fathers down to A.D. 325. Original Supplement to the American Edition, ed. and tr. Allan Menzies (New York, 1906), IX.

————, *Selections from the Commentaries and Homilies of Origen,* tr. R. B. Tollinton (London, 1929).

Philo, *The Works of Philo Judaeus, the Contemporary of Josephus,* tr. C. D. Younge (London, 1890), I.

Plato, *The Dialogues of Plato,* tr. B. Jowett (New York, 1937).

Plotinus, *Select Works of Plotinus,* tr. Thomas Taylor (London, 1911).

Quasten, Johannes, *Patrology* (Westminster, Md., 1950–60).

Rajan, B., *Paradise Lost & The Seventeenth Century Reader* (London, 1947).

Robbins, Frank Egleston, *The Hexaemeral Literature* (Chicago, 1912).

Saurat, Denis, *Milton: Man and Thinker* (London, 1946).

Sewell, Arthur, *A Study of Milton's Christian Doctrine* (Oxford, 1939).

Staley, Vernon, *The Catholic Religion: A Manual of Instruction for Members of the Anglican Communion* (London, Oxford, and New York, 1948).

Svendsen, Kester, *Milton and Science* (Cambridge, Mass., 1956).

Taylor, George C., *Milton's Use of Du Bartas* (Cambridge, Mass., 1934).

Thorndike, Lynn, *The Sphere of Sacrobosco and Its Commentators* (Chicago, 1949).

Tillyard, E. M. W., *Milton* (London, 1956).

————, *The Miltonic Setting Past & Present* (London, 1957).

————, *Studies in Milton* (London, 1955).

Tuve, Rosemund, *Images and Themes in Five Poems by Milton* (Cambridge, Mass., 1957).

Visiak, E. H. *The Portent of Milton* (New York, 1958).

Waldock, A. J. A., *Paradise Lost and Its Critics* (Cambridge, Mass., 1947).

Werblowski, R. J. Zwi, *Lucifer and Prometheus* (London, 1952).

West, Robert H., *Milton and the Angels* (Athens, Ga., 1955).

Whiting, George W., *Milton and This Pendant World* (Austin, Tex., 1958).

Willey, Basil, *The Seventeenth Century Background* (New York, 1953).

Williamson, George, *Seventeenth Century Contexts* (London, 1960).

ARTICLES

Adams, John R., "The Theism of *Paradise Lost,*" *Personalist,* XXII (1941), 174–80.

Adamson, J. H., "Milton's Arianism," *Harvard Theological Review,* LIII (1960), 269–76.

————, "The War in Heaven: Milton's Version," *JEGP,* LVII (1958), 690–703.

Allen, Don Cameron, "Milton and the Sons of God," *MLN,* LXI (1946), 73–79.

Bell, Millicent, "The Fallacy of the Fall in *Paradise Lost,*" *PMLA,* LXVIII (1953), 863–83.

————, "The Fallacy of the Fall in *Paradise Lost,*" *PMLA,* LXX (1955), 1187–97, 1203.

Broadbent, J. B., "Milton's Hell," *ELH*, XXI (1954), 161–92.

Campbell, Lily B., "The Christian Muse," *The Huntington Library Bulletin*, VIII (October, 1935), 29–70.

Childers, Charles Louis, "Milton's Doctrine of God, Studied in the Light of Historical Christianity," *Dissertation Abstracts*, XX (1960), 1781–82.

Cope, Jackson I., "Milton's Muse in *Paradise Lost*," *MP*, LV (1957), 6–10.

Curry, Walter Clyde, "Milton's Dual Concept of God as Related to Creation," *SP*, XLVII (1950), 190–210.

Dahlberg, Charles, "*Paradise Lost* V, 603, and Milton's Psalm II," *MLN*, LXVII (1952), 23.

Diekhoff, John S., "Eve, the Devil, and *Areopagitica*," *MLQ*, V (1944), 429–34.

Dodge, R. E. Neil, "Theology in *Paradise Lost*," *University of Wisconsin Studies in Language and Literature*, II (1918), 9–21.

Emerson, Everett H., "Milton's War in Heaven: Some Problems," *MLN*, LXIX (1954), 399–402.

Fiore, Amadeus P., "The Problem of Seventeenth Century Soteriology in Reference to Milton," *Franciscan Studies*, XV (1955), 48–59, 257–82.

Fisher, Peter F., "Milton's Theodicy," *JHI* (1956), XVII, 28–53.

Fletcher, Harris Francis, "Milton and Yosippon," *SP*, XXI (1924), 496–501.

Gilbert, Allen H., "Critics of Mr. C. S. Lewis on Milton's Satan," *South Atlantic Quarterly*, XLVII (1948), 216–25.

———, "The Problem of Evil in *Paradise Lost*," *JEGP*, XXII (1923), 175–94.

———, "The Theological Basis of Satan's Rebellion and the Function of Abdiel in *Paradise Lost*," *MP*, XL (1942–43), 19–42.

Green, Clarence C., "The Paradox of the Fortunate Fall in *Paradise Lost*," *MLN*, LIII (1938), 557–71.

Hanford, James Holly, "The Chronology of Milton's Private Studies," *PMLA*, XXXVI (1921), 251–314.

———, "The Date of Milton's *De Doctrina Christiana*," *SP*, XVII (1920), 309–19.

———, "The Temptation Motive in Milton," *SP*, XV (1918), 176–94.

———, "That Shepherd Who First Taught the Chosen Seed: A Note on Milton's Mosaic Inspiration," *UTQ*, VIII (1938–39), 403–19.

Henry, Nathaniel H., "Milton and Hobbes: Mortalism and the Intermediate State," *SP*, XLVIII (1951), 234–49.

Howard, Donald R., "Milton's Satan and the Augustinian Tradition," *Renaissance Papers* (University of South Carolina, 1954), pp. 11–23.

Howard, Leon, " 'The Invention' of Milton's 'Great Argument': A Study of the Logic of 'God's Ways to Men,' " *HLQ*, IX (1945), 149–73.

Hughes, Merritt Y., "Myself Am Hell," *MP*, LIV (1956), 80–94.

Hunter, William B., "Holy Light in *Paradise Lost*," *Rise Institute Pamphlets*, XLVI (1959–60), 1–14.

———, "The Meaning of 'Holy Light' in *Paradise Lost* III," *MLN*, LXXIV (1959), 589–92.

———, "Milton on the Incarnation: Some More Heresies," *JHI*, XXI (1960), 349–69.

————, "Milton's Arianism Reconsidered," *Harvard Theological Review*, LII (1959), 9–35.

————, "Milton's Materialistic Life Principle," *JEGP*, XLV (1946), 68–76.

Huntley, Frank L., "A Justification of Milton's 'Paradise of Fools' (*P.L.*, III, 431–499)," *ELH*, XXI (1954), 107–13.

Joseph, Sister Miriam, "Orthodoxy in *Paradise Lost*," *Laval Théologique et Philosophique* (Quebec, 1954), VIII, 243–84.

Kelley, Maurice, "Milton and the Third Person of the Trinity," *SP*, XXXII (1935), 221–34.

————, "Milton's Debt to Wolleb's *Compendium Theologiae Christianae*," *PMLA*, L (1935), 156–65.

————, "Milton's Use of 'Begot' in *Paradise Lost*, V, 603," *SP*, XXXVIII (1941), 252–65.

————, "The Theological Dogma of *Paradise Lost*, III, 173–202," *PMLA*, LII (1937), 75–79.

Kivette, Ruth Montgomery, "Milton on the Trinity," *Dissertation Abstracts*, XXI (1960), 189–90.

Larson, Martin A., "Milton and Servetus: A Study in the Sources of Milton's Theology," *PMLA*, XLI (1926), 891–934.

Lovejoy, O., "Milton and the Paradox of the Fortunate Fall," *ELH*, IV (1937), 161–79.

Lumpkin, Ben Gray, "Fate in *Paradise Lost*," *SP*, XLIV (1947), 56–68.

Maxwell, J. C., " 'Gods' in 'Paradise Lost,' " *N&Q*, CXCIII (1948), 234–36, 242.

McColley, Grant, "The Book of Enoch and *Paradise Lost*," *Harvard Theological Review*, XXXI (1938), 21–39.

————, "Milton's Technique of Source Adaptation," *SP*, XXXV (1938), 61–110.

Mineka, Francis, "The Critical Reception of Milton's *De Doctrina Christiana*," *University of Texas Studies in English* (Austin, 1943), pp. 115–47.

Mosse, George L., "Puritan Radicalism and the Enlightenment," *Church History*, XXIX (1960), 424–39.

Parish, John E., "Milton and an Anthropomorphic God," *SP*, LVI (1959), 619–25.

Patrides, C. A., "Milton and the Protestant Theory of the Atonement," *PMLA*, LXXIV (1959), 7–13.

————, "*Paradise Lost* and the Mortalist Heresy," *N&Q*, n.s., IV (1957), 250.

Pritchard, John Paul, "The Fathers of the Church in the Works of John Milton," *Classical Journal*, XXXIII (1937–38), 79–87.

Reesing, John, "The Materiality of God in Milton's *De Doctrina Christiana*," *Harvard Theological Review*, L (1957), 159–73.

Rice, Warner G., "Fate in *Paradise Lost*," *Papers of the Michigan Academy of Science, Arts, and Letters*, XXXI (1945), 299–306.

Robins, Harry F., "Milton's First Sonnet on His Blindness," *RES*, n.s., VII (1956), 360–66.

Samuel, Irene, "The Dialogue in Heaven: A Reconsideration of *Paradise Lost*, III, 1–417," *PMLA*, LXXII (1957), 601–11.

Saurat, Denis, "Two Notes on Milton," *RES*, XII (1936), 324.

Scott-Craig, T. S. K., "Milton's Use of Wolleb and Ames," *MLN*, LV (1940), 403–7.

Sewell, Arthur, "Milton and the Mosaic Law," *MLR*, XXX (1935), 13–18.

Shumaker, Wayne, "The Fallacy of the Fall in *Paradise Lost*," *PMLA*, LXX (1955), 1185–1202.

Stein, Arnold, "Satan: The Dramatic Role of Evil," *PMLA*, LXV (1940), 221–31.

Stoll, E. E., "Give the Devil His Due: A Reply to Mr. Lewis," *RES*, XX (1944), 108–24.

Summers, Joseph H., "The Voice of the Redeemer in *Paradise Lost*," *PMLA*, LXX (1955), 1082–89.

Tillyard, E. M. W., "The Causeway from Hell to the World in the Tenth Book of *Paradise Lost*," *SP*, XXXVIII (1941), 266–70.

West, Robert H., "Milton's Angelological Heresies," *JHI*, XIV (1953), 116–23.

———, "The Substance of Milton's Angels," *SAMLA Studies in Milton* (Gainesville, Fla., 1953), pp. 20–53.

Whiting, George W., "The Father to the Son," *MLN*, LXV (1950), 191–93.

Williams, Arnold, "Milton and the Renaissance Commentaries on Genesis," *MP*, XXXVII (1939–40), 263–78.

———, "The Motivation of Satan's Rebellion in *Paradise Lost*," *SP*, XLII (1945), 253–68.

———, "Renaissance Commentaries on 'Genesis' and Some Elements of the Theology of *Paradise Lost*," *PMLA*, LVI (1941), 151–64.

Wolfe, Don M., "The Role of Milton's Christ," *Sewanee Review*, LI (1943), 467–75.

Woodhouse, A. S. P., "Notes on Milton's Views on the Creation: The Initial Phase," *PQ*, XXVIII (1949), 211–36.

Wright, B. A., "Masson's Diagram of Milton's Spaces (a Note on *Paradise Lost*, I, 73–4)," *RES*, XXI (1945), 42–43.

INDEX

Adams, Robert: Milton's reading, 9

Alexandria, Egypt: description of in Origen's day, 31

"All in all": God in Origen and Milton, 108–9

Ammonius Saccas, teacher of Origen and Plotinus: teachings, 32

Angels: have bodies and take nourishment according to Justin Martyr, 20; hierarchically ranked by the pseudo-Dionysius Areopagiticus, 109–10; Milton's: concerned with affairs of men, 113; created before the world, 112; feast with men, 112; not ordered hierarchically, 110; Origen's: achieve rank through merit, 110; concerned with affairs of men, 113; created before the world, 111–12; feast with men, 112; not ranked hierarchically, 109; in *Paradise Lost* achieve rank through merit, 110–11; Victorinus of Pettau says one-third fell, 27

Ante-Nicene Fathers: accept Philo's teachings, 18; character of, 18; climate of opinion among, 27–28; how educated, 18; as judges of orthodoxy, 28; shapers of the Church, 28

Anthropomorphism: Milton warns against, 68–69; Origen warns against, 68

Anti-Trinitarianism. *See* Subordinationism

Athenagoras of Athens: subordinationist, 20–21

Attributes. *See* God

Azazel: in Origen, 133

Barnabas. *See* "Epistle of Barnabas"

Byron: "Cain" reviewed, 5

Cadiou, René: says Rufinus does not do violence to Origen's works, 36

Celsus: attacks on Christianity, 29

Chaos, 93–94

Chiliasm: in ante-Nicene times, orthodox, 154; in Commodianus, 26; in "Epistle of Barnabas," 19; in Justin Martyr, 20; in Lactantius, 26; in Methodius, 27; in Papias of Hierapolis, 19–20; in Tertullian, 23; in Victorinus of Pettau, 27; not in Origen, 154

Christ: anointed, 147; in ante-Nicene Fathers, existed before the world, 28; ascension, 54; "Christ," two meanings for, 147; "Christ" not used in *Paradise Lost*, 147; dies body and soul, 54; in "Epistle of Barnabas," 19; incarnate, 147; judge, 153; millennial reign, 54; in Origen, 148–49; orthodox hypostatic union, 147; as prophet, priest, and king, 54; risen not ubiquitous, 54, 150; second Adam in Milton, 151; second Adam in Origen, 151; second advent, 54. *See also* Logos; Son

Christian Doctrine. See De Doctrina Christiana

Clement of Alexandria: father of speculative theology, 22; the Log-